W. L Blamires, John B Smith

The early story of the Wesleyan Methodist Church in Victoria

W. L Blamires, John B Smith

The early story of the Wesleyan Methodist Church in Victoria

ISBN/EAN: 9783743464032

Manufactured in Europe, USA, Canada, Australia, Japa

Cover: Foto ©Lupo / pixelio.de

Manufactured and distributed by brebook publishing software (www.brebook.com)

W. L Blamires, John B Smith

The early story of the Wesleyan Methodist Church in Victoria

THE EARLY STORY

OF THE

WESLEYAN METHODIST CHURCH

IN

VICTORIA.

BY THE

REV. W. L. BLAMIRES,
(PRESIDENT OF THE VICTORIA AND TASMANIA CONFERENCE, 1886),
AND THE
REV. JOHN B. SMITH,
OF THE SAME CONFERENCE.

A JUBILEE VOLUME.

Melbourne:
WESLEYAN BOOK DEPOT, LONSDALE STREET EAST,
A. J. SMITH, SWANSTON STREET; W. THACKER,
GEELONG; WATTS, SANDHURST.

SOLD BY ALL BOOKSELLERS.

MDCCCLXXXVI.

ALL RIGHTS RESERVED.

PREFACE.

This volume is a contribution to the history of the Wesleyan Methodist Church in Victoria. The authors, years ago, saw the importance of preserving documents and records, which would give authentic data concerning the early times of this Church. In the year 1881, the Victoria and Tasmania Conference directed them to collect such materials, and this request was repeated by the General Conference of the Australasian Wesleyan Methodist Church. That trust has been considered a positive and sacred duty by them, and they have fulfilled it with some success, having been largely aided by numerous friends and Circuit authorities, who possessed such records. They sought also to obtain oral or written statements from such of the early pioneers who survive to the present time, and they are greatly indebted for such information kindly given by the Revs. W. Butters, J. Harcourt, J. C. Symons, M. Dyson, and Messrs. Witton, Beaver, Stone, the Tuckfield family, Mrs. Caldwell (formerly Mrs. Hurst), and many others. Their obligation is greatest of all to the representatives of the late Rev. Joseph Orton, for the loan of his manuscript journals, which are full of important materials relating to the founding of Methodism in South Australia and Victoria.

The collection of records, etc., was an official duty, but the writing and publishing of this book is a private undertaking, so that the Wesleyan Conference is not to be considered as having given its *imprimatur* to it; at the same time it is believed, that the members of the Conference and of the whole Church look with favour upon the issue of such a book; and it is hoped that the public generally will concur in this view. The Christian enterprise of the Wesleyan Church in this land deserves a permanent and appropriate record, whether this volume be an adequate representation of it or not. The sons and daughters of Methodism would not willingly allow the work of God in the rise and progress of their Church to pass from their memory, or go into oblivion. This book is an attempt to embalm and preserve some of the vital facts and salient features of its story. The Jubilee year seemed an opportune time for its issue. Then especially the grateful Methodist heart eagerly devoured accounts from the lips, or records from the press, which told of the mighty works that God had done for their fathers, and "in the old time before them," as tending to make their joy the more intelligent and deep. So this book is designed to make the strains of grateful joy the more abiding, as it may aid not only the present, but another generation to show forth the "high praises of God." The volume is, therefore, a Jubilee Memorial, and an offering to the Methodist public.

Like the Banyan tree, whose branches spread out, then incline towards, and eventually reach, the earth, where they strike root until vigorous offshoots become both a progeny and support to the parent stock, so there are innate forces in Methodism which cause it to spread out in all directions, till a cluster of Churches is formed, in time becoming selfsuporting, but yet maintaining a vital and glad connection wh the parent Church. The truth of this has been vefied and illustrated in this land.

The plain narrative of this growth is given in this volume. Th authors are not historians, but more like annalists They ha? not exhaustively studied the facts, interrogated the spit, and deduced the important lessons, which Methodism in iis land presents to the historian. They have compiled an put into a succinct form the facts and annals of the early M(hodist story. Their plan has been, of set purpose, to be ful when writing about the first and pioneer work of the Chrch, but to be brief and summary when relating its mo? recent achievements. They could not enlarge upon the recent, as they felt at liberty to do upon the earlier stor. The work was too delicate, and the perspective too nea for them to attempt it. They preferred sketching the mo? distant landscape, and have dealt with the nearer foreground in a few outlines. This may be disappointing to >me, but worthy deeds and lives in recent years will be !ealt with in due time, when we are considerably old(, but by other hands than the writers of this volume.

'his work seeks to fulfil in respect to Victorian Metodism, the inspired injunction, " Walk about Zion, and o round about her ; tell the towers thereof. Mark ye well her bulwarks, consider her palaces ; that ye may tell it t(the generation following. For this God is our God for rer and ever."

W. L. B.
J. B. S.

CONTENTS.

	Chap.	Page
Introductory	I.	
Foundation	II.	
First Advances	III.	32
Transition	IV.	45
Gold and Change	V.	61
Extension	VI.	70
Precursors of Revival	VII.	81
Revivals	VIII.	89
Church Institutions, Movements, Memorials (1863-85.)	IX.	106
Suburban Methodism	X.	115
Geelong and Ballarat District	XI.	137
Castlemaine and Sandhurst Dist.	XII.	160
Maldon, Maryborough, and Adjacent Circuits	XIII.	186
Sandhurst Circuit	XIV.	205
Kyneton and Daylesford Circuits	XV.	228
The Dunolly and Tarnagulla, and Inglewood Circuits	XVI.	233
Northern Areas.—The St. Arnaud Charlton, Echuca, and other Circuits	XVII.	241
Gippsland District	XVIII.	247
Western District	XIX.	251
Ovens and Murray District	XX.	273
North-Western Circuits	XXI.	285
Missions and Miscellaneous	XXII.	291
Conclusion	XXIII.	303
Appendix, Table A		314
,, ,, B		315
Index		316
Errata		End.

VICTORIAN METHODISM:
Its Origin and History.

INTRODUCTORY.
CHAPTER I.

THE chronicle of Wesleyan Methodism dates back to the year 1739. The rise and organization of the United Societies which developed into the Wesleyan Church began with the crisis in the religious history of the Revs. John and Charles Wesley, when they clearly apprehended the Scriptural doctrine of justification by faith alone in Christ Jesus our Lord, and entered into the experience of a conscious salvation; and when with fervent zeal they preached such doctrine and life unto others. The germ of the whole body of Christian life and activity found in the widespread Methodism of the several continents may be found there. God gave it life, and that life has formed its own body of a compact, well constructed, vigorous organism, or Church, which is known in the world as Wesleyan Methodism. And yet also, the form it now possesses, the functions it now fulfils, and the blessing which it now works, are owing to the constant Providence of God, and the ever present grace of the Holy Ghost. Far be it from us unduly to vaunt the agency of man, but we give the praise of the good that is done on earth wholly to the Lord our God.

The great Head of the Church, however, has deigned to bless the Scriptural teaching, and the enthusiastic zeal in the cause of Christ, of the Wesleys, their helpers, and their successors; and it is the story of that blessing as it has unfolded and exhibited itself in one province of the Southern World that we purpose to write.

The principal events in the Methodist Calendar are the Conversion of John and Charles Wesley, their open air preaching, and the formation of the first societies; the organization and enrolment, by the Deed of Declaration, of the Methodist pastorate as having oversight of the Methodist Societies; the calling into activity of so many agencies and institutions which are somewhat, yet not altogether, peculiar to Methodism, such as the Local Preacher, the Leader, the Class Meeting, the Lovefeast, &c.; the death of John Wesley and the transition of the societies into a distinct Church having all the marks, privileges, and ordinances thereof; and the epoch of the formation of the Missionary Society in 1813. The era of its missions does not date from that year, for Methodism was essentially Missionary from the first. Its first public collection in the Conference at Leeds, in 1769, and its first agents sent beyond the British Islands, Messrs. Boardman and Pilmour, mark, however, the beginning of its Foreign Missions. Those missions were for a long time under the charge of Dr. Coke, who brought to the fostering care of them a sublime self-denial, and a tireless activity of oversight truly Apostolic. But, just subsequent to his decease and the immediate formation of the Wesleyan Methodist Missionary Society, came the event, which is marked in the Methodist Calendar in this hemisphere, as the founding of Rome in hers, the birth of Australian Methodism, the founding of that Church in these fair lands. The Rev. Samuel Leigh, our devoted pioneer, was the first authorized Methodist agent sent to these shores by that Missionary Society, and he landed in Sydney in 1815. From his labours and those of his immediate fellow-helpers sprang the early Methodism of New South Wales and Tasmania. Victorian Methodism is the child of these parents.

The boy has grown, and it is our duty to tell of his growth into lusty manhood, and to speak to the generations to come of the wonderful works of God in his nurture and blessing. Some details of his early story may appear to others as trivial, but they will not be so to the children that owe so much to him. They will prize the smaller incidents that may be preserved from oblivion, even as they treasure the stick, or the fly, whose life was centuries ago, that may be preserved in amber. But the great principles of the Gospel as they are illustrated in this story, are the heritage of the whole Christian Church, and many will delight to know how they had form and development, idea and embodiment in the rise and progress of Victorian Methodism.

A colonising and convict element fused somewhat together in the early days of the older colonies. Wool, grain, and gold, have been leading motors in the settlement, both of the older and the younger colonies. Victoria owes most to the wool and gold. These brought to the land a hardy and adventurous race, who settling at first on the Southern and Western coasts, eventually overspread the whole land. Of the immigrants, most were of the steady habits and colonizing instincts that mark the Anglo-Saxon race; and religion, if it assumed not the stern type of the Puritans in New England, had yet a home and welcome amongst them, and toned down the rough asperities, and developed the better elements, of colonial life. Methodism had a mission to them from the first, and has been a prime factor in what is best and noblest in Colonial history, and the national life. There was a much smaller portion of society that had the convict taint in it than in adjacent lands to the South and North. The number of these persons grew beautifully less as the days passed on, but they were not despised by the Methodist agent, who, by his hopeful theology, Christian zeal, and Divine charity, sought to raise them; and, happily, many jewels were plucked out of the mire by his instrumentality, and many outcast pariahs of society were brought into the family and fold of God.

FOUNDATION.

CHAPTER II.

THE rise of this Church is not lost in antiquity. Its sources are not like those of the Nile, unknown or matter of dispute, because shrouded in the dim distance. Facts, figures, names, events, are given to particularize the origin and advance of this Church in very modern times— within the present century. Wesleyan Methodism in Victoria is coeval with the founding of the colony. The first settlement of whites took place when Messrs. Edward and Stephen Henty landed at Portland Bay in November, 1834, with servants and stock of cattle and sheep. But that settlement had no such history and made no progress like to those pertaining to that City which, founded a little later, has long ago eclipsed the other place in all material growth and prosperity. Mr. J. P. Fawkner's party was the first to settle on the site of Melbourne. The vessel *Enterprise* with these settlers and founders of the colony on board, arrived in the Yarra on 29th or 30th of August, 1835, and forthwith they occupied the river bank and the adjacent slopes of land on which now is found the magnificent City of Melbourne. But the infant settlement had only two weatherboard houses, eight or ten sod huts and tents occupied by about fifty persons, as the whole strength of the white population, at the end of 1835. The infant City of that time gave but small augury or prophecy of the giant it has become.

That year, 1835, witnessed the first religious service conducted by Methodists, owing to the zeal of a remarkable

man who has left his mark upon the religious history of
Tasmania, and also upon certain places and classes in
England. Henry Reed, Esq., then a zealous Local
Preacher in Tasmania, having the welfare of the native
population in view, went over to Port Philip in 1835 with
one of the earliest bands of settlers, and in one of the only
two sod huts that had then been extemporised for shelter,
read and expounded a portion of Sacred Scripture, and
offered prayer to Almighty God. The congregation had in
it William Buckley, the escaped convict, who, as most
readers of Colonial history know, had been living in a state
of wildness and barbarism with the natives for over
thirty years; the brother of Mr. John Batman (who
afterwards, we believe, became the chief constable of the
settlement); and three natives from Sydney, who but
imperfectly understood the English language. Such was
the beginning of Methodist work in Victoria. It was but
a feeble effort, and Mr. Reed's was but a short visit, but
that service, even though it was of the nature of family
prayer, dates the first of many that Wesleyans have held in
this Colony, and was the earliest attempt to bring the land,
and both its white and dark-skinned people, to the feet of
King Jesus. Mr. Reed's sole object in visiting the country
was to try to be useful to the natives and the few English
people who were there. A like benevolent motive—to
Christianize the natives, and preserve them from destruction
by any demoralizing influence that might be brought by
the Colonists—prompted the visit to Melbourne of the Rev.
Joseph Orton, in the following year. His voyage across
Bass Straits was a prolonged and unpleasant one in a small
craft. The weather was rough, and the tossing of the
vessel caused sickness amongst the passengers, and great
loss amongst the cattle that were on board. Mr. Orton,
because of effluvia from dying and dead cattle, which,
through stress of weather, could not be thrown overboard,
was necessitated to keep on deck through the ten days of
the lengthened passage, subject to the worst sickness,

inconvenience, and annoyance that he had known on ship board. He sailed up the River Yarra on April 20th.

This is his account of the services held on Sabbath, April 24th, 1836.

"Sunday, 24th April.—At eleven o'clock the people of the settlement were assembled for Divine service . . . . . . [This was on Batman's Hill, and on the premises of Mr. John Batman. The liturgy was read by Mr. Orton, the responses were led by James Simpson, Esq. The tunes were raised by Dr. Thomson, afterwards of Geelong.]

"I addressed the company from the young ruler's question, 'What shall I do to inherit eternal life?' At the conclusion of my discourse I took occasion to show the propriety of a consistent deportment on the part of the European settlers in the new settlement, especially enjoining them to acknowledge God in all their ways, that they might insure the divine blessing with their undertaking, otherwise they might expect His curse with all they undertook.

"In the afternoon the people again assembled, to whom I preached from John i. 12. The number of Europeans was greater than in the morning, but the larger proportion of my congregation consisted of natives—about fifty—who sat very quietly, and seemed particularly interested by the singing. I took the opportunity to make an appeal to the intelligent part of my audience on behalf of these poor degraded creatures, among whom they have come to reside, and whose land (which is comparatively flowing with milk and honey) they have come to possess, endeavouring to show their incumbent duty, on the principle of common equity, to use all means to promote their temporal and spiritual welfare.

"I have not been more interested by any sight than the one presented this afternoon. My soul truly went out after their best interests; I felt as if I could have sacrificed every personal comfort for their benefit; I longed to be able to communicate my views and feelings to them. I could but anticipate the happy time when these poor creatures, degraded below the brute, will come to a knowledge of the truth.

"Several of what is called the Jagger Jagger tribe came in from a hunting excursion, and brought news that more would be in soon. One of those who came in to-day is one of the chiefs with whom Mr. Batman first had an interview upon landing, and with whom he entered into a treaty for a certain portion of land. The treaty will be nullified, I apprehend, by the British Government, as forming a bad precedent."

This is creditable to the heart of the good minister. His compassion was for some of the blackest, and his yearning over some of the most degraded, of the human race. Buckley's account given to Mr. Orton stated that the natives, upon occasion, ate their own offspring. Here certainly Methodism was going, in the person of her representative, according to the injunction of Mr. Wesley himself to his helpers, "not to those who want you, but to those who want you most." This religious concern for the natives brought over the first layman and the first minister who conducted public service in the new settlement, and it brought from England the first two ministers of the Wesleyan Church, who took up their abode in the land. This seed sowing had a larger harvest in the course of time among the whites, but had some fruit also among these sable sons of the soil, whose land was coveted by the early settlers, but whose salvation was sought by these first agents of the Gospel.

The representations made by the Rev. Mr. Orton induced the Wesleyan Missionary Society in London to appoint the Rev. Benj. Hurst and the Rev. F. Tuckfield, as the pioneers of a Mission to the Aborigines of the land.

The memorandum concerning the rise of Wesleyan Methodism in Melbourne which is entered in the minute book of the Melbourne quarterly meeting, states "The nucleus of the Wesleyan Methodist Society was formed by a few members who emigrated from Tasmania about the latter end of 1836 and the beginning of 1837, consisting of Mr. George Lilly, Mr. J. S. Peers, Mr. W. Witton, and a few others, who, after their landing on these shores, availed themselves of the advantages of Christian Communion, for which purposes, as well as for holding prayer meetings and other religious services, they met at stated periods in a wattle and daub hut. Soon after the arrival of Mr. W. Witton, in March, 1837, by mutual consent he was appointed to take charge of the members, then seven in number, of which he became their recognised leader."

Messrs. Lilly and Peers occupied very respectable positions in social life.

Mr. Peers was an enthusiast in music. He led the singing at the first Wesleyan Church erected in the colony, a small brick building 30 x 16 at the corner of Swanston Street and Flinders Lane, of which he bore the first outlay of expense, stipulating only that he should be repaid when the congregation moved to more commodious premises. He was leader also of the choir in the small Church constructed of weatherboard, 20ft. by 16ft., which was the first building used for worship by the Church of England, and which stood on the site since occupied by St. James' Church. Amongst his helpers were Messrs. John Caulfield, Mr. Edward Peers, and Mr. John Sutch. Afterwards he had a similar office in the Wesleyan Sanctuary erected in Collins Street; and, mainly through his exertions, a large and effective choir was formed, a harmonium procured, and afterwards a fine organ which long remained the best in the colony. This was presided over by Mr. Clark, senr., afterwards gold broker.

At or about the time of the erection of the Wesleyan Church in 1838, the following were active members of the Church or congregation. The gentlemen named in the above extract from the minute book, also Mr. E. Peers, Mr. Thomas Jennings, Mr. Ralph Walton, Mr. Overton, Mr. James Candy, Mr. Howell, afterwards of Geelong,

Mr. Charles Stone, Mr. John Burgess, Mr. Thomas Watson, Mr. John Lobb, Mr. James Fenton, Mr. T. Trotman. Several of these did good service to the Wesleyan Church for years subsequently. Mr. Charles Stone (who came in September, 1838) is the only survivor of these worthy fathers of Victorian Methodism last named. Shortly after Mr. Thomas Wilkinson must have joined the godly band. He had been a devoted worker in the East end of London for many years, subsequently a fellow worker with Mr. Henry Reed, of Launceston, in his efforts to convert and Christianize the degraded convicts of Tasmania. He could tell many a thrilling tale of human depravity, but also of brutalized humanity changed by the power of the Gospel. He became a pioneer of Methodism in Portland, a member of the Legislative Assembly of the colony, and a grand old veteran of Christ's cause in Brunswick, where in 1881 he peacefully died.

The first class was held in Mr. Witton's house, situate in Lonsdale Street. A prayer meeting was early held in T. Trotman's house, south of the Yarra. These ordinances were kept up by these earnest men. On the Sabbath day, if no Local Preacher could officiate, they worshipped with other congregations of Christians. A Sabbath school was formed at an early date, in which some of the first teachers were Miss Howell, afterwards Mrs. Silas Harding, of Geelong, Miss Wilkinson, daughter of Mr. Thomas Wilkinson, and Messrs. Peers, Trotman, Mr. and Mrs. Smith. The first school building was a rude structure at the end of Russell-Street, near the Yarra bank. When open some months it had but twelve children. The first Anniversary Tea Meeting was held at the time of the Rev. Mr. Simpson's visit.

Mr. Tuckfield sailed from Hobart on June 30th, and arrived in Hobson's Bay in July, 1838. Several members of the Wesleyan Church hearing of his arrival, went to welcome him. So soon as the first greetings were over, Mr. William Witton, who had been resident in Melbourne for a short time, but had formerly been an active member of the

Society in Launceston, presented his credentials as a Local Preacher, which were found satisfactory. Then the minister and layman, walking arm in arm, proceeded from Sandridge to Melbourne, accompanied with others of the deputation, exchanging Christian salutations and talking over the prospects of Christian enterprise amongst the white settlers and the aboriginal population. It was a time of great joy and delightful intercourse, when for a short time, pastor and people in the small number that then represented Methodism in the land, could mingle together their prayers and praise in acts of worship, hear God's word expounded, and plan the beginning of the godly work and goodly Church which were afterwards to be accomplished facts in their midst. The stay of Mr. Tuckfield was but short, but it was a spiritual feast time to the people in Melbourne. Mr. Hurst came early in 1839. The story of their arduous self-denying labour amongst the natives at Buntingdale is of great interest. Till the arrival of Rev. Mr. Orton, they appear to have supplied services to Melbourne once a month.

The benevolent action of the authorities at the Colonial Office in London brought some important help to the infant Church in Melbourne. They appointed Mr. Robinson as chief protector, and other gentlemen, Messrs. Sievewright. Parker, Thomas, Dredge, and Le Sœuf, as assistant protectors to the Aborigines. Of these gentlemen, Messrs. E. S. Parker, and James Dredge were active Wesleyans. The former was a man of cultivated intelligence, considerable force of character, and with a style of speaking remarkable for its clearness, chasteness, and fluency. His apparently impromptu speaking in committee, on the platform, or from the pulpit, as the writer who has heard him frequently can testify, had an even flow of choice, picked words and neat sentences, which, if reported verbatim, would read like the finished style of a practised writer. Not a word out of place, not a word used for which one could readily suggest a better, no high flown phrases, his speech was a well of pure "English undefiled." He was one of the few speakers that one hears in a life-time to whom it is always a pleasure to listen for the musical flow and clear utterance of fit language in our native tongue. He had been for a short time a Wesleyan minister in England, and continued to the day of his death a most acceptable Lay Preacher in the pulpits of our denomination. Mr. James Dredge was a holy man, a brother like to Barnabas, "a good man and full of the Holy Ghost," a man of prayer and power, who was in labours more abundant for the spread of His Master's kingdom during the early years of this colony's history.

Mr. Orton's journal, under the date April, 1839, records that Messrs. Parker and Dredge resided near Melbourne, and had been ministering the Word of Life to the people. They had kept the Society together, and had conducted public services, but had received instructions from the Government soon to go on their respective stations in the interior. Shortly after the arrival of Messrs. Parker and Dredge they made a house to house visitation of all professing Wesleyans in Melbourne. This visit was stimulating to the piety and zeal of the little flock of Wesleyans which had somewhat drooped through the lack of leaders, and through too much eagerness in money-making. The little Society much regretted that these devoted men could remain but a short time with them; but as their official work was with the blacks, they soon departed up the country. Mr. Parker formed a station for the blacks near Mt. Franklin, where he met with some partial success in defending them from the encroaching habits of degraded whites, and in teaching them some elements of commercial and industrial knowledge and of Christianity.

As the congregation in Swanston-street grew, the Society set about two things—making a clamour for an appointed and settled minister for them, and securing a better site and church building. Their repeated letters obtained the consent of the Rev. Mr. M'Kenny, at that time Superintendent of Wesleyan Missions and resident in Sydney, that the Rev. Mr. Orton should transfer himself to Melbourne for a few months, prior to carrying out his intended departure to England. Mr. J. J. Peers was again the principal agent in securing the amount wherewith to build a new church. He collected with unwearied energy most of the money for the building; when it was completed the Quarterly meeting acknowledged by its vote and gave him thanks "for his indefatigable and continued exertions on behalf of the Melbourne chapel." Mr. Symons justly says that "Methodism in Melbourne is indebted to few men more than to Mr. Peers." According to the same writer: —"For some time before his death his health was delicate; his sickness was borne with Christian submission and fortitude, and in peace he passed away to join the chorus of the redeemed, who unceasingly sing the song of Moses and of the Lamb." The site of the new church in Collins-street was not obtained without difficulty. Mr. Witton was instrumental in persuading the Trustees to ask for this half acre of land, in preference to a piece on Eastern Hill, which was of larger size, but removed farther from the centre of population. They sent off their application to the Government at Sydney, but, as soon as the report of it got abroad, some citizens got up an opposition memorial, yet the petition of the Trustees was granted ere the counter petition was received by the Board of Land and Works. The grant had attached to it the condition that £300 should be raised by the Trustees and lodged in the bank in proof of *bona fides* in this Church undertaking, which was accordingly done, as we have seen, chiefly by the energy of Mr. Peers. The land, with building thereon, was in 1857 sold for nearly £40,000.

The statement of Mr. Orton speaks of his again visiting Melbourne in 1839, landing on April 10th, when he found the wilderness which he had left on his previous visit, converted into an extensive town, containing four or five hundred houses. When the settlement was first formed, swamp lands adjoined the few miles of the Yarra's course below Melbourne, ti-tree scrub was plentifully skirting its banks, sod huts, and houses of wattle and daub were its best tenements; but now the land had been cleared from the scrub on the river banks, and the sloping rises which extended back from the river had been covered with houses, some of which were substantial and handsome buildings. He records, at this visit, that "the Methodist Society has swelled to the number of thirty members, a commodious place of worship has been erected by their liberality, in which two or three persons officiated as Local Preachers." The cost of the first church was £250, nearly all paid by the time of Mr. Orton's visit. As far as circumstances would allow, this Society was organized by Mr. Orton, a Sabbath school put in order, prayer meetings established, and the distribution of tracts, which had previously received the attention of a few individuals, zealous for the cause of God, was stimulated and extended.

He records also the "zeal, assiduity, and careful attention of several leading members of the Society to the cause which lay near their hearts, under whose nurturing regard the Society and congregations had not only maintained their position, but had encouragingly progressed."

Mr. Orton preached twice in Melbourne on the 21st April. On the 28th the preachers were—Mr. Hurst in the morning, Mr. Tuckfield, afternoon in the open-air, Mr. Orton in the afternoon, at Mr. Langhorn's (or Langham's); evening at church, Mr. Orton preached, and administered the Sacrament of the Lord's Supper. On the 19th, Mr. Dredge took him to an assembly of natives, 400 to 500 being present. He spoke to them through Mr. Dredge as interpreter. He subsequently preached at Mr. Robinson's (Protector of Aborigines), and notes that six Tasmanian natives from Flinders Island were present. These understood English, and sang several hymns correctly. On May

2nd, he left Melbourne for a lengthened tour in the interior, desiring to learn more about the natives, and about any opening for mission work amongst them. His first week was spent in journeying around by Macedon, to Geelong, which he reached on Saturday. On the Sunday following he preached in Mr. Fisher's barn. Then he journeyed to Barwon and Buntingdale, and spent the rest of the month to the westward, amongst the stations of the squatters. On May 30th he was among the Stony Rises, and arrived in Geelong on June 1st. He records sad cases of ill-treatment of the blacks by some few of the whites, and makes grave charges against one or two. On his arrival in Geelong, he received imperative orders from the London Committee to proceed to the Friendly Islands to investigate some allegations of a traveller which turned out to be groundless charges. But Mr. Orton did not reach the Friendly Islands. He left Point Henry on June 3rd, and after a time reached Sydney, where he was delayed till the end of January, 1840, thence he proceeded to Mangungu, N.Z., awaiting the *Triton*. When the *Triton* came in May, 1840, he found that he had been superseded, and his mission of inquiries entrusted to another. These delays, the suspense, the vacillation of the Committee, the detention from his family for so many months, with no regular work done, preyed heavily upon the good man's mind, but he bore up bravely and nobly. He had, on Rev. John Waterhouse's arrival in Hobart in 1838, received leave from the London Committee to return to England. The execution of that project had been deferred because of his short visit to Victoria in April and May, 1839, and now might well have been carried out. But in heroic self-sacrifice, anxious for the welfare of the Melbourne Society, at this time without a Minister, despite his depression of mind, he proceeded to Sydney and volunteered to Mr. M'Kenny to take charge for a while of the Melbourne Circuit, and to delay his intended departure to England. That offer was gladly accepted, and we shall find him again in Melbourn in October 1840, welcomed with glad delight by the infant Church.

The Christian care of the Aboriginal race was brought prominently forward on the occasion of the meeting to form a local branch of the Wesleyan Missionary Society. Methodism is essentially Missionary; and it has carried the doctrines of the Cross not alone among English-speaking races, but amongst people strange in tongue to, and far distant in location from, the inhabitants of the British Isles. Some pulsations of the Missionary spirit in the breast of British Methodism reached to the extremities of the body in this distant land. Those pulsations, perhaps, beat feebly, as compared with the life in the mother country, but they are here, nevertheless. Because the mission spirit, caring for the benighted, and the despised of other races, was present in this Southern hemisphere, the earliest Methodist ministers came here, and the first Missionary meeting was held. That meeting took place in the Wesleyan Church, on Monday, September 16th, 1839. A statement of the rise and progress of the Wesleyan Aboriginal Mission was read. As usual in such meetings, resolutions were proposed, speeches made, a committee was formed, contributions were solicited, and a collection was taken up. Amongst the speakers were the Revs. B. Hurst, W. Waterfield, James Clow, James Forbes, and F. Tuckfield; also, Dr. Patrick, and Messrs. Robert Reeves and E. S. Parker. The first Committee consisted of the Rev. B. Hurst, Messrs. E. S. Parker, J. E. Dredge, J. Fenton, J. J. Peers, W. Witton, J. T. Smith, with A. Thomson, Esq., treasurer, for Geelong; Mr. George Lilly, treasurer for Melbourne; and the Rev. F. Tuckfield and Mr. W. Willoughby as secretaries.

The Rev. William Simpson, a Wesleyan minister, then stationed in Launceston, paid a visit to the young colony and the rising church in 1839, and thus records his impressions in a letter, headed, " Melbourne, December 19th, 1839," which was written to the Rev. John

Waterhouse, of Hobart:—"Melbourne is situated two or three miles above the extreme head of Port Philip Bay, and possesses the advantage of a stream of fine fresh water. It occupies two very gentle hills with the valley between them, and contains, perhaps, from 3000 to 4000 inhabitants, a large proportion of whom are Scotch, and, of course, Presbyterian. They have the largest place of worship in the town, although the Independents have a chapel in course of erection which will be much larger. Our chapel is much smaller, but literally crowded at each service on the Sunday, especially in the evening, and, were I going to remain here, I think that instead of suffocating myself and congregation in so small a place I should turn out of doors. If we had a man to fix here, a chapel might be commenced immediately. Ground has been reserved by Government in a most eligible situation, but it will not be secured until the parties concerned have raised £300, and actually deposited it in a bank, forwarding the receipt of the cashier to the Colonial Secretary. So says Mr. M'Kenny, of Sydney. In consequence of this, I met the provisional Trustees, who agreed to raise the money at once, and get a grant of the land. This is of the more importance just now, as this very piece of land is applied for by the gentlemen in town for the erection of a Post-office, and if we do not lay in our claim, it is possible that they might deprive us of it. We could raise pretty nearly £1000 to commence, which would enable us to build half a chapel, running a temporary partition behind, so that we could complete it when we had funds. In the meantime we are getting sadly behind for want of some one being permanently settled here. . . . From all I have seen I should say we want a man here with his eyes open, and who will be prompt in adopting, and firm in carrying out, his measures; and the more I think of it, the more I am convinced of the propriety of our District appointment, for a man more fitted than Mr. Manton, I don't think we have, and a better field for missionary exertion I don't think we have in either colony. I am quite confident that in Van Dieman's Land there is is no place equal to this in importance, exclusive of Hobart Town and Launceston, and my opinion is that *this place ought to be occupied at once*, if possible, though some other place might be only partially supplied in consequence. I regret very much that a journey to Buntingdale is impracticable, as I should feel considerable pleasure in paying it a visit. It would keep me from my own circuit too long. The shop of poor Mr. Blanch was blown up on Tuesday last, and himself and wife killed, and three other persons seriously injured. Young Shoobridge narrowly escaped and has lost a good deal of property."

I have already stated that the first anniversary tea-meeting of the Sunday school was held at the time of Mr. Simpson's visit. The school at its organization had as superintendent, Mr. Thomas Forster; secretary, Mr. Theodore Dredge, junr.; Mr. Andrew Crockett, treasurer. Mr. and Mrs. Thacker, Mr. Webb, Mr. Alley, Mr. Lobb and family from Hobart, are mentioned as being present at the tea meeting, in active sympathy with the school. The Brunswick-street Sunday school is said to have been commenced a short time after this with four scholars.

Mr. Orton came to Melbourne on Saturday, October 3rd, 1840, to take for a time the pastoral charge of the Society, which now consisted of eighty members, under the care of four Leaders, having also seven Local Preachers. The small Church in Swanston-street was then crowded to excess. His account says that the new Church in Collins-street was in course of erection. Under his administration the several parts of the Methodist economy and services were soon in vigorous operation. Two additional classes were formed, and by December the number of members had increased to 109.

Mr. Orton preached in Melbourne on Sunday, October 4th, and again on October 11th, but on the 12th he has recorded in his journals one of those cruel and despicable

B

proceedings against the black natives, sometimes by arbitrary and unwise officials, more frequently by merciless individuals in private stations, which blots the history of the treatment of natives by the white immigrants in the early years of our colonization. A charge of plunder and murder of white persons had been laid against some natives (the latter part of the charge apparently groundless). This day (the 11th) natives from several tribes, a hundred or two, were reported to be near the town. The officials ordered out soldiers and police for their capture. The natives were surrounded, but as one attempted to run away he was shot dead by a sergeant, without any orders to fire. The rest were driven into town, about a hundred drafted off to prison, and others confined in a shed. During the night some escaped by undermining the foundation of the place; the alarm was given, indiscriminate firing took place, and another native (said to be one of the quietest, and not attempting to escape) was shot by the police. Mr. Orton's own comment is in these words:—" Thus, on the mere ground of suspecting two or three individuals, several tribes are forcibly and cruelly made prisoners, without any warrant of justice, nearly all of whom (if not all) are innocent of their offence, deprived of their liberty, and some murdered into the bargain. And yet these unhappy beings are declared to be Her Majesty's liege subjects. . . . How would such conduct be borne by British subjects at home, and how would it be tolerated by the British Government, if fairly represented to the authorities in England." Upon the trial of these prisoners who could not understand the depositions and evidence, only the shadow of a charge could be brought against twelve persons, the rest were set at liberty. Early in January, 1841, ten were brought to trial, the evidence showed plunder of food, and firing or threatening to fire, by the natives, but upon great provocation, and no person was wounded. They were found guilty and sentenced to ten years' imprisonment in the hulks. One native, attempting to escape afterwards from the vessel, was shot and severely wounded. But he and the rest were ultimately set at liberty, as Judge Willis discovered that the whole of the proceedings had been illegal.

This farce of justice occurring in other cases, the fact that native evidence was not received by the Court throughout this period, the arbitrariness of the authorities, and the repeated cruelties of the white settlers vexed the soul of this righteous man, and indignant and repeated are his entries and comments on these unrighteous proceedings. He has seven cases of violence and massacre particularly specified in his journal, founded not on hearsay evidence, but on the depositions shown to him by the Protectors, officers of the State; some of the cases showing wholesale slaughter. In one instance eighty natives were slain in exterminating massacre, apparently because when the firing commenced on the part of the whites, one of the assailants had been shot by a person of his own party, which rendered the whole desperate and merciless. No legal proceedings were of avail in a Court of Law, because native evidence was rejected, and the testimony of the miscreants themselves was the only direct evidence on the part of the whites. Mr. Westgarth has stated:—"In one neighbourhood, near Mount Rouse, during the years 1842-4 not less than two hundred natives were shot by the settlers." There will be a day of reckoning for these things in a higher court. We are not prosecuting, nor prisoner's counsel, but merely annalists, who have to refer to these dark pages of Colonial history, as they touch upon the Methodist story, and portray the sympathetic yearning for the preservation, uplifting, and salvation of the Aborigines possessed by this good Methodist pioneer. The unhappy condition of the natives weighed heavily upon the good man's mind, the mission at Buntingdale was not the success that he had strongly hoped for, many harassing events transpired which tried his spirit, fortitude, and patience, and his health began to give way.

The first Quarterly meeting of the circuit was held at the Minister's residence, situate in Russell-street, on Friday, January 28th, 1841. This is a meeting which manages the financial affairs pertaining to the support of the Ministry, reviews and initiates measures for the supply of Christian ordinances and carrying on the conservative and aggressive work of religion within the bounds of the Circuit. The Circuit may be one congregation, but is usually an aggregate of congregations, united in a spiritual and financial bond for Church work and enterprise. The record of this first Quarterly meeting states in ink (although the writing has been crossed out in pencil) that Mr. Abel Thorpe and Mr. R. E. Bourne, were unanimously elected Circuit Stewards. Churches were required for Newtown and Williamstown, and Building Committees were appointed for the two places respectively. It further states that the meeting was one of unanimity and affection, attended with prayers and "confident expectation, that this infant Society would become a praise in the earth; and, under the direction and fostering care of the Head of the Church, would prove a blessing to the rapidly-increasing population of the land." We presume that the funds of the Circuit were aided by a Government grant, as in the estimates for Port Philip for 1840, a Wesleyan Minister had an allowance of £150 placed to his credit. The members at this first Quarterly meeting were the Rev. Joseph Orton, and Messrs Dredge, Thorpe, Witton, Wilkinson, Peers, Forster, Wellard, Crockett, Willoughby, and Smith.

Mr. Orton was a man of medium size, with dark hair and pale features, earnest and somewhat fiery in his style of preaching. We suppose that he was of nervous temperament, as he had a habit of twirling his fingers in the curly locks of his hair, or of winding his watch chain around one finger, when speaking to an audience. That individuality which is betrayed by a man's favourite forms of speech was marked in him. Few sermons were preached without this phrase coming into use, " darkening counsel or words without knowledge." Other marked phrases are retained by those who listened to him, and who have survived him to this day. His sermons in the body and bulk of them have passed away from living memory, but the favourite quotations or phrases remain to memorize the sermons and the man. He was a disciplinarian, and had love of order. He was very intent on doing good while his day of work lasted, for at this period of his life his physical frame was considerably shattered, needed rest, and was giving premonitions of that speedy dissolution which shortly afterwards took place. Whilst he stayed in the Melbourne pastorate, services were established at Brighton, Brunswick, Williamstown, and other surburban villages, as they were then, but which are populous municipalities now.

Mr. Orton records in his journal that "the first stone of a chapel, two-and-a-half miles from Melbourne, was laid to-day," December 27th, 1841, whether at Newtown or Brunswick we cannot decide.

On Mr. Wilkinson's arrival, Mr. Orton stayed a while in Victoria, then went to Sydney to consult Mr. M'Kenny, there saw a doctor who forbade his preaching again because of an affection of the throat, came back to Victoria, and finally determined, in January, 1842, to make the voyage to England.

The Melbourne Methodists took leave of him at a farewell meeting, held on February 28th, where a written address, warmly appreciative of his pious care of them in the start and infancy of the cause, was presented to him. He could not speak to them, and his reply was written out and read. It was modest, grateful, trustful, but had the laboured, somewhat involved style of his writings. The good man's heart, however, warmed towards the people, and they parted from him with sadness and grateful love. The electricity latent in the human heart has certain special times of manifestation.

" 'Tis when we meet, 'tis when we part,
    Breaks forth the electric fire."

On March 2nd he went on board the *James*, Captain Todd; Rev. J. M'Kenny conducted a service on the deck at which crew, passengers, and visitors were present. The friends, taking leave, "sorrowed most of all, that they should see his face no more." His journal records many discomforts on the voyage, and the gradual failure of health in the cold latitudes. His earthly career closed on April 30th, 1842, and his mortal remains were committed to the deep, while the vessel was rounding Cape Horn. We may well count that a saintly and useful life was finished by a peaceful end.

We look back to him with reverence for the part he took in planting the Methodist Church in Victoria. He had some notion that his tender plant would grow into a giant tree with wide-spreading branches, and bearing abundant fruit. But neither he nor his compeers saw what a halo of imperishable renown would surround his name amongst future generations of Methodists; because, given the hour, he was the man, under Divine Providence, to seize the early opportunity of planting on these shores, and in this fertile land, so vigorous an offshoot of the Methodism of this Southern world.

> "To those who walk beside them, great men seem
> Mere common earth, but distance makes them stars;
> As dying limbs do lengthen out in death,
> So grows the stature of their after fame."

We remark concerning his early helpers, less known and less prominent in the work than he, laymen who were early identified with the Melbourne Wesleyan Church. Mr. Wellard was a native of Essex, who had joined the Methodist Church in early life, came to Tasmania with some intention of employment as a religious teacher, then migrated to Victoria, and laboured long and usefully as a Methodist Local Preacher, having won the esteem of many for his unblemished Christian life.

Mr. Crockett was an Irish Methodist, straight, stalwart, industrious, hospitable; resident afterwards in the interior at Mansfield. Mr. Thorpe was in a good social position, and was much respected.

Mr. Thomas Forster was afterwards a prominent member and official of the Church in Geelong. A pillar of the Church, stout, sturdy, strong, reliable.

Mr. James Smith was a saintly man, wearing in youth and manhood a genial smile, that seemed almost like heavenly radiance when his head grew grey, and his heart ripe in holiness in after years. He was long a witness by lip and life of perfect love, most indefatigable in his private labours for the good of his fellows, acceptable as an occasional preacher, although having no wide range of thought or vocabulary; generous, bountiful, a lover of prayer and of good men, devotedly attached to the Church of his choice, but mostly a lover of Christ, and hence having a catholic spirit towards all who love the Lord Jesus.

Mr. William Witton is the surviving member of the first Quarterly meeting, and one whose Christian course has been coincident and contemporaneous with the rise and progress of Methodism in Victoria. He is a stout, robust man of middle stature, with grey eyes, somewhat florid complexion, and of manly address; a father in our Israel, the patriarch of the whole family of Victorian Methodists; among the first to unfurl and plant the Methodist flag in this land—a flag which has not yet been hauled down, nor shall it be while time shall last, for it is designed to show that the land is a heritage of King Jesus. He was a pioneer in the Western District to thread the whilom wilderness, and in different spots to turn up the virgin soil and scatter broadcast the seeds of life, which are now bearing a grand harvest; a man, who, long ago, was of our good brethren, the Lay Preachers, classed A1 in the register, and now, after years of service, he has no lower classification. He is still hale and hearty, sound in the faith, strong for labour, and carrying about the glad tidings of the kingdom of God in the Warragul Circuit in Gippsland. In the commerce which truth carries on, he yet goes to and fro laden with the precious commodities of the Evangel of Christ, and with those choice products which piety and prayer alone can secure for ourselves and carry to others.

FIRST ADVANCES.
CHAPTER III.

WE sketch in this account, chiefly the outer phenomena and manifest workings of Methodism in its rise and progress within the colony; but those outer manifestations have an inner life which we have no wish to hide from mental view. Yet, to discover and disclose those hidden springs of action is no easy work. Can we trace up the streams of benevolence and beneficence to their fountain head? Can we analyse and show the superior and inferior motives and aims which prompted and governed this religious movement? Can we note the life germs which in their development and growth have given existence to this body of institutions, members, adherents, specialties, and activities which we call Victorian Methodism? We do not desire to make any subtle analysis of this work, nor give any far-fetched reasons to account for the growth and spread of this section of the Church of Christ. Our simple explanation of it is "the Divine life in the soul of man." Its leading motive of action has been, and is, Christian "faith which works by love." That chief motive may have been in part adulterated here and there with partizan feeling, desire for Church aggrandisement, or the multiplication of a sect. Human works are imperfect, and some dross may have mixed with the fine gold of Christian spirit and action. Yet, we think, that unchallenged, or at least not successfully to be controverted, is the claim for the leading spirits of Early Methodism and the great bulk of its members, that they were actuated by a pure desire for the glory of God in the spread of religion, and the salvation of men. Our creed in this matter is a short and simple one. He that loveth God will love his brother also. We do not go into minute dissection in order to find out life. No scalpel is used to find out human life. Let the reality of it discover itself. It has its subtleties, which evade your research. It has also its vitalities and its evidences, which make themselves plain enough to the learned mind or common understanding. Religious life has a few simple elements. Those primitive forms appear in almost endless diversity in the complicated matters of Church movement and action. We give some of these, but we cannot pretend to trace out their diversified combination and ramifications, for in religious life the relations existing between the inner and the outer, the spirit and body, the effort and the success are so subtle, far reaching and complicated, that the cleverest man on earth would be at fault correctly to delineate or fully to describe them. You have in libraries, thousands of books, but twenty-four letters in their combination are the elements of all the words, sentences, paragraphs, that they contain. So faith, hope, joy, love, peace, purity, patience, obedience, and a few other graces of the Divine Spirit are the letters from which are made the volumes and virtues of Christian lives, and the incidents and annals of Christian history. The reader will bear in mind as he goes on with this story, that we assume the existence and working of these graces and this Divine spirit, even though our account may not throughout keep the facts and truths in especial prominence. We believe such agencies to have wrought in these good men and grey fathers of our Church, the story of whose lives, so far as it affects Victorian Methodism, we briefly rehearse.

We make no apology for taking account of some small matters, which to others may appear trivial and unimportant, nor can we pass by the course of regular circuit occurrences, though the record of figures and routine may be voted dry. In these small matters of the present are signs of the important future. The straw on the surface is an index of the direction of the current, the leaf is a type or pattern of the whole tree; "the child is father to the man."

Resuming the thread of narrative, and detailing the second portion of our story from the time of Mr. Wilkinson's becoming the resident Superintendent to the discovery of gold in the land, we chronicle the holding of the second Quarterly meeting of the Melbourne Circuit. The Rev. Samuel Wilkinson had arrived, as the first Minister regularly appointed, by arrangements made in Sydney, to occupy the post of Wesleyan minister in Melbourne. He came on March 9th, 1841. He is a genial kind-hearted man, with no brilliancy as a preacher, yet sound in doctrine, and steadfast in his work. He still lives, and is pursuing his honourable and unblemished career as a Methodist preacher, and a servant of Christ. He presided over this Quarterly meeting held in May 14th, 1841, at which were also present:—Rev. J. Orton, and Messrs. Witton, Wellard, Dredge, Crockett, Forster, Peers, Overton, and Thomas Wilkinson. Some forward steps had been taken for the erection of the Newtown (Fitzroy) Church, and it was proposed to place one at Brickfield, believed to be at South Melbourne. The number of members had increased to 105, and a further increase to 118, was reported at next Quarterly meeting on July 23rd. Mr. Marsden was appointed to succeed Mr. Bourne as Circuit Steward. Land for a Church at the place now called Coburg had been promised, and a Committee was appointed to get means for its erection. But the event of this quarter was the opening of the Collins-street Church. It was situate on half an acre of land, was 60 or 65 x 45ft., with a gallery at one end, and cost £3000. Subsequently it was lengthened by 25 feet to 90 feet. The materials were of brick. It was in the Grecian order of architecture, and was an ornament to that part of the town. All its appointments were in keeping with that chaste and useful style of building. It has been a hallowed place to many. The regular worshipper counted it as his home nearest to heaven. The youths of Methodism revered it as " our holy and beautiful house where our fathers worshipped Thee." Immigrants, after months of privation of religious ordinances, regarded it as a harbour of refuge and place of rest ; and we have known such to shed tears of joy as they stood in the porch of the temple, or entered to enjoy anew the feast of Christian sociability and truth, to which they had been accustomed in former days. Did not God also regard it as the place of His feet made glorious with proffered worship and imparted blessing, as His earthly alter from whence arose to heaven the incense of devotion and praise, and His sanctuary of grace, musical with the voices of worshippers, and irradiated with the beams of His everlasting truth and love. Did not God look on it as a witness for truth and Divine things, amid the surging world of bustle and deceits and sharpness that was around ? A witness for religion amid the tumult of commerce ? A structure pointing to heaven 'mid the multiplied affairs which were binding to earth ? We may certainly do so, as hundreds of our fathers have done.

"For it is well amid the whirr,
Of restless wheels and busy stir,
To find a quiet spot, where live
Fond pious thoughts conservative,
That ring to an old chime
And bear the moss of time."

The first offerings of praise and worship within its walls were on Thursday, 24th June, 1841, when the Rev. W. Waterfield preached in the morning ; text, " Thy kingdom come"; collection, £17. Rev. J. Orton preached in the evening from Psalm cxxxii., verse 7, 8, and 9 ; collection, £35. The opening services were continued on Sunday, 27th, by Mr. Tuckfield preaching in the morning from Psalm lxxxvii., verse 5. Rev. Mr. Forbes in the evening from Acts viii. chapter, verse 5 ; collections at two services, £70.

The Rev. Samuel Wilkinson continued as the Circuit Minister until the end of 1842, and the Circuit, under his administration, was blessed with a steady progress. In April of this year the membership numbered 162 full members, and 11 on trial, an advance of 55 on those reported at the first Quarterly meeting held in Mr. Wilkinson's time. The first steps were also taken for a preacher's appointment at Geelong, hitherto visited occasionally by the Ministers resident with the natives at Buntingdale. At the Quarterly meeting held on April 8th, and again by adjournment on May 20th, so good a field did Geelong appear, that Mr. James Dredge was requested to labour there. The promising youth of Geelong Methodism has been amply fulfilled in later days. Rev. J. C. Symons states that " Mr. Dredge was a man of superior mental endowments, great excellence of character, and an able preacher. This appointment was most satisfactory to the people, and most opportune for the interests of the Church. His services were highly valued, and were very useful." They were continued from June, 1842, until 1846, when, as health failed, he sought recovery by a voyage to England. Captain Dalgarno, who commanded the vessel in which he sailed, speaks in the most glowing terms of his saintly spirit, and the suasive power, on behalf of religion, which he exercised on all round. He was maturing for heaven, for he fell asleep in Jesus ere the vessel reached the English shore. "His memory is warmly cherished by those who were favoured with his ministry ; and his name is perpetuated by many members of his family, who have been, and still continue, identified with the Wesleyan Church in Victoria."

In Mr. Wilkinson's time, the progress of the church was quietly and steadily going on. The colony did not suffer from the depression of its secular interests, which took place in the years immediately subsequent to this time, nor were the people stirred with such a rage of excitement as came about in the time of the gold fever. As the colony was making quiet progress, so in Church affairs, there was an even step, a steady march onward. The Church had rest, and the members "walking in the fear of the Lord, and the comfort of the Holy Ghost, were multiplied." This was owing, in human agency, not only to the urbanity, wisdom, and quiet power of the pastor, but also to the fervour and activity of Christian helpers and members then living in Melbourne. Who that calls to mind the cautious wisdom and firm integrity of Charles Stone, the sunny warmth and cheeriness of James Smith, the fire and firmness of Oliver Parnham, the power in prayer, and glowing ardour of soul possessed by Robert Galagher, and of others then in connection with the Melbourne Church, whose lives have been lengthened to or near this present date, but would know that spiritual forces were at work in them (such as Methodism has prized and utilized in her godly laymen), that would tell immensely for good in the circle of their acquaintance and in the whole [community? These were men not given to rant and rhapsody in devotion, nor making great stir in public life; but nevertheless, by their consistent piety, their well-ordered homes and families, their honest upright walk in business affairs and daily life, and their conscientious work in Church lines, they accredited the Church of their choice. They were pillars in the Church, epistles and exponents of the faith, and mainsprings of religious movement and activity felt to the outmost circle of Melbourne life. The beautiful regularity of their Christian lives was to be seen not only in conscientious attention to public duties and ordinances, but in the wise government of, and harmonious action in, their Christian homes. The sunniest, best fenced, most fertile spot in God's vineyard is a Christian's home. These abounded in the Methodism of that time. The counterpart of the Cotter's Saturday night, celebrated in Scottish songs and by Northern bard, could have been found in such homes. Their interiors would have presented no luxuries, nor many decorations by æsthetic art, but the plainness of furniture becoming the home. Simplicity of dress befitting the men and women, and homespun virtues that adorned them most, were readily to be marked in them. Quiet thrift, with cordial hospitality; plodding industry, with open-handed beneficence; reverence for authority, for religion, for God. The Bible having the chief place on the book-shelf, its pages wide open at the family altar, its living truth enthroned in the heart. Other books, such as, "Lives of Early Methodists," the numbers of the "Methodist Magazine," or the "Christian Miscellany," "Foxe's Book of Martyrs," "Bunyan's Pilgrim Progress," "Baxter's Saint's Rest," would have a place by the Book of Books, for family reading and for religious nurture. The time for rising and for rest, for private devotion, for family worship, for secular duties, would be as regular as the clock, and less noisily pursued. But the cheer would come in at the visit of a friend, the calling in of a neighbour, the birthday anniversary, the pastor's call, when would be the uplifted voice in holy song, for these Methodists loved music, and Methodist tunes were lively and lustily sung. The exuberance of spirit, and religious joy would flow for the most in strains of joyous song. The almost quaker-like simplicity of garb, the homely virtues, the meek and quiet spirit wore well in the rubs and duties of everyday life. They were a salt to conserve and flavour the piety of the Church! May they be long continued!

The Rev. William Schofield succeeded Mr. Wilkinson as Minister. He was present at the Quarterly meeting of January 24th, 1843. He did not neglect the business arrangements of the Church, but was an adept in figures. The details of Circuit income are now recorded. They furnish the items of "Class and Ticket money, £36 12s.; Quarterly collections, £15; marriage fee, £5; arrears, £1; from District Treasurer, for Mr. Schofield's travelling expenses, £26 1s. 3d.; total income for the quarter, £121 7s. 6d. Mr. Schofield was of medium height and of build inclined to stoutness. A man of shrewdness and energy, sometimes directed into secular channels more than was deemed fit by some of his flock; but, nevertheless, in the main attending to the best interests of his people. He had the faculty of interesting young men in religious truth, gathered them around him by sympathy and fatherly kindness, formed many into a Bible class, and was the agent of spiritual good to a number. The Hon. F. E. Beaver, then a youth, was by him led to the Bible class, to the class meeting, and to Christ. A notable and widespread revival of religion occurred in this minister's time. Methodism has been remarkable for these health-giving epidemics. Where has not Methodism, which is the child of revival, been signalised in its history in any place by those heart-stirring times, when multitudes, as with one consent, turn from the ways of worldliness and sin to the paths of righteousness? Where in outlying British provinces and possessions has not the pious British soldier been the means of a like active propagation of Christian truth, Methodist ordinances, and religious blessing and success? A soldier, named Rudkin, one in a detachment of troops then stationed in Melbourne, was a leading instrument in this revival. He was a man of prayer, and, therefore, a man of power. A flame of fire himself, he kindled the holy fire of religious love and enthusiasm in others. Although labouring in a private station, and sustaining no public office, he was of eminent use in leading sinners to Christ; and in increasing the interest in experimental godliness in both soldiers and civilians.

In Mr. Schofield's term we note the appearance of these official Laymen at the Quarterly meeting, viz., Messrs. P. Dredge, Parnham, Grimshaw, Thompson, Fenton, Horton, indicating that these were leading and active members in the Church. Messrs. Jones and Forster were Circuit Stewards in 1844, and Messrs. Sidney Stephen, and Burns in 1845.

The specialties of religious services were open air meetings, some of which were very successful, and a prayer meeting at 5.30 a.m. determined on for every morning, but we know not how far this latter meeting was kept up in interest and attendance. We, however, give the good fathers credit for all that this early devotion implies. In the few entries respecting the number of members, we find the return of 181 full members, and 22 on trial at the meeting of April 11th, 1843, and the largely increased number of 360, with 9 on trial in January 11th, 1846, about three or four months after Mr. Schofield left. Some of the outlying places were growing, but were not strong, if the financial test be applied, for the income for the last quarter of 1844 was from Collingwood, 10s. 10d. quarterly collection; Brunswick, same collection, 3s. 1d., and class money, 16s. 8d.; and from Williamstown, collection, £1 3s.; and class money, £1 1s 10d. However, as the income from the Circuit exceeded, in 1845, the expenditure by £62, the Quarterly meeting felt strong enough to apply for a second Minister, and also to apply for the appointment of one to Portland. An increase of the Ministerial staff took place in 1845, as the Rev. E. Sweetman was the presiding officer at the Quarterly meeting held on October 14th, 1845, and the Rev. W. Lowe was present at the succeeding one held in the Minister's house, Bourke-street, on January 6th, 1846. The writer had no personal acquaintance with the Rev. Mr. Sweetman, but had heard about him from early boyhood, owing probably to the singular coincidence, that from the Windsor Circuit in England, where his parents then resided, two men, bearing the names of Dove and Sweetman, had been recommended to the Methodist ministry, and had been sent out to the Mission work, one to Sierra Leone, and the other to Australia. Both were men of placid, amiable disposition, of courteous, gentlemanly bearing, and their whole temperament and behaviour corresponded with their names. Rev. Edward Sweetman was the effective and beloved superintendent in

Melbourne until January, 1850. Many stories are current of the calmness and self-command of the man, of his affable spirit towards others, and of his unruffled temper under trying circumstances. He had a colleague, full of fire and energy, in Mr. Lowe. Under their labours, with those of their fellow helpers, Methodism made steady progress, so that the number of members mounted up in October, 1847, to 412, with 51 on trial; and in December, same year, to 436, with 36 on trial. The Quarterly meeting repeatedly expressed by invitation, its desire to retain Mr. Sweetman, "an enlightened, faithful, and able minister of the Gospel," as its superintendent; and Mr. Lowe was again and again invited to remain. These were true yokefellows in the work of the Lord. As the income increased with the membership, application was made in 1846 for a third minister, and for one also to be stationed in Geelong. This was repeated in 1847, when the following resolution was added: —"That Mr. Symons of the *Maitland*, and Mr. Flockhart of the *Arbuthnot*, having preached at Melbourne with very great acceptance, this meeting has respectfully to request the Rev. W. Boyce to communicate with the Wesleyan Committee, and represent the wants of the colony with reference to Ministerial aid, and that the Melbourne Society would have great pleasure to receive either of the above brethren, should it be practicable to send them out." These gentlemen were eventually received into the Methodist Ministry in these lands. In these years Mr. J. R. Pascoe's name appears at official meetings, and for some time he was an influential layman in connection with the Melbourne Society. Mr. Walter Powell's name appears in the minutes of the Quarterly meeting on October 5th, 1847; also that of Mr. Wills in 1846, and that of Mr. Guthridge in 1848. The Rev. W. C. Currey was present at that held on January 4th, 1848. This, we presume, indicates the reinforcement of the Ministerial staff so much desired; and the formation of Geelong and places adjacent into a separate Circuit.

c

The return of members is thenceforth divided as pertaining to the respective Circuits, the numbers given in the British Minutes of Conference for 1848, being:—Melbourne, 295; Geelong, 129; Buntingdale, 2; and for the year 1849, being:—Melbourne, 294; Portland Bay, 34; Geelong, 134; Buntingdale, 2." The appointments named, in the British Minutes of those years, to stations in Victoria, were not regularly carried out in practice.

The cause at Newtown (afterwards Fitzroy) commenced with open air service in the bush, near what is now Moor-street and Carlton gardens. Messrs. Beaver, Morris, and others remember attending such services in the years 1841-2. The first Church was on the south side of Moor-street, near its intersection by Brunswick-street. This was followed by a stone Church erected in 1849, on the site of the present in Brunswick-street. The first Sunday school started at Newtown, had Mr. James Webb as superintendent; Mr. Beaver, secretary; Mrs. Westlake, Mr. South, and others as teachers. The Rev. Nathaniel Turner mentions his landing in Melbourne in December, 1846, and further records "I enjoyed the early Sabbath morning walk to the home of my friend Mr. Bell. On attending a delightful service in Collins-street, at which I heard Mr. Sweetman preach, I found myself surrounded by several Tasmanian friends, who were right glad to greet me. After dining, I visited Collingwood, where Mr. Lowe preached a profitable sermon. The congregation was good and deeply attentive, but the Chapel is a miserable affair. Here I found one of my greatly endeared spiritual children, Mr. Walter Powell, formerly of Launceston, in charge of a very interesting Sabbath school. I addressed a few words to encourage and stimulate the congregation before they parted. Several souls have lately been converted to God. At the evening services I assisted Mr. Sweetman in the administration of the Lord's Supper." The visit of this venerated man would be much prized, not only by his spiritual children, but by the Methodist congregations generally, to whom his name was as a "household word."

The cause was likely to grow that had connected with it a sage and able administrator such as Mr. Sweetman, a fervid preacher like to Mr. Lowe, staid and earnest men in middle life, like to Mr. John Wills and others, and intelli‧ gent, pious, enterprising young men, as Messrs. F. E. Beaver and Walter Powell. Accordingly, under God's blessing, with the influx of population and the spread of this suburb of Melbourne, this infant Society made rapid growth in numbers and influence, until it became a stronghold of Methodism. It has been, and remains to this day, a choice and fruitful field of Methodist culture, signalized as much as any place in and around Melbourne, for the steadfast piety of its members, and the liberality of its people, for the success of its school and mission enterprises, for the noble‧ bands of young people of both sexes, that have thrown themselves with zeal and thoughtfulness into the work of the Church, and for the influence for good that this Society has wielded upon the surrounding communities; as also for the many agents that it has sent out to leaven with the Gospel other places and lands. This religious fruitfulness can be traced back to the preparations and solid work of the period we have now in review. The ground was trenched deeply by faithful preachers, fervid prayers, holy living, and by the power of the Spirit of God upon the consciences and hearts of men, and it has proved itself a right fruitful soil. The blessing of Jehovah has rested upon this vineyard, as set forth in the prophet's words, "I the Lord do keep it, I will water it every moment, lest any hurt it, I will keep it night and day."

The period of which we are treating was marked more by steady advance than by fitful leaps of progress. The judicious superintendent worked well the ordinary means of Church life and activity, but he could travel out of beaten paths at times, and try new methods of aggression on the territories of darkness, and of accumulation of electric power in the Church. A camp meeting was appointed for Good Friday, 1848, and watch-night services were held quarterly in that year. Special services were held in 1849, and inaugurated by sermons on Sunday, January 14th, preached by the Rev. John Harcourt. At the April Quarterly meeting, resolutions were passed, enjoining a more strict attention to the reading of God's word, to private prayer, and family devotion. Mr. Harcourt proved himself an earnest preacher, a diligent pastor, and a most acceptable colleague. He is the soul of honour, with a sensitive and fervid temperament, somewhat precise, but courteous and gentlemanly, a good man, exact in his business habits, and throwing no mean talent and no fitful energies into the work of building churches. He did much pioneer work in the bush, in the newly-settled parts of the Western seaboard, and upon the goldfields, as well as contributing to the consolidation and growth of the Church in and around Melbourne. The Rev. E. Sweetman found in him a hearty colleague, and a kindred spirit. That Barnabas of our early Church, Mr. Sweetman, was truly a son of consolation, and continued through these years to knit hearts to himself, and win souls to Christ. He had a noble presence, and great suavity of manner; a most kindly heart, and a winsome piety; so that the man commended the message which he delivered in the name of the Master, and attracted many to the ways of piety. His pastoral wisdom is embalmed in the memory of many early colonists. Mr. Symons has paid tribute to his charm and power in the pulpit, and we give a part of his sketch:—" He was a preacher of a very superior order, and would have taken high rank in any place, where sense is esteemed more than sound, and where thoughts are more valued than words. There was a thoughtful vigour and an elegance of diction in the pulpit performances of Mr. Sweetman, which gave a great charm to his sermons, and which, added to a deep but quiet earnestness, made him a most interesting, useful, and profitable preacher." Mr. Symons must surely have taken for his model and ideal, a man in whose praise he is so enthusiastic. But a still better portraiture of him is given in that sweet English classic, the "Deserted Village." Mr. Sweetman was as fair a copy of Goldsmith's Village Preacher, as this Southern world has seen.

TRANSITION.

CHAPTER IV.

A NEW ecclesiastical period began with the years 1850 and 1851. The Victorian Church had become of such importance as to warrant the formation of it into a new District, and the appointment of the Rev. W. Butters as its first Chairman. Its title was at first "The Victorian Section of the Australian District," but it was really from this time a new District, distinct and separate from those of adjacent colonies, yet bound to them by their common relationship to the Home Connexion and the British Conference. The manhood of Victorian Methodism had come, it donned its ecclesiastical toga, as being of full age; and it had cause soon to use its best wits, and show itself worthy of its responsibility, for strange, unexpected, and extraordinary circumstances were soon to environ it. The upheaval and disorganization of society, and that irruption of numerous hordes of immigrants from other lands, marking the epoch of the goldfields, were soon to take place. It wanted a good pilot to guide the ecclesiastical ship, amidst the seething rush of waters and boiling deluges of events, that were soon to try the best skill of the steersman, and the utmost strength of the ship. These events would be more severe and critical than any passage through " The Rip " or " Narrows," or any voyage down rapids, almost as bad as " shooting Niagara." Where was the skilled pilot to be found? He was providentially at hand in the person of the Rev. W. Butters. Can we put him before our readers? Can we justly describe the man? Let us not be considered offensive or bizarre in our account, when we say that his was the name of a person, not of a thing; and of no inconsiderable person; he was a man, and a great man too. He, with his excellent wife, conjugated "to do" in all its tenses in his active life here, and he did not decline to suffer when privation, inconvenience, hardship, could promote the cause of his Master. He was a Hercules in his strength, a giant in intellect, a Saul in stature, a great man in our Israel. He used to speak of himself as a "buttress" to the Church; we think that he was a pillar; not an external support merely, but a strong internal column. He exerted a Samson's strength, not to pull down the temple, but to build it up. He lived and spoke, and acted for its edification. No one had more shrewd sense, or more sterling honesty. He was a man of understanding "to know the times." And when stirring times came, he was found sagacious in his counsel, far-seeing in his views, comprehensive in his grasp, prompt in his decision, and widely active in the employment of men and measures that would best serve the interests of religion and the permanent welfare of the people. He was a power in the pulpit. For the strength and cogency of his arguments, the lucid exposition of his subject, the fervour and almost white heat of his impassioned appeal, few men in Victorian pulpits can compare with him. He did not, even before a village congregation, bring a slip-shod manner, and an unprepared jumble of thoughts and words; but he was truly grand on great occasions. Sermons on "God's Inquest on the Lost Soul," "the Power and Work of the Holy Spirit," from Zech. iv., verse 6, 7, and other sermons that could be named, cannot be forgotten by those who heard them. In his instruction he was a master-builder in the city of God, laying a good foundation of Christian doctrine, building a solid superstructure of Christian experience and holiness. He had come hither as a man of renown. He had laboured among the degraded convicts of Port Arthur, the vilest of the vile, the hardened of the hardened, and from chain gang and manacled desperadoes, had won some trophies for the Redeemer. His zeal in his youthful ministry in Launceston had been signally owned of God in the conversion of sinners, and in the bringing many from among the socially respectable classes to the feet of Christ. After nearly 17 years spent in Tasmania, he came in the prime of his manhood and strength to conduct the affairs of the Methodist Church in Victoria, and to make full proof of his ministry. A sentence which dropped from his lips, on the first occasion that the writer heard him, well sets forth his spirit and his style of public address. Talking of Christian missions as individual, as well as collective work, he said, "I would read or pray, give or speak, go or stay, as God directs and helps me, so that I might in any wise add strength to the pinion, and speed to the flight of the angel flying in the midst of heaven, having the everlasting Gospel to preach unto them that dwell on the earth." Rev. xiv., verse 6.

Mr. Butters presided at the Melbourne Quarterly meeting on April 2nd, 1850, when a Wesleyan Immigrants' Friend Committee was formed for the purpose of rendering assistance in any practical way to new arrivals; for a stream of immigration was setting in. This was another step in the work that culminated in the well-known "Wesleyan Immigrants' Home." Amongst new names at the Quarterly meeting this year and the next, appear those of Messrs. Hyde, Cameron, Little, Head, Baldwin, and Thomas. Messrs. J. R. Pascoe and Henry Jennings were Circuit Stewards for these two years. A chapel at Richmond was projected, as Mr. Henry Miller had given a piece of land for that purpose—a small one had previously been built. The Day school movement received a great impetus through Mr. Butters' direction. The first mention of a Wesleyan Day school in Melbourne was at the Quarterly meeting of October, 1845, when it was determined to establish one.

This was shortly after in efficient operation. A school house was built in Lonsdale-street on the present site of the Wesley Church, and a school started during the pastorate of the Rev. Mr. Harcourt. The building was used for religious service on Sunday afternoon and evening in the year 1851. Other new schools were founded in the suburbs of Melbourne and in other parts of the colony, so that when the statistics were tabulated at the time of the first District meeting, the return gave 20 Day school teachers, and 699 scholars on the roll. This movement received a great extension on the gold fields. The popularizing of Day schools permeated with religious instruction, was brought about by Church enterprise, and was fostered largely by the liberality and care of the Methodist pastorate and people.

When the first District meeting was held, which was on September 9th, 1851, the Rev. W. Butters was chairman; Rev. F. Lewis, secretary; and Rev. W. Lightbody, John Harcourt, and Samuel Waterhouse were present. Mr. Waterhouse had been recommended to the work of the Ministry by the Tasmania District Meeting, and entered on the work in Victoria in October, 1850. The Bush Mission, extended to Bacchus Marsh, Kilmore, Kyneton, Mount Franklin, was largely under his care. Many families dwelling on farms and stations scattered in the newly-settled districts, received and valued his ministrations. After some months of earnest labonr in this colony, he departed to the Fiji Mission, on which his heart was set. This first District meeting made its station sheet as follows: —*Melbourne*: W. Butters, John Harcourt; *Collingwood*: S. Waterhouse; *Geelong*: F. Lewis, W. Byrnes; *Belfast*: W. Lightbody; *Portland*: W. C. Curry; *Kyneton*: Vacant for the present. N.B.—Rev. Joseph Morris expected from India.

The schedule of property at this time, showed:—Church and School at Collins-street, with ministers residence built during the year; school house at Lonsdale-street; stone church at Collingwood (Fitzroy); Brunswick, brick church;

Williamstown, small church; churches at Great Brighton, Little Brighton, East Brighton; a small one at Richmond; and a stone church at Pentridge. The Class Leaders were: —*Melbourne*: Mrs. Wilson, Messrs. J. R. Pascoe, Horton, Powell, Hyde, Wellard, Little, Waitt, and Galagher; *Collingwood*: Messrs. Lowe, Abbey, and Wills; *Pentridge*: Mr. Sidebottom; *Brunswick*: Mr. Lobb; *Brighton*: Messrs. Webb, Cameron, Stone, Head, and Barker; *Richmond*: Messrs. Guthridge and Parnham; *Plenty*: Mr. Ordish; *Kilmore*: Mr. Chambers; *St. Kilda*: Mr. Jennings. For the colony the yearly return showed Local Preachers to be 39; Class Leaders, 50; Members, 712; on trial, 45; sabbath scholars, 1283; and about 5000 attendants on public worship. The Church made satisfactory progress in the quiet times immediately succeeding. That the Sabbath school work was not in every school as efficiently conducted as might be desired is shown by the following advertisement which appeared in a Melbourne paper:—"Wanted several parties of both sexes, competent to undertake the duty of Sabbath school teachers in the school recently formed in connection with the Wesleyan Chapel, Lonsdale-street. Persons wishing to engage, will please send in their names to the Rev. J. Harcourt. For terms, see Eccles. xi., verse 1." This probably was an appeal made at the beginning, or early in the life of the school. The number of Churches being more than that of Ministers, reminds us that the service of the outlying Churches was largely, and of the principal Churches occasionally, conducted by the devoted and self-denying body of men, the Local Preachers, who, through the last decade, had been diligently plodding on their way to the different appointments under summer heat and in winter rains, sometimes with the simmering sky blazing on them almost as in torrid zone, at other times threading their way through open bush, or over sinking sand or swamp, so that the people gathered for Sabbath service might have preached to them the Word of Life. The swamps and sands, which even now skirt the Yarra, remind us of the difficulties for the pedestrian who would reach Williamstown by Spottiswoode's Ferry, or any near route. In the forties, the track to Brunswick and the Plenty was through open bush, and it was easy to lose one's way. In 1852 new comers lost their way when journeying between Melbourne and the Brightons. Sometimes one might chance to meet a footpad there. The journeys to distant appointments, nine, ten, and twelve miles, for the Local Preachers were mostly on foot. Yet they minded not fatigue, extremes of weather, nor perils on the road, that they might be messengers of grace to their fellow men, and might "save some." Those who comfortably and swiftly travel from the centre to the suburbs of Melbourne in this day, can have little idea (unless they are old colonists) of the difficulties of transit in former days. There were open spaces by the University, between Lygon-street and the Wesleyan Immigrants' Home, and in other parts of the city, that were in winter sticky with soft mud and clay, and seamed with deep and open gutters. Crossing the space where now stand the Treasury Buildings, the writer of this, walking in the dusk of the evening, (in 1855) fell into an open drain, scored by nature, some five or six feet deep, and had an impromptu bath, as well as a severe shaking, before he could flounder out on the other side. Those were the days of rough travel and primitive ways in the city and vicinity of Melbourne.

Before the second District meeting, the discovery of gold in several parts had upset and revolutionized the whole state of affairs in the land—material, social, economical, commercial, religious—and had spread its wave of influence to near and far distant shores.

Gold had been discovered in large quantities in California in 1848. It was found by Mr. Hargreaves in New South Wales in 1851, and by Mr. Esmond in Clunes, Victoria, in the month of June or July, 1851. and shortly after at Ballarat, at Buninyong, at Forest Creek, Mount Alexander, and other places.

When the news spread abroad respecting the rich finds of gold on these newly-opened diggings, the people of all ranks and classes, flocked hither in thousands. Each was hopeful for a good slice of luck, and a good share of the plunder. A few weeks of toil, not severely hard to one accustomed to the use of tools, was to bring him a fortune for life. The gold was there, hundreds were getting large quantities, why should not he? The hard handed son of toil was the best equipped for the labour, but many, unaccustomed to manual work, found sufficient incentive to dig and delve, and a large number were successful. The riches of the goldfields were marvellous, and came into many hands. In the month of October, one ton weight of the precious metal was forwarded to Melbourne by the gold escort from the Mount Alexander district, and this was followed from time to time by almost similar quantities. An exodus took place from the farms, towns, cities, and colonies adjacent. Stores were shut, farms forsaken, ships deserted by their crews, towns almost depopulated of their male inhabitants, clerks, mechanics, labourers, storekeepers, policemen, sailors, professional men, Government employés, whoever could get away, went off to the diggings. The settled districts became for the time, like a Sahara, and the living population crowded to the new Eldorado, thick as "leaves in Vallambrosa." When the sire went, the son would go too. The aged men had the vigour of youth come back in the new fever that had seized them. Of course, miners went from the copper regions of South Australia; stalwart farmers, free labourers, and expiree convicts came over from Tasmania. New South Wales sent its thousands. Soon, many were migrating from islands of the South Sea, and ship loads came from distant California, bringing, many of them, their experience in digging, cradling, and sluicing, to bear upon these new fields. But the British Isles, as soon as the news reached there, poured forth their thousands upon thousands in one continuous stream of passengers and immigrants to the golden shores. They came, thick as flies in summer, dense as clouds of locusts upon the fields of autumn. The influx of immigrants, and the departures from old lines of occupation by the colonists soon disarranged prices, and disorganized society. Prices of commonest articles advanced with fearful rapidity, and rents in Melbourne become enormous: the waves of population were coming in, and could not be provided for. Tented life was necessary on the goldfields, it became necessary as a supplemental provision, for accommodating the swarms of people that came to Melbourne. People coming from other parts were only too glad to get, at almost fabulous prices, shelter for the night in outhouses, huts, schoolrooms, vestries, and churches. The inns and houses could accommodate but a small portion of the new arrivals. Presently diggers, favoured with ample funds, or gold that could get friends and funds, poured back again into the city, and multitudes spent their newly-acquired wealth with extravagant recklessness. At the hotels or in the shops they parted with scores or even hundreds of pounds in a few days or weeks, thinking they could readily replace what they were squandering. Some ate bank notes, sandwiched between slices of bread. Some "shouted" for bottles of champagne. Others were free with their money in riding or driving about with the most costly vehicles to be obtained. Alas! many spent large sums in gambling, rioting, and debauchery. Lightly come, freely wasted, was the order of the day with the money and the gold. The demon drink was abroad in a terrible form, and let slip the dogs of moral havoc amongst the thoughtless people. The result with many was the head turned, and the life depraved. Through these events society was in a state of flux, and no one could predict how and when it would settle down. Tradesmen and merchants were at first in great alarm, but soon saw that new openings for trade presented themselves, and that the circulation of gold would be the life of business and commercial prosperity. Presently wealth came rolling in upon tradesmen, importers, merchants, farmers, as well as upon prosperous diggers. This restlessness and excitement upset the calculations of ministers and church officials, and tried greatly the religious steadiness of the members. To keep sobriety of thought and earnestness of devotion, amid the whirl and war of interests, and fever of exciting, stirring events was almost as difficult as for a swimmer to pass safely through the rapids and whirlpools below Niagara. Numbers of them were carried on the prevailing stream of migration to the goldfields, and some of them, we fear, were lost in the vortex of worldliness. But the bulk of Church members from Victoria, South Australia, Tasmania, who were the first Methodists on the goldfields, stood firm to their Church and their religious principles. When in December, 1851, it was estimated that 20,000 persons, mostly men, were resident on the goldfields; it was also calculated that 4000 were adherents of the Wesleyan Church, and these formed an important, and we may confidently say, a conserving element in the population there gathered. When such numbers of convict expirees, and desperadoes, the wild, dissipated and reckless from many parts, had assembled, and reckless tendencies were fed by so many incentives, many feared lawlessness and anarchy would come similar to what had taken place in the early days of California. Some turbulence took place; but law and order were maintained, largely by the support given to the authorities, and the moral influence exerted by so strong a proportion of order-loving, godly people, as represented the Methodist and other Churches. Some of the action of constituted authorities was open to debate and exception; it appeared arbitrary and imprudent, but those were difficult times. They tried the nerve and the wisdom of officials greatly. But in all right and considerate action they could count on the support of miners and diggers who represented the Methodist body. There was plenty of prodigality, gambling, dissipation, and riotous living on the diggings, but there was a strong leaven of sober virtue also, a salt to season the whole body corporate and to save it from overspreading corruption. The

Puritans being so strong in number in the days of founding the American commonwealth, gave complexion to the hardy, sober thought of New England, and largely shaped the social and national life of the United States. North America has been all the better for that important element in its society. So it was good for this land, when the rush of mixed characters, different classes, and varied nationalities, took place to the goldfields, that Methodism had previously taken such a hold of the soil, and so many of its virtuous, sober-minded citizens were found in the population of the goldfields—the remnant that the Lord had sent with others like-minded of the sturdy British stock to save from the horrors of rapine, anarchy, and recklessness of human life that marked the early times in the goldfields of California, and from the desperate wickedness and " depths of Satan" found in demoralized communities.

Now Mr. Butters' capacity for wise administration shone forth. When Leaders, Local Preachers, and members were leaving the city in shoals, he did his best to supply their lack of service, and save the Church from loss and wreck. He put into harness other promising agents, kept ordinances going as best he could, closed up the ranks of his workers, and stayed off any wide disaster. Soon he was overwhelmed with work in his oversight of Churches already planted, and his endeavours to supply some Christian services to the new clusters of people on the goldfields. He had to answer the thousand and one questions of new arrivals, some of whom appeared disappointed if he could not tell them where to pick up gold in the street. Provision of some kind must be made for the shelter and housing of Methodist adherents or families flocking here by the hundred, and such shelter was hard to get. He was assisted nobly by such active, intelligent men as Messrs. Walter Powell, Pascoe, Guthridge, Beaver, and others. Writing under date of January 21st, 1852, Mr. Butters states that "about one thousand arrived from Tasmania and Adelaide yesterday, and we are told that thousands more are coming. I suppose that multitudes may be expected from the home country." As the opening of schoolrooms and other places afforded not sufficient room for nightly shelter, and when incidents like the following pressed upon them the urgent expediency of finding more accommodation as also some Christian homes, for the influx of people, then the Wesleyan Immigrants' Home was erected. At a meeting convened in Collins-street, to devise means for obtaining more Ministers from England, presided over by Mr. Butters, and attended by many influential laymen, Mr. W. Powell rose to speak under strong emotion. He stated that on that day, whilst passing on the street, he met a woman, a Wesleyan, in great distress, and unable to obtain lodgings or shelter, because every place had been so crowded, and she had been compelled to pass the night previous on the wharf under the shelter of a cask. She was a respectable woman, on her way from Tasmania to join her husband in Ballarat. He proposed that an Immigrants' Home be built, and offered £50 towards it. This being warmly taken up by others, led to the erection of that Home in Melbourne. Mr. Butters made several trips to the goldfields to see the exact state of things, and to give them the occasional ministry of the word. The Rev. John Harcourt and F. Lewis went also, as did the Ministers of other Christian Churches. Mr. Butters soon saw the urgency of more ministerial aid and agents. By September, 1851, he had collected £100 to send for two additional Ministers from England and to defray the cost of their passage; but by the end of the year he concluded that was altogether an insufficient addition to the ranks, if promising and needy cases, clamouring for ministerial supply, were to be met. Supported by the December Quarterly Meeting he made urgent requests for more Ministers to the Rev W. B. Boyce (General Superintendent of Missions) and to the Missionary Committee in London. Mr. Butters' letter to the latter is worthy of transcription and permanent record. It is dated Melbourne, January 21st, 1852:—"Some weeks ago I posted the minutes of our First Annual (District) Meeting. Since then, however, great changes have taken place among us with which I think you ought to be made acquainted. From other sources you will have learned that large portions of this vast country have been proved to be immense goldfields of surpassing richness, and that already several tons of the precious metal have been brought into Melbourne. The news of our wealth has brought thousands of persons from the adjacent colonies, who, with many of the inhabitants of our towns and villages, are now congregated where the rich deposit is found.

It is impossible to imagine the wild excitement which has been induced, and the effects which have followed in every department of our work. At the date of the discovery, everything was in a healthy and flourishing condition. Our chapels were filled to overflowing, our class and prayer meetings were well attended, and our numbers in society were steadily and rapidly increasing. Our Sunday and Day schools were in great prosperity. . . . But the gold has, for the present, sadly deranged our plans. Many of our members, and more than half of our Local Preachers are scattered over the length and breadth of these extensive goldfields. Some of them have become suddenly and unexpectedly rich, while others have been greatly inconvenienced by the changes which have taken place, and there is a manifest danger lest the all-absorbing subject should turn away their minds and hearts from things unseen and eternal. We confidently hope, however, that this state of things will soon pass away, and that the wonderful events that are transpiring around us will be made subservient to the extension and establishment of the Redeemer's kingdom. What the ultimate effect of these may be the shrewdest among us dare not guess. It seems reasonable, however, to expect that an immense population will be attracted to the place. . . . We shall require a proportionate increase of Ministerial strength. At our September Quarterly Meeting, held before anything important in reference to the gold was known, the propriety of requesting the Committee to send out help was earnestly urged, and twelve of those present engaged to contribute or collect £5 each towards paying the passage and outfit of two Ministers from England. The thousands that have been added to our population since then have rendered the case increasingly urgent. We require at least four Ministers in this Circuit. . . . At a distance of about eighty miles is Mount Alexander, where there are between twenty and thirty thousand persons digging for gold, among whom are hundreds of our own members without any Wesleyan Minister, except as they are visited from Melbourne. The Brethren feel the circumstances of these persons at the mines to be so urgent that about a fortnight ago we met together and determined that though Melbourne itself required additional help, yet one Minister should be sent from its staff to devote his undivided attention to that part of the country. (He states further, that application had been made to the Lieutenant-Governor for aid from the gold revenue towards the Minister's support, which had been readily granted). You are aware that for many years the Trustees of our principal chapel have been all but overwhelmed with a large debt. Last year Mr. Boyce generously promised us £500, if we raised £500 to pay off £1000 from our debt. A few evenings ago the friends met together and added to amounts which had been previously promised, sufficient to pay off the entire debt of £1300. I probably ought to add that of the large amount so generously contributed several of our successful gold finders gave most nobly, some of them in cash, and some of them in gold, just as it was got out of the earth."

In the year 1852, trade made such rapid strides, that small tradesmen became prosperous merchants, and artisans and journeymen who remained in the city or returned to it, found their services in request at a high wage and premium: some of them became contractors on their,

D

own account. These for the most part put their wealth into good channels in extension of their business, and in ready support of philanthropic and religious institutions. Amongst those who gave munificent sums may be named Messrs. Walter Powell, James Webb, N. Guthridge, F. E. Beaver, Pascoe, and others. They were free with their donations to build churches, secure Ministers, build the Immigrants' Home, relieve the destitute, and to aid the struggling. There was great strain upon business men; 1852 and 1853 were years of general prosperity; but some reaction came in after years, which brought down some establishments with a crash. At this time, 1852, the head of a large business said, "I must work as I do or close up my business: there is no middle course." This was the era of enterprise and push, the former quiet times had passed away, and competitors, for even a living, as well as for riches, were on eager stretch, and at high pressure speed. It told unfavourably for meditative religion, and for quiet waiting upon God, but it enabled some to give with a princely liberality. Any enterprises needing money, set on foot by the Chairman of the District, the Pastor, or the Church, met with a hearty support.

The District meeting met on September 22nd, 1852, and was attended by the Ministers, Revs. Butters, Lewis, W. C. Currey, Symons, Byrnes, and Chapman. The Rev. John Harcourt had removed to South Australia; Mr. Whewell was introduced into the Ministry by the recommendation of this meeting, and was placed as a colleague with Mr. Butters. Other changes in stations were:—Mr. Symons to Collingwood, Mr. Currey to Mount Alexander, Mr. Byrnes to Brighton. The meeting apportioned Government grant of £600 to the goldfields, reviewed the work generally, recorded the erection of a Church of wood at North Melbourne (Hotham), and deplored the lapses of immigrants on the voyage out from England and other countries. It stated that few out of the multitudes that in lands on the other side of the world had been Church mem-

bers identified themselves on their arrival here with
their Church. The greater number, it was feared, had
fallen away from religion. This unhappy result was
only too true at the time, but many in subsequent years
were recovered to Church fellowship and a religious life.
Among the arrivals of this year were some choice spirits,
who became pillars of our Church, Henry Cooke, and
Captain Matthews, etc. Mr. Benjamin Cocker is mentioned
as present at the April Quarterly meeting. He had been
a merchant in Launceston, was a wonderfully gifted and
persuasive preacher, and after varied experiences in these
lands, the South Seas, and America, he settled down as
Professor of Moral Philosophy, etc., at Ann Arbor University, State of Michigan. He acquired great influence and
renown as a teacher and writer of important books, and
was held in high esteem by the Church of which he
had become a Minister, the Methodist Episcopal Church
of America.

The Wesleyan Immigrants' Home was opened on November 24th, 1852. It had cost £3000 to £3500, of which
the Government gave £1000. It was a well-conducted
home, a shelter for sojourners, a centre for the orderly
and sober immigrant, a register of information, a substitute
for their own home to the young men who by hundreds
came to it, and a safeguard from the prowlers and the dens
of the city. One or other Wesleyan Minister was Chaplain
for years, conducted family worship, and gave information,
advice, and help to the crowds which frequented it. Mr.
Courtney first, and afterwards Mr. Thos. Fielding, did
good service as the superintendents of the institution.
It subsequently came into the hands of Mr Joseph
Lowe as a private enterprise, rented from the Church as
proprietors. A cottage was built on the site, which was
for years the residence of a Wesleyan Minister. Mr.
Butters stated at the time of the opening that "such
had been the crowded state of Melbourne for some time
past, that on several occasions the vestry and schoolroom

had been used as places of nightly shelter to newly-arrived members."

The remaining debts on existing chapels were swept away; but the frightful cost of materials and labour deterred the Church authorities from any buildings in this year, 1852, save those mentioned as the "Home" and North Melbourne Church. But a scheme was launched for obtaining iron chapels from England; the sum of £4000, it would appear even £6000 was raised to pay for six or seven buildings of these materials. The matter succeeded as a commercial speculation, but was a failure in respect to Church accommodation. That was a fortunate thing, as iron is not the material suited to this warm climate, as the only Church of iron, that at Prahran, built at this time, soon made manifest. Those who pry into these antiquities, represented by the scheme for iron chapels can consult Symons' "Life of Draper," p. 157-9.

The enterprise was well meant, and gave Mr. Butters, Mr. Powell, and others, a great deal of anxiety; but, happily, was set aside by more suitable structures. Churches were erected during 1853, at Prahran, cost £1400; St. Kilda, cost £1300; Brunswick, cost £1600. In 1854, at Richmond, cost £3000; and the Church at Brunswick-street enlarged at a cost of £2000. The prices were extravagantly high, as carpenters wages ranged from 20s. 8d. to 30s. per day; stone masons and bricklayers, 25s. to 40s.; and material and other labour in proportion. In a letter of date November 25th, 1852, Mr. Butters wrote of the moral state of the colony, and the resolute spirit of the Methodist people in grappling with the work and difficulties before them :—"I wish I could write more favourably in reference to the spiritual condition of our society, and the moral condition of the country; but the state of excitement in which we have been for the past year, has been most unfavourable to spiritual prosperity. Melbourne is in a very different state now to what it was before gold was discovered. We are resolute, however, to endeavour by distribution of tracts, the re-establishment of out-door preaching, and the employment of every other means within our power, to stem the torrent. I have a deep conviction that if the Church of Christ does not do its duty at this time, the land will become a proverb and a reproach. We, as a people, have a great work to do. May we have grace to do it! Amen and amen!"

GOLD AND CHANGE.

CHAPTER V.

THE event of the year 1853, in Methodist circles, was the visit of the Rev. Robert Young. He was the deputation sent by the Missionary Committee and the English Conference to inquire and report respecting the expediency of organizing the Wesleyan Methodist Connexion in Australia, New Zealand, and the South Seas into an Affiliated Conference. The many questions connected with this broad subject were to be reported on by the Rev. Robert Young. The view that lands colonized by British subjects, and growing fast in wealth and population, would soon become ecclesiastically self-supporting, had been for years entertained by the Mission authorities. They had given practical effect to their views by sending the Rev. W. B. Boyce to Sydney in 1846 as General Superintendent, to prepare the way for such a consummation in this part of the world. He had diligently attended to his trust. Then in December, 1851, the Missionary Committee expressed its opinion that the Australian Church could act for itself, and was hopeful that other portions of the Southern Mission field could be incorporated with it. On their recommendation, the British Conference determined to send two Ministers to consult with the Ministers and Churches in the lands of the Southern Hemisphere, respecting the principles and features of the Plan for an Australian Conference, and generally to report on the practicability of the plan, and the state of the Churches. The Rev. Robert Young, and Rev. John Kirk were appointed as the deputation. Their first attempt to reach here was defeated. The steamer *Melbourne* was disabled and put into Lisbon, having narrowly escaped wreck. Mr. Young returned to England, and re-embarked December 19th, 1852, this time in the *Adelaide*; but Mr. Kirk withdrew from the Mission, returned to England, and remained there. Mr. Young reached Adelaide early in May, 1853, after an eventful and perilous voyage, and on May 11th, landed in Melbourne. He was welcomed at a breakfast meeting held on the 14th, and made a statement of the object of his visit. Another meeting was held in Collins-street Church, when, in view of the urgent need of Ministerial help, six hundred pounds were promised to pay for the passage of six Ministers, and the money was shortly after sent home. Another hundred pounds was obtained from some other place (? Drysdale or Indented Heads), and entrusted to Mr. Young for the same purpose. Mr. Young remained about three weeks, when he passed on to other parts, but returned to the colony at the end of the year.

In response to Mr. Butters' first appeal after the discovery of gold, the Missionary Committee in London resolved that four Ministers should be sent forthwith. The Rev. John Kirk was to have remained in Australia. The Revs. Isaac Harding and Richard Hart were appointed to Melbourne on the stations for 1852 of the British Conference, and the Rev. Thomas Raston, formerly of Sierra Leone, was also selected. The Rev. Isaac Harding came by the end of June, 1853, and was retained in Melbourne. The Rev. Richard Hart arrived during the year, and was appointed to Geelong. The Rev. Thomas Raston suffered shipwreck on the coast of Brazil, but eventually reached the colony, and was at his circuit on Bendigo by the end of August. Mr Harding busied himself as Chaplain of the Wesleyan Home, and by going on board newly-arrived immigrant ships to search out Wesleyans and other Christians, together with the pressing duties of the Circuit in those eventful times. He also took charge of affairs in Melbourne, whilst Mr. Butters left in the end of the year for an extended visit to the goldfields. Mr. Harding was strong, healthy, able to ride hard and endure fatigue, and had the spirit and qualifications of a pioneer. His ministry was acceptable, and his pastoral visitations were much valued. After a few years in Victoria he laboured in New Zealand and Queensland. The Rev. E. Sweetman came over from Launceston, and for a time took charge at Brighton, which had been formed into a new Circuit, and where a Minister's residence was being built.

The Annual District meeting was held in Geelong on August 9th, 1853. There were present :—Revs. W. Butters, F. Lewis, J. Harding, Thomas Raston, Richard Hart, W. C. Currey, William S. Byrnes, John C. Symons, and Joshua Chapman. Messrs. Byrnes and Symons had completed their probation. Messrs. Chapman and Whewell retired for want of health (the latter resumed after a season). Stations were arranged which are noted in other pages. A note of regret was sounded that comparatively few of those who were members in England could be as yet induced to meet in class. It was stated that Melbourne Society was in a "state of fusion, and in what particular form it would come out of the furnace we dare not guess." The difficulties had increased, because the Superintendent had been single-handed—his colleague had been out of health—but this was partially remedied by Mr. Harding's arrival. Through house rent in the city becoming so dear, most of the official Laymen had gone to reside in the suburbs, and their attendance at services and meetings on the week night could not well be secured. Collingwood had been unsettled, but was recovering the healthy tone of former times. A few conversions had taken place, and it was projected to meet the wants of a dense and growing population by more Church buildings and services. Ten places of worship had been purchased or erected, of canvas or slabs, on the goldfields. Meanwhile a great increase in the population was going on. The numbers had advanced by 161,631 between March 2nd, 1852, and April 26th, 1854. The population had more than trebled.

The report for the year 1853, emanating from Mr. Butters, records the continued straits for house room for the influx of people; that Church accommodation was sorely insufficient for the crowds who would attend; that 5000 persons took up their abode in tents on the south side of the Yarra (Canvastown); that a large tent was set up by the Wesleyans outside the encampment in which they conducted public worship, and held a Sabbath school for some months. The removal of this temporary population caused the removal of the tent to Emerald Hill (South Melbourne) where a class had been formed, a Sunday school begun, and regular services were held. A reviving influence had fallen upon Brunswick, which had multiplied one class into three, led to the erection of a schoolhouse and a master's residence; and the commencement of a subscription for a new chapel. At Pentridge the Church was full to overflowing, and steps were taken for its enlargement. At Williamstown, the Chapel which had been shut up, was reopened and improved; a class and Sabbath school again commenced, and the friends were applying for a Minister to be stationed. At St. Kilda a Church of wood had been erected, and there and at Prahran were two Sabbath schools and five Society classes. It was proposed to commence service at Sandridge. Brighton and Collingwood had been formed into separate circuits, and the prosperous issue of the measure during the year, had fully justified its wisdom. Throughout the province the Day schools were well reported of, and five Sabbath schools on the goldfields were in flourishing operation.

The year 1854 opened with the holding of a Special District meeting, as the Rev. Robert Young had returned from his extended tour through the South Seas, and wished a definite opinion from the Victorian Church respecting the proposals with which he was charged. Mr. Young spent the closing part of 1853 on the goldfields, in company with Mr. Butters, and we have given some account thereof in other pages. The Ministers gathered in the District meeting fully concurred in the wisdom and necessity of forming the Australasian Conference, having the Polynesian Mission within its bounds. They honoured the deputation by their resolutions, hospitalities, and appreciation of his services. He was a man of mark in the Home Connexion, and had exercised a Ministry that had been singularly successful. Without any shining talents, he was a good specimen of the English Wesleyan Preacher devoted to His Master's work. The British Conference of 1854 thanked him for his valuable services, and accepted the plan for the Affiliated Conference as submitted to them.

The other noteworthy business of the District meeting was the requests to retire from active work and return to England, preferred by Mr. Lewis on account of his own health, and by Mr. Sweetman, on account of his wife's health. These requests were acceded to, with resolutions expressive of the value of Mr. Lewis' services during twenty years, and Mr. Sweetman's for about the same time. The Minutes for the British Conference for 1855, state that Mr. Sweetman had withdrawn from the ministry of the Wesleyan Church, but Australian Methodists strongly assert concerning him, that he is, if "lost to sight, to memory dear."

Mr. Lewis had become a great sufferer through dyspepsia, and was physically incapacitated for the arduous work of an itinerant Minister. He returned to England; but days and years of suffering were appointed to him, until he fell asleep in Jesus on 12th March, 1864. His name is graven on many hearts in these lands, for he had won many to righteousness, and had helped them much who had believed through grace. It was proposed by the District meeting to build Churches at Sandridge, Williamstown, South Melbourne, Collingwood Flat, Hawthorn,

Heidelberg ; also, to raise £5000 for Day school purposes ; and further, to found or erect a Grammar school for education of the youth of the more respectable classes, the first germ of the project of Wesley College. Melbourne reported an addition of 120 new members in four months ; and other places were having accessions to the membership. The Chairman of the District was relieved from Circuit engagements, that he might have a more extended oversight of the general work. Other appointments in the forecast of this meeting were :—*Melbourne West:* John Eggleston (he was present at this District gathering); James S. Waugh and W. Byrnes ; *Melbourne East:* John C. Symons and W. Hill ; *Geelong:* J. Harding and R. Hart ; *Williamstown:* W. C. Currey ; *Port Fairy:* Joseph Albiston ; *Portland:* W. Lightbody ; *Castlemaine:* W. P. Wells ; *Sandhurst:* Thomas Raston ; *Ballarat:* Theophilus Taylor ; *Beechworth:* Charles Akrill. It will be observed that in this list are new names of Ministers. These were the Ministers who left England by the ship *Beulah.* This vessel had, even for those times, a voyage unusually prolongèd. Starting from England in September, 1853, she did not cast anchor in Hobson's Bay until February 3rd, 1854, having been 139 days in the passage. But she brought with her men of mark ; some of whom have done as much as any of their brethren to mould and serve the Victorian Methodism of the third quarter of this century. Messrs. Waugh, Wells, and Albiston continue to the present as leading Ministers of the Church. The Rev. William Hill rendered distinguished service, until his tragic end in Pentridge Stockade. A despicable ingrate took his life. Theophilus Taylor was in delicate health, but was a forcible preacher and energetic man. His career in the colony was a brief, but useful one. Mr. Akrill failed in health. Taken together, this was a notable and valued reinforcement of the Ministerial staff. There had been also a valued addition to the active Laymen in the Circuit, by the arrival of many tried and true men from England. Messrs. Pascoe and Beaver were Circuit Stewards during the changeful year, 1853, and Messrs. W. Powell and Cooke, in the years 1854-5; when Mr. W. Powell removed, Mr. O. Parnham took his office. In those years we note on the list of officials:—Messrs. R. Hodgson, J. Bromley, Gardiner, Stevens, King, Davis, A. Fraser, Radcliff, Roden, Kendall, Bell, Marshall, the most of whom had come from Tasmania or the old country, and became men of influence in our Church in these and after days. Others could be named, as Leonard Robinson, J. M'Cutcheon, W. G. R. Stephenson, J. K. Powell, who came about this time, and gave valuable support by their abilities and means to the rising cause. The Rev. James Bickford had arrived and succeeded Mr. Sweetman in the Brighton Circuit. The Rev. John Eggleston took the Superintendency of the Melbourne West Circuit in March, 1854, and the services of the Rev. B. S. Walker were secured, about the middle of the year, for the oversight, more particularly, of the growing societies of Brunswick and Pentridge (now Coburg). The number of members for this circuit was 528 at the end of 1854, with 31 on trial. The finances were flourishing. Dr. Cutts came to the colony, and began the practice of his profession at this time. He, with Mr. R. Hodgson, has been identified with the interests, burdens, and affairs of Wesley Church for a greater length of time than any other layman. He has also represented our Church at the University Council, the Denominational School Board, The Trustees of Savings Banks, and on several Royal Commissions. His influence, time, and professional skill have been ungrudgingly given to forward the interests of our Church in Melbourne and the colony. He has also sustained most offices that a Layman can hold. His friend, Mr. R. Hodgson, a devoted Class Leader, effective Local Preacher, and most steady worker, has recently gone to his heavenly reward. He was in most respects a model of the trusty servant of the Church, who, like "the beloved Gaius," "doest faithfully whatsoever thou doest." He passed away to the land of rest in 1885.

The Rev. John Eggleston's name is greatly revered by all who knew him. We do not regard his first term in Melbourne as his most successful years; but he was a devoted man and earnest preacher of the Gospel. He was of the School represented in England by men of the second and third generation of Methodists, such as W. Bramwell, D. Stoner, and John Smith. Much given to prayer, and living in close communion with God; diligent in studies and pastoral duties; concentrating thoughts and energies into the one groove of soul-saving, and that in the Revivalist forms, these men were living flames of ardent zeal, and very successful in turning sinners to righteousness. John Eggleston was one of them. His preaching probed the conscience, and searched the heart. His fidelity applied the moral law as a rule of life, and test of conduct, and sounded the alarm of its terrors to those who came short of its standard. Some thought he dwelt too much on its fiery judgments; but he could comfort as well as terrify. His Gospel notes were sweet as angel's music. His sermons were well thought out, and very forcible in their closing appeals. As he was a witness of entire sanctification, gifted above the average in those qualities of a preacher which have most prevailed in Methodist communities, and knew right well how to use the "Sword of the Spirit, the Word of God," some have wondered that he was not uniformly successful. His term in some Circuits was comparatively barren of those striking results, which came in other Circuits in rich abundance. In the fire and fervour of his youth, he had been made a signal blessing in Hobart and South Australia. His middle life was spent in Victoria and New South Wales. His later period, whilst full of mental and physical vigour, yet afflicted by failing sight, was given in the ripe maturity of sanctified wisdom and sterling piety to Circuits in Victoria. Like another John, he was a Boanerges, and a saintly Divine. His youthful friend, who, in the outset of his Ministry, was said to have much of his spirit and style, the Rev. J. W. Crisp, was his colleague in Ministerial work in the year 1855, and then girded himself for that Christian warfare, which he has boldly and successfully carried on through many years. With strong men like Messrs. Butters, Eggleston, Waugh, Symons, and Bickford, leading and marshalling her hosts, through God's gracious blessing, Methodism was recovering from the shocks which the onset of Mammon's impetuous forces had given, was turning the tide of battle, and winning some victories, but was also preparing for more pronounced and signal ones in the future. Under the guidance and management of Mr. Butters, and through the support of his coadjutors, both clerical and lay, Methodism had passed safely through the throes of a social revolution, and emerged, not only unharmed, but more powerful for good than before. In this eventful crisis of affairs, she had proved her sound qualities and great capabilities to those who tried her, and to those who watched her. No Church had shown greater adaptability to the times in meeting the spiritual wants and emergencies of shoals of persons, thrown into unwonted circumstances, and placed in altogether new conditions of social life. The body politic underwent a convulsion, which tried the foundations of law, order, morals, and social economics; and the ecclesiastical body was put into a fiery crucible, but came out the purer and stronger through good qualities inherent in it. It was like passing through a period of sickness, and a sound constitution getting the better of it, when not only are bad humours thrown off, but the vigour of youth comes back, and health, more robust than before, is gained. This renewing of youthful strength to the Church was because her sources of supply and fount of life were in the heart of God. Through the Divine mercy the Church had been preserved, increased, blessed; yet had also been made a great blessing unto others. She was an ark of safety to many, when an inundation of greed, mammon-serving, disorder, outrage, drunkenness, and bad morals, threatened to overflow the land. Like our Australian gum-tree, in its remedial qualities, the Church was a means of purifying in a pestilential atmosphere, and a purveyor of health in some death-dealing regions. The districts where it was planted, were all the better for its presence, and notably where moral miasma was rife.

EXTENSION.
CHAPTER VI.

THE wheels of time and of the itinerancy had gone round, bringing a new Minister to the head of affairs in Melbourne in 1855. Mr. Butters had departed to Adelaide in the month of March, bearing with him flattering testimonials to his Ministerial worth, and the hearty prayers of the people for his prosperity in his new field of labour. His successor had arrived in the person of the Rev. D. J. Draper, who was every way fitted to rank beside him in shrewd sense, and careful management of men and things; but was scarcely as effective in his pulpit services. Nevertheless, surrounded by good men, trained in a good school, habituated to the direction of Methodist affairs, which had prospered very greatly under him in South Australia, Mr. Draper wisely directed the machinery and measures of the Church, and was largely the agent of its consolidation and increase in the immediately succeeding decade of years. He had attended the first Australasian Conference, in company with his compeers and brethren, which had been held in Sydney in January of this year of grace, 1855. That had been a memorable Conference, which affected materially Victorian Methodism in the arrangement of stations, and in the first exercise of self-governing control and power in the newly-constituted Church. Nevertheless, as it was not held within the bounds of this colony, this reference to it may suffice. It made the transfer of Mr. Butters to Adelaide, and Mr. Draper to Melbourne; and the latter proved himself worthy of his important trust, as the ecclesiastical head, for the time being, of the vigorous Methodism of the land. The arrangement, which had been tried in 1854, of setting the Chairman of the District free from Circuit affairs, was not continued in the succeeding year, hence Mr. Draper had charge of the Melbourne East (Collingwood) Circuit, and was chaplain at the Wesleyan Home, but in 1856, he was freed from Circuit work. His frequent journeys in the interior for the oversight of the rapidly spreading Church, which was entering on new fields of labour month by month, are narrated in Mr. Symons' "Life of Mr. Draper." The book contains a good review of the Methodist story of these years 1852-64, and is a painstaking compilation.

We can well understand that these Ministers would be true yokefellows in the work of the Collingwood Circuit. Mr. Symons, as the junior, duly reported "that the roof of Northcote Chapel had been blown off during the terrific gale" of May 27th. Then a short time afterwards Mr. Draper " rode to Northcote, and visited several families and solicited money for the enlargement of the Chapel." He would get a cheery response to his solicitation as Northcote then had, as now, several respectable, affluent, and liberal families connected with its Wesleyan Methodism, and the two Ministers rejoiced together in bringing subsequently to a successful issue, the projected enlargement of the Chapel. The two colleagues were both possessed of good "common sense," and duly prized it in themselves and others. They were both instructive preachers, and clear-headed men. They were both blessed with excellent wives, ladylike, cheery, active, good. They both loved music, and promoted good instrumental music and congregational singing in the Church service. A man, like Mr. Spensley, who was superintendent of Brunswick-street Sabbath school, and, by his gift and love of song, was putting new tone and tune into that school, and thereby making it (with other means) very attractive to the young people, had in that method, the warmest encouragement from the two Circuit Ministers. Mr. Symons showed also his shrewd wisdom in dealing with unruly scholars. In that school, about this time, were three brothers two of whom gave great trouble to their teachers and the superintendent by their misconduct and insubordination, and seemed almost incorrigible. Their expulsion was discussed in the Teachers meeting, but Mr. Symons' great influence went on the side of a longer trial of them, and he prevailed. The sequel showed the wisdom of a patient dealing with them. For, one became a promising Wesleyan Minister, but died after a short career of Ministerial service; another has been a pillar of our Church and representative member; the third has been a most efficient State school Teacher and Local Preacher, steady, talented, and trusted. During the time of Mr. Symons' labour in this Melbourne East Circuit, a youth was converted to God, who afterwards became a Wesleyan Minister, and for the year 1885 was the respected President of the New South Wales and Queensland Conference. Mr. Nolan stated, at the time of his ordination to the Christian Ministry, "that when Mr. Symons was pastor of the Brunswick-street Church, he became first a scholar in the Sunday school, then a regular hearer in the Church. Before long he was led to feel his need of a Saviour. One Sabbath evening, on retiring from the prayer-meeting, one of the Church members who had noticed his seriousness, entered into conversation with him. As they walked up Brunswick-street, his friend explained to him the faith of the man with the withered hand, and he assured him that if, like that man, he made the effort, like him he should receive the power. His friend left him at the end of Brunswick-street, and in crossing from thence to Collins-street, where there were then no buildings, except the Church and the school, he (Mr. Nolan) resolved to take the advice just given; and taking off his cap, he cast his soul on Jesus.

He made the effort, and he did receive the power." The teacher's *penchant* for minute detail, appears to have seized the disciple when he gave this description, and this illustration (possibly of his reverence of spirit), in taking off his cap. But the disciple is a man of whom any teacher might be proud: genial, earnest, warm-hearted, a faithful friend, a successful Minister, beloved by both Ministers and people. We cannot state how Mr. Draper would have felt had he seen a young convert tossing up his cap out of joy or reverence, nor whether he himself had given any example in that line; but we can surmise how he felt when his own hat blew off in Collins-street, and a young friend ran after it for a good distance and brought it back to him, for then Mr. Draper, with a twinkle in his eye, and a peculiar tone in his voice, said, "I do not know, Mr. Stephinson how to thank you sufficiently, for of all the sights that appear to me ridiculous, that of a stout man, with short legs, chasing his hat along a crowded street on a windy day, beats all, and you have saved me from cutting that pretty figure." Mr. Draper was glad to be spared from exhibiting on foot, as observed of all observers in crowded Collins-street, any of the peculiarities of John Gilpin's ride to Edmonton. He had a rich vein of humour, as well as a keen sense of the ridiculous. When Mr. Draper was in South Australia, although he was a good horseman, yet on one occasion, when riding in company with Mr. Dare, he was thrown from his horse. He fell on a sand heap, from which rising immediately, he, pointing to the impression which his stout figure had made on the sand, exclaimed, "Look here, Dare, D. J. Draper, his mark." The man who was so calm and heroic when he and others were afterwards in awful perils on the deep, had been full of mirth at his own somewhat ridiculous adventures on the land. He used to tell with great glee about an anonymous letter which he had received, commenting on his style of preaching thus:—
"Dear Mr. Draper—Permit me to give this unasked for advice respecting your preaching; condense! condense!

condense! more thoughts, fewer words! A Well-wisher." The good man's style on Sundays, and when he had carefully prepared, was somewhat open to criticism, yet, strange to say, on the week night, when he gave a sermon, he would talk in a quiet, fatherly, somewhat conversational style, which differed greatly from the verbose and involved sentences which at times marked his more elaborate efforts. This man, who could be grave and gay, lively and severe, was a distinguished leader in our Israel in this progressive period of its history. His *fidus Achates*, Mr. Symons, was his counsellor in all public questions, as well as helper in all Circuit work. On questions of City or Chinese Missions, Home or Foreign work, Grammar school or Day school education, temperance or literature, the Book Depôt, or the Wesley Church, discussed in these years by Mr. Draper, in committee or in public, with fellow Ministers, the Government of the Day, or the general public, this faithful henchman and colleague was at his elbow, and a sound adviser was at his ear; when wanted for public controversy a more ready combatant could not be found. Mr. Symons is of a pugnacious disposition, self-reliant, and dogmatic; and can give vigorous blows in the polemics of theological warfare, or in the discussion of civil strife. He was dubbed by a facetious brother, " our senior wrangler." But whilst he is hard-hitting, tenacious in his opinions, rather intolerant towards those who differ from him, he is a fair, and, often, a generous adversary. He may be rough on you in his speech, but is very kind in his acts. War is frequent in his words, brotherly love is in his heart. No one is more free to do a service, or to put himself to greater inconvenience in doing so. It may be to take an appointment at a moment's notice, travel a great distance, lecture, preach, write, put his hand in his pocket for help, and make a munificent gift, cover with a forgiving mantle your sins, or stand with his shield to defend you in all these and other ways of brotherly service, no one is more free than Mr. Symons. He is also painstaking in finances, Circuit business, and general affairs.

The yearly Conference was held in 1856 in Melbourne, and commenced on Thursday, January 24th. The President was again the Rev. W. B. Boyce, and the Rev. W. Butters was secretary. Twenty-six Ministers were present, amongst them as new arrivals in Victoria, Revs. William L. Binks, Geo. B. Richards, and also Thomas Williams appointed to South Australia, for the time being. Five were received as probationers in Victoria :—Revs. Henry Chester, John Catterall, Martin Dyson, Thomas James, and John Mewton. In the stations Mr. Binks was appointed to Collins-street; Mr. Bickford to Brighton; Mr. Albiston to Williamstown; Mr. Richards, as the colleague of Mr. Harding, at Geelong; Mr. Waugh continued at St. Kilda. Amongst the reinforcements of Ministers which had arrived from England within the last two or three years past, were several who had seen Foreign service in the Mission field. Messrs. Bickford and Binks had been in the torrid heat of the West Indies, and with the coloured races of British Guiana; Mr. Hill, among the balmy breezes, but enervated population of Ceylon; Mr. Wells, amidst the Arctic regions of Newfoundland; and Messrs. Raston, Hart, and Richards, in the deadly climate of Western Africa. The numbers reported were :—Melbourne West, 222 ; East, 425 ; South, 124; Brighton, 159 ; Williamstown, 29; Pentridge, 146 ; and for the colony, 2328, being an increase of 373 members on the year. The Australasian Church had now 8338 members of the white races in the colonies, and 12,830 of the dark races in the Mission field. In Victoria were 72 Sabbath schools, with 4497 scholars, and 54 Day schools, 3517 scholars. The cause of Day school education had made great extension, and the Wesleyan Church exceeded any other denomination in her efforts to provide it. But now great trouble arose from the action of the Government of the day in returning to a former basis of distribution of the Government aid, it being proportioned according to the number of adherents of the Church returned in the census. This acted very prejudicially to the Wesleyan Church, as she had about one fourteenth of the population, but about one-fifth of the scholars in schools under the Denominational Board. After great efforts on the part of the Chairman of the District and the Wesleyan Education Committee, some concession was obtained, which enabled the bulk of the schools to be maintained, but other schools had to be abandoned, and efforts for extension were greatly crippled. The inequities in distribution of the grant, gradually brought the Wesleyan authorities to favour the supersession of the two Boards which had been constituted (the National and the Denominational) by the one Board, which was established by the Heales "Common Schools Act" in 1862. The question of support to Day schools occupied much of the time of the Education Committee and the District Meeting in 1856. In 1856 Messrs. Parnham and F. Cooper were Circuit Stewards, and Messrs. Woodfin and Curtis appear on the Official list in the Melbourne West Circuit. In 1857 appear Messrs. Tapley, M'Gregor, Jamison, Pentland and Hadley. In the early part of 1857, Revs. Edward King, C. Dubourg, and C. Lane arrived in the colony, and have since given much devoted service to our Church. Churches in Flemington, Footscray, and Albion, were erected; also one of stone at North Melbourne, the former one being used as a school. Messrs. Hadley and M'Gregor in due time became members of the Legislative Assembly in Victoria. Mr. Pentland entered the Ministry in another Christian Church. Mr. Jamison has been a most valued and useful officer in Moorabbin. Messrs. Baird and W. G. R. Stephinson were recommended to the Ministry from the Melbourne Circuit. After a year or two Mr. Baird entered the Presbyterian Church, and has been the respected Pastor of a Church in Geelong. Mr. Stephinson has spent a long and useful career in the Friendly Islands and in New South Wales. The active mind of Mr. Binks, as Superintendent·in these years, found full scope in the ordinary Circuit work, and in many projects for building Churches, and in this he had valued assistance in Mr. Crisp for one year, and experienced counsel and help from Rev. W. P. Wells, his colleague in the following year. Soon the minds of Messrs. Binks and Wells, in conjunction with Mr. Draper, engaged in a scheme which told greatly upon the extension of the Church in Melbourne, the sale of the Collins-street property and the subsequent building of the present Wesley Church.

Mr. Binks has made a name for his Church buildings, having, as much as anyone, the credit of the erection of Wesley Church, Brunswick-street Church, and (with the Rev. John Cope) of the present Lydiard-street Church, Ballarat, three of the finest ecclesiastical edifices belonging to our Church in Victoria; but he is also, in other respects, a beloved and faithful Minister, and a wise Superintendent. He is shrewd, active, vivacious, a ready speaker, with a clear and emphatic delivery, keen in reading character and men, ready in resource in the management of measures, sagacious in counsel, and much resorted to by others in perplexity and difficulty, and, therefore, he has been a leading man in piloting the affairs of the Church in this last thirty years. He has much unction and power in prayer, gives a thoughtful sermon which, though it may not rise into eloquence, always tells upon the ear and heart, because of the clear tones of his voice and his forcible utterance of appropriate Gospel truths, takes care of the young men of his congregations, and by his firmness, readiness, tenderness, and activity, is almost the beau ideal of a judicious Superintendent. He laid his hand upon the writer of this chapter, and sent him into the Wesleyan Ministry. This year, 1857, besides Messrs. Baird and Stephinson, three others, Messrs. John Atkin, W. L. Blamires, and F. Langham stood together at the District Meeting for examination, as to their call to, and qualifications for, the Christian Ministry. Mr. Blamires has spent the intervening years in various Circuits of Victoria, Mr. Langham has given the flower of his days, and the best energies of his calm, yet active mind to the Mission work in Fiji, where for years past he has been virtually the Wesleyan Bishop, and has won a name for self-denying zeal, sanctified wisdom, and a devoted Christian life, acknowledged by all classes who know him, and second to none who have laboured for this last third of a century in that interesting portion of the South Sea Missions. He is of the best type of Christian Missionaries. The staff of Ministers was also reinforced by the arrival of Revs. W. Hopkins, W S. Worth and William Woodall, in the early part of 1858. The Rev. J. S. Waugh, who had been to Ireland on a visit, and married his estimable wife, had returned to the colony in March, 1858.

The Wesleyan *Chronicle* was started in July, 1857, and was a small monthly magazine of Church and miscellaneous literature, designed for Methodist and other readers. The editorship was first in the hands of the Rev. Isaac Harding, who was succeeded in April, 1858, by the Rev. James S. Waugh. Under their care it has been a good defence against assailants of Methodism and of Christianity; and a record of contemporaneous events which is proving most valuable to the writers of this narrative. Expositions of Scripture, a rich fund of anecdote, brief biographies of departed worthies, accounts of Church movements, critiques on national and ecclesiastical affairs, vary its interesting pages. Its literary ability varies, but maintains a good standard on the whole. In the first three or four years of its existence, we note contributions from the pens of Messrs. Draper, Waugh, Harding, Wells, Taylor, Symons, Hutchison, Dodgson, Blamires, and others. This Church, from Wesley's days, has been active in spreading literature, as well as promoting education. "More light" is a cherished motto with it, whether the "more sweetness" comes or not. Of set purpose, it diffuses knowledge, accounting that then a better kind of devotion and religious life, other things being equal, will follow. So in a year or two onward, the Wesleyan Book Depôt was established, being aided both in the building and stock accounts, by the wise and munificent liberality of Mr. Walter Powell. This same gentleman had a large share in promoting a splendid bazaar which was held in February, 1858, in aid of the contemplated Wesley College Building. He gave a large contribution, £500, and laid it out to good advantage in purchase of articles in the home country, which augmented considerably the value of his donation in the sales afterwards effected here. This effort in the hands of leading Ministers in Melbourne and of Messrs. N. Guthridge, A. Fraser, J. Webb, W. Little, J. Whitney, T. Vasey, S. Finlay, Dr. Cutts, and A. Anderson, was brought to a successful issue, realising £1925, a most substantial aid to the institution.

But the event which was the most notable of this period was the provision of Churches for the increasing population of the city and suburbs. The census of March, 1857, showed the population of the colony to be (exclusive of Chinese), 385,342, a great leap from the numbers of 77,345 in 1851, and of 238,776 in 1854. The Wesleyan Methodists had increased from 15,284 in 1854 to 28,000 in 1857. At this time, 1857, the Methodists bore nearly the same proportion to the city population, as was shown by the relative percentage of the whole colony—about 7 per cent. To make a suitable provision of Church accommodation gave continued concern to the leading Ministers and other officials. A happy suggestion of Mr. D. Macarthur's, taking form and activity in the fertile brain of the Rev. D. J. Draper, put them in the way of a most excellent scheme for an increase of Church buildings in the metropolis, which should be of finer architectural appearance and of larger space than those already built. It was to sell the Collins-street property, and with the proceeds build, or help to build, several Churches. This was accordingly done, for the land with house and building thereon, except the Church, sold for £40,000. By this sum the Wesley Church and Parsonage was erected, and important aid was given in the building of Churches at North Melbourne, Emerald Hill, St. Kilda, Brunswick-street (Fitzroy), and elsewhere. The site for the Wesley Church has proved an unfortunate one, not well to be discerned at the time of its erection; but the building is a handsome commodious structure in the decorated Gothic style, with a tower at one front entrance rising to the height of 100 feet, and surmounted by an octagonal spire, 75 feet high. It is estimated to seat 1700 persons, and is one of the finest ecclesiastical buildings in the Southern Hemisphere. Of late years, it has not been a success as a parish Church, but it has served grandly as a central Church and Cathedral. Owing to the movement, taking place in large cities, of respectable families farther from the centre to the suburbs, the ordinary congregation is small for the size of the building, but it is swollen to vast numbers upon important occasions, and at Connexional services. It is a central spot, to which masses of Methodists come from the radiating suburbs, when a service of more than ordinary interest takes place. Good Mission work has been faithfully done amongst the demoralized classes which are not far from the Church. The opening services were marked by a high tone of spirituality and blessed results. The officiating Ministers were Revs. Dr. Cairns, Isaac New, William Butters, and Joseph Dare, who gave impressive and eloquent discourses. August 26th and 29th were red letter days in the Methodist Kalendar, as this beautiful edifice was set apart for Divine worship. This was the epoch of substantial Church building. One was opened at Fitzroy-street, St. Kilda, on September 19th, 1858; another at North Melbourne on June 5th, 1859; another in Brunswick-street in 1860; one at Emerald Hill in 1864; and yet another at Prahran, September 20th, 1864; besides minor ones at Sackville-street, 1857; Fitzroy-street, 1858, in the Melbourne East Circuit, and at other places. The transfer of the Collins-street land was not effected without the trouble and expense of an Act of Parliament. Some difficulty was met in obtaining the full amount of purchase money; harassing anxieties and additional outlay were occasioned by the failure of contractors in those trying times, in the erection of the Wesley and St. Kilda Churches; but the result repaid the toil, anxiety, and cost in the stately and commodious structures, which in so many centres of population made such extended provision for the public worship of God. Wesley Church has been often the place of gathering for our solemn feasts, and the praises of God in festival joy have gone up therefrom to the vaulted arches of heaven. It has been to many an altar of consecration to God; a place of ordination to the Christian Ministry for our young and God-commissioned men; a Bethesda of healing to numbers that have come within its porches, and a Bethel of God's presence to multitudes gathered together in its temple worship—"None other than the house of God, and the gate of Heaven." May the pointed spire of this Church be long an index and symbol of the heavenward aspiration of the worshippers assembling under the roof; be as a conducting rod which shall take harmless to the earth, heaven's lightning wrath, that might otherwise scathe the surrounding population for the abominations of the city; be the outward sign of the invisible grace of earnest pleading, offered within the walls, like to those of Abraham on behalf of guilty Sodom, to deprecate and turn away the deserved judgments of God; be a height which, like the mountain peak, shall arrest the clouds of heaven's blessing, and precipitate their fatness of fertility upon the adjacent lands; be as a minaret from whence shall issue the Christian's daily call to prayer; be as a pointer to the polestar, guiding many a heaven-bound mariner over life's tumultuous waves; and be as a staff, heaven-pointing and heaven-piercing, from whence shall be borne aloft the flag of heaven's kingdom, the rallying point of those who strike for spiritual liberty, and of those who would mount by Christian worship on earth to a place near the throne of God in heaven!

PRECURSORS OF REVIVAL.

CHAPTER VII.

THE period 1858 to 1865, inclusively, was pre-eminently one of revival. But ere we recount any summary or details in revival work, let us remark on some other events worthy to be noted. The Ministry had received additions to its ranks in Revs. Thomas Williams, George Daniel, J. S. H. Royce, and Alfred Rigg, who had been Missionaries in the Fiji, Friendly, and Navigator Islands, and by their faithful service had largely contributed to the spread of Christianity and the growth of Christian Churches in those fair isles. Mr. Williams was already in well-deserved repute for his graphic and picturesque account of "Fiji and the Fijians," which is the great authority on the subject. The Rev. John G. Millard had been transferred from New South Wales. He is an eloquent and popular preacher. His *bonhommie* and facetiousness make him good company. If wit and apt repartee belong to the cloth, surely he has wrapped himself in a large mantle of it. Traditions of these things, which cling to such men as Sydney Smith, Rowland Hill, and Jesse Lee, will probably in our after times cling to John G. Millard. But he has also been successful in the great Master's work. Francis Neale, coming from the home country, immediately after his arrival commenced his active Ministry, which has been continued to this time. Mr. Neale, with a physical frame in strong contrast to Mr. Millard's, is somewhat akin to him in popular eloquence. Choice, well-balanced sentences, set in poetical form, given forth with clear tones and attractive style, serve to convey good ideas and sound Scriptural instruction to their hearers. Both write poetry, and Mr. Millard's fertile brain has composed some rhymes in dreams of the night. He is the author of a Victoria Jubilee Ode. The Rev. James D. Dodgson came to these shores as an invalid, having been for some time in the Ministry in England. He has regained his health, and has been a most acceptable preacher in Circuit work. Thoughtful, sound, keeping close to Wesleyan theology in his sermons, fairly energetic in his delivery, with a pleasing address; he, nevertheless, is precise, wanting in abandonment to the enthusiasm of the moment, slavishly keeping to a prepared line of thought and verbiage which mark a memoriter preacher. We are not positive that Mr. Dodgson is the latter style of preacher; but we think so. God has employed him as a winner of souls. The Rev. Edwin I. Watkin, Jesse Carey, R. Osborne Cook, Edward B. Burns, are Colonial men, who have for the most part spent their Ministerial career in this colony, and have been a credit to Victorian Methodism. Mr. Watkin is of superior gifts as a preacher, very genial in spirit, plodding, and painstaking in his diligent labours as a Circuit Preacher and Pastor, has won great popularity, and is now the respected President of Wesley College. He has not taken up the ornate style of some Ministers mentioned before, but is known for his terse, pregnant sentences in speaking and composition, his homely common sense, and his abundant, often quaint, and humourous anecdotes. He answers more to the model of Samuel Coley, than any other prominent man in our Victorian Ministry. Entering the Ministerial ranks in these years, and beginning to try their powers, are— Ebenezer Taylor, Robert S. Bunn, Andrew Inglis, Henry Baker, Francis E. Stephenson, W. Weston, Thomas Edmeades, A. R. Fitchett, Albert Stubbs, Lorimer Fison, M.A., James A. Taylor, David Annear, James. W. Tuckfield, Jabez B. Stephenson. With varying gifts, they have been earnest labourers in the vineyard of the Lord. Some of them were connected with Victoria but a short time. Three went to New Zealand, three to South Australia; others have given part of their Ministerial service to Tasmania and Fiji.

Laymen worthy of some place in the Church's roll of remembrance are Mr. Hyde, a Class Leader at Lonsdale-street and in Fitzroy, who could not be beguiled to the diggings, but stood firm at his post in that exciting time. (1851-5) Mr. William Ellis was a Secretary and Superintendent, much beloved in Wesley Church Sunday school. Mr. John M'Cutcheon, talented and active, was a labourer with him in the school. His brother, Robert, younger than he, has occupied a good place in Methodism. "Grandfather" Joseph Lowe, with his many sons, ought to have a niche in any temple of Methodist fame or story. He was the spiritual father of the Rev. Nathaniel Turner, and was always on the outlook to do good to young men. Kindly, genial, sterling, prayerful, "an old disciple." His sons, James and Joseph, are steady pillars of the Church, and of this family, William, the son, and James and David S. Lowe, the grandsons, are useful Ministers. Mr. Samuel G. King came into prominence as the Superintendent of the Sunday school at Hotham, and the Trustee most active in bearing the financial burdens of that Church. With some masterful style, probably acquired at the head of a large business, he is yet intelligent, hearty, most generous and free in his gifts, a good Committee man, a most earnest supporter of our institutions, an active friend to young men. Mr. Hotchin, his brother-in-law, has been an acceptable Local Preacher, and is the present courteous manager of our Book Depôt. Mr. A. J. Smith, has been a Class Leader for many years in Melbourne and vicinity, the first to start a class in Carlton, and in many departments of work he has brought to bear a kindly intelligence, and a warm Christian heart. Mr. James T. Harcourt, as an officer of the Church, and Member of Parliament, has sympathised with religious growth and social advance. Mr. T. J. Crouch is the man, with the Hon. Alexander Fraser, who has been longest identified with our interests, in the St. Kilda Circuit. He apparently likes debate, as the war horse the battle, is ready as a speaker, and enterprising as a man. The Hon. A. Fraser has been an influential Layman, as a Class Leader, Church Treasurer, Member of Legislative Council, and for a short time the Minister of Public Works. Space fails to tell of other good men and true, Messrs. Bee, Newman, Whitford, E. John, Allan Nicol, Parr, Martin, Bedggood, Pollard (of Richmond), Courtis, M'Callum, John Webb, N. Wimble, E. Oakley, H. Cornell, Patterson, E. Stranger, J. Swan, Johnson, and others, who for a greater or less lengthened period have stood by, in activity and fidelity, the cause of God, as represented in the Methodism of Melbourne and its immediate neighbourhood. The van standards of the host may have been borne aloft by the Ministers, but these worthy Laymen also stood by the colours, and led on the marshalled regiments to contest and victory.

We may refer to two welcome visitors from the British Conference, whose stay for a short period was in the years under review. The Rev. Dr. Jobson came as the representative of the Home Conference, being known by face or fame to many Methodists, and bringing with him a high repute as a fervent Minister, with a picturesque style of description, who had exercised for years a successful, soul-saving Ministry. He arrived in Hobson's Bay on December 14th, 1860. His stay was a fortnight, during which, mostly in the company of Mr. Draper, he visited Ballarat, Geelong, and other places in the interior; besides looking at the Churches and places of interest in and around the metropolis. His platform addresses were not, in our opinion, up to the level of his sermons. His sermons were evangelical, full of fire, searching, practical, hortatory, and persuasive, and that preached at the opening of Brunswick-street Church, on March 10th, 1861, will live in the memory of many, and was instrumental in leading some souls into the enjoyment of Christ's salvation.

The Rev. E. E. Jenkins, M.A., was a Minister of a different intellectual mould. He never uttered in public a slip-shod sentence, nor indulged in much of small talk, although he was genial, free, and sociable in private. His sentences were crisp, clear, and incisive, made up of vigorous thought, in picked, packed words. His is a master mind, and he brought gifts and resources of no mean order to the elucidation of Gospel truth in all his discourses. They attracted large numbers of hearers of all denominations, who invariably declared they had a rich treat and feast of the bread and marrow of Gospel doctrine, promise, and precept, in the repast he set before them. His lectures on India, and his platform speeches were all of that first-class character. Original and profound thought, with a suitable and masterly style of expression, marked almost every sermon that he gave. His published discourses, some of them heard with great profit in Victoria, rank with Dr. Pope's subtle, strong, beautiful expositions of Holy Writ, as of the best class that the Methodist Ministry and Press have sent forth in these later days. He came to this colony in June, 1863, and stayed until the end of January, 1864. The Rev. E. E. Jenkins is one of the General Secretaries of the Wesleyan Missionary Society in London, and was in 1872 the President of the British Conference.

The changes in Ministerial appointments had brought the Rev. John B. Smith from Tasmania to Victoria in 1860, and this Minister has since that year laboured in various Circuits with diligence and fidelity. He is well-known as a frequent contributor to the Methodist Press, having given choice products of his sympathetic spirit, fertile mind, and pastoral habits to various Circuits, and picturesque articles of his writing to the Methodist Press. The Rev. James Hutchison, who had been transferred from the Irish Conference, and had given two years of valuable pulpit service to the Melbourne East Circuit, was in 1861 appointed to Launceston. The Rev. Peter R. C. Ussher came from South Australia in 1865. Young Ministers were received on probation :—Mr. James Burchett in 1864, and Messrs. Bolton S. Bird, Thomas F. Bird, Edward Davies, Robert M. Hunter, W. Jennings, in 1865. Several of these are talented Ministers, and all of them have obtained a good report as earnest servants of God and his Church. Messrs. Burchett and W. Jennings joined other Churches.

Some Ministers passed from the muster roll of the Victorian Church. The Rev. W. Butters, in consequence of failing health returned, by leave of the Conference, to England in 1863, and has spent the eve of life in a suburb of London. His hard toil and pioneer work had well earned a period of comparative repose, in the midst of troops of friends in the land of his birth. The Rev. W. Hill had exercised a most acceptable Ministry in the Melbourne Circuits, and at Geelong, and was appointed to the charge of the Castlemaine and Sandhurst District in 1863. His friend, Mr. E. I. Watkin has rightly and beautifully said of him :—"As a preacher, his praise is in all the Churches. He had clear and comprehensive views of Divine truth ; his mind was richly stored with theological and general knowledge ; his language was perspicuous, elegant, and eloquent. In his mental constitution there were harmoniously blended the elements of strength and acuteness, taste and imagination. Easy, engaging, dignified in his address, he excelled as a platform speaker. Some of his public addresses were noble specimens of sanctified eloquence." Most that are acquainted with the history of this colony know that he was struck by the murderous blow of a prisoner in the Pentridge Stockade, into whose cell he had gone to give spiritual advice, and died therefrom on May 13th, 1869.

The decease of other Ministers of the Wesleyan Church in Victoria had preceded Mr. Hill's. The Rev. Walter Tregallas' name is the first on the obituary roll. He laboured but a short time in Portland, when he became afflicted with disease of the brain. He was removed to Melbourne, and had some lucid intervals, but died on July 3rd, 1856.

Another faithful Minister was taken to his reward after a short but successful career in this colony. The Rev. Theophilus Taylor died in Ballarat on January 4th, 1859. Ballarat Methodism owes most to him of any Minister, as with enfeebled strength, he laid the foundations, broad and deep, of the structure of Methodism in that important city and goldfield. His health suffered through the strain of excessive labours, and for a year or two he held a Supernumerary's position. His last days were eminently peaceful. His wife and child have, since his decease, been closely identified with our Church in Sydney. Mrs. Taylor was a noble helpmeet to her husband in his beloved work.

The Rev. James Odgers was a young Minister, who laboured for fifteen months in the active work, was then called to suffer during a prolonged sickness, which he bore with great patience, and eventually slept in Jesus on August 26th, 1862. He was a youth of considerable promise. These having served God in their generation, deserve a record in the annals of the Church.

In 1863, Australian Methodism celebrated the Jubilee of the Wesleyan Methodist Missionary Society. The daughter owed much to the mother, and rejoiced with her when her Jubilee was celebrated. The occasion served to raise a fund which was applied mainly to Colonial purposes. The promises to this fund exceeded £5000 in Victoria. Some portion went to augment the resources of the Church Building Fund, and another portion was held in reserve until such time as the Theological Hall should be erected. The interest of this reserve fund has aided to meet the cost of training Theological students in Victoria. The meetings held throughout the breadth of the land were joyous and enthusiastic in their character, and developed a great liberality in the people. The lists of subscribers show the names of men who were the brain, and bone, and sinew of the Methodism of that time, and are a permanent record of the men of mark and worth in the different Circuits. We could wish that there had been a strong increase of the Missionary spirit following this celebration; but as yet, Colonial is behind English Methodism in its zeal for the Foreign Mission cause. Would that we could write more to the credit of Victorian Methodism in this matter! When shall the example of large hearted and perennial liberality evinced in this cause by the British Churches be followed by us ? We have Mission fields almost at our door, grand in the successes won, and in the openings for further enter- prise. Shall we do a commensurate part towards the Christianizing of the nations, and colonizing of the lands of the Southern world ?

REVIVALS.
CHAPTER VIII.

THE tide of Revival mercy, which in 1858 spread with such a swift progress over the United States of America, which was attended by many unwonted phenomena in Ireland in the following year, and which beneficially affected the religious life of England and most Protestant countries of Europe, visited also these southern shores. It came in lessened energy, yet in that which carried spiritual health and salvation over the Churches of the land. The Wesleyan Church was largely blessed by it. She had been no stranger to Revivals. She is the child of Revivals, and has a strong liking and affinity for sound and Scriptural ones. These times of refreshing had come to Circuits and Churches, here and there, during the gold excitements, and had not been altogether absent from the first planting of the Church in the land, but were not so widespread as in this later period. The increase of members, which had been continuous in the seven years preceding 1858, was then largely swelled by the influx of Methodist people from other lands. The increase from that cause should have been much greater ; though it was undoubtedly large. Now, in the years 1858-64, whilst the stream of immigration continued, it was in a much decreased volume, and the exodus taking place in some years from Victoria to New Zealand, New South Wales, and Queensland was large, and consisted almost entirely of adult and able-bodied men.

F

The impressions made on Mr. Draper's mind by this large migration of people are shown by remarks of his in a letter of the date, August 28th, 1861 :—"The population has been most unsettled, and the incessant removals are prejudicial. Many of our members are off to New Zealand, and numbers are about to follow them. The miners are the most unsettled class of persons I ever knew. I expect that a great many will never return to the colony." Again, an entry in his diary of September 21st, runs thus :—"The people here are mostly Otago monomaniacs. The rush to New Zealand exceeds anything I could conceive of. About two thousand left here in one day, and still they go. It is supposed that 20,000 or 30,000 men will remove to the goldfields at Otago." So that at this time the increase of Church members, occasioned by the balance of immigrants over emigrants in favour of the colony, was a small one. But notable and large additions came through God's blessing upon ordinary services, and the Revival movements which now took place.

That at Brighton may be placed in the front of our notice, as it was one of the earliest in order of time. The rising cloud of blessing appeared at a lovefeast held at Great Brighton, on May 22nd, 1859. The sorrow for sin shown by numbers expressed itself in tears and prayers for mercy. The Sanctuary became a Bochim, a place of weeping. Nine persons professed that night to have their mourning turned into joy, by the sweet assurance of God's reconciling love, and others went to their homes "sorrowing after a godly sort," and seeking the conscious salvation of Christ. Then special services were held daily, and private devotions increased in intensity and spiritual power, so that soon there was "a sound of abundance of rain." The work went on amazingly, affecting all classes, the tender child and the aged sire, the educated man and the unlettered peasant. Answers to prayer were swift or immediate in a wife's conversion, a husband's decision and prayerfulness, and in whole families brought to love and serve God.

"Showers of blessing" came on devout worshippers, and on most of the congregations in this Circuit. The Rev. E. King, the Superintendent, wrote, "fools may have mocked, devils howled for rage, as they witnessed their empire invaded, and the prey delivered from the mighty, devotees of order may have rebuked us for confusion and irregularity, icy stoics gazed unmoved on scenes which filled angelic bosoms with rapture; but servants of the Heavenly King 'must speak their joys abroad,' and say, 'Praise the Lord, call upon His name, declare His doings among the people, make mention that His name is exalted; sing unto the Lord for he hath done excellent things.'" The Minister, who had the lead of this movement is, in temperament, calm, placid, even; in manner and spirit, courteous and kindly; not given to rant, nor favouring unseemly extravagancies in public worship; but he is a devout man, a faithful preacher, a diligent student of the Greek Testament, of sterling piety, a witness and embodiment of Christian holiness, and has been favoured, not so much with the smiles of the populace, but by the praises of good men, and with the benediction of several notable revivals under his ministry. Mr. Henry Baker, afterwards a Wesleyan Minister, was a leading and active instrument in this revival, a man filled with perfect love, a burning flame. The President of the Conference and other Ministers, came to the help of the Circuit Preachers, so that the good work spread to Little Brighton, Moorabbin, and the other places adjacent. The results of this religious revival were peace and goodwill where brethren had been at strife; the greatly quickened piety of professed disciples of Christ; the spirit of praise, prayer, love, self-denial, benevolence, triumphant in them; scores of careless, hardened sinners brought to seek the everlasting welfare of their own souls and those of their families and acquaintances; many trained in godly families taking the important steps of religious decision and surrender to Christ; between one and two hundred new members added to the Churches; and the fruits of good living thereafter manifesting the genuineness and power of the work.

The Melbourne Circuits shared in the blessing. In Wesley Church many conversions took place; at Brunswick-street Church, a great ingathering of converts was reported, and scenes of Pentecostal power were witnessed. Brunswick, Richmond, and other places near, were similarly favoured, in more or less degree, so that it was computed that in the city and suburbs 200 persons had recently professed that faith in Christ which bringeth personal salvation. The Castlemaine and Sandhurst Circuits were the scenes of like revival movements and power.

At the end of the year 1859, Drysdale was visited with a similar work of grace. The religious awakening and fervour caused groups of men and youths, who had idly lounged at the corners of streets and roads, or in the taprooms, to frequent the house of prayer. Families were converted. Two, four, and nine persons at a service, professed to find the Lord Jesus as a personal Saviour, Life, and Comforter. The moral aspect of the district became astonishingly changed. A Local Preacher, Mr. S. Stoneman was greatly honoured of God as the means of leading many to His footstool, and into the enjoyment of this salvation, by his pointed, but quaint preaching and fervent prayers. The Rev. J. D. Dodgson brought his lengthened experience of such work in the home country, to bear upon the conduct and extension of the Revival. The first Revival, and others that have succeeded it, have made Methodism the strongest religious denomination in the Drysdale and Bellarine District—about 42 per cent. of the population returning themselves at the last census as Wesleyans.

In 1860 and the following years, the Geelong Circuit had great prosperity under the powerful ministrations of the Rev. Joseph Dare, with the Revs. Joseph Albiston, and F. Neale and his other colleagues. Mr. Dare was singularly well qualified for leading on to good results those exciting times and scenes of popular religious fervour. He had a strong and mellow voice, a cheery commanding presence, and an enthusiastic spirit. He could enlist the power of sacred song, and be a leader of the liturgy which deprecates deserved wrath, and swells out in bursts of joyous praise. He was powerful in declamation, and was the most acceptable popular orator that has yet appeared in Victoria. He could not be compared with Bishop Moorhouse in that strong mastery of his subject, power of rejoinder, and wealth of knowledge which the latter applies to his pulpit and platform utterances. He was not so finished an elocutionist as the Rev. Charles Clark, but he could put far more heart into his sermons. Dr. Kelynack can excel him in word pictures and fascinating imagery, whilst on a par with him in his resounding voice, and wonderful inflexions of it. But still, Dr. Dare (as he afterwards was called) was, for mastery of an audience by commanding eloquence, and impassioned powerful appeal, the prince of preachers that we have yet had in Victoria. We do not think his mental grasp was wide or strong; he dealt chiefly with commonplace truth and modes of presentation of it, yet as Lowell says of the poet Gray, that in his "Elegy," commonplace thoughts have been lighted up with genius, so ordinary, homely truths were made forcible by Mr. Dare, through the clothing of graceful expression, the charms of style, and the genial heartiness with which he could convey them to his hearers. He had rounded, well-balanced periods, figures of speech, illustrative anecdotes, pertinent allusions to passing events and celebrities of the day; but, although these are common arts of the rhetorician, yet he gave them with a swing, fire, and inspiration, all his own. We fear that young Victorians will know little about him, and that to after generations his may be but a shadow of memorial, as oratory is so fleeting, and he has left nothing in print worthy of him. A sermon on the "Trinity of Persons in the Godhead," preached at the Round Lake Camp Meeting is in an American volume, and may be the exception to the general remark that nothing is extant in print equal to the orator's reputation. A few sermons and speeches are scattered in Connexional periodicals, but these will scarcely preserve his fame. The orator's speech, like the beauty's face, is a quick passport to favour; but it is also short-lived, passing away after a brief day, living in memory of contemporaries only, lasting mostly for one generation, having no such abiding influence as the writer's page, or the poet's verse. The orator must get something worthy of himself in print, if he is to live in after times. If the burning thoughts be only put into spoken words, these fly away, and are lost to sight; but if they be fixed in type, or circulate in the printed sheets, their currency will be to after generations. Dr. Dare was not only an eloquent man, but he was also a winner of souls. Many were the seals of his Ministry in all parts of the land.

Revivals are, in these later days, somewhat exceptional phenomena, or recur at irregular intervals; but they were the normal state of things in the earliest age of the Christian Church. But the day will come when they shall be constant and continuous, as in the brightest days of Church history. Instead of exciting wonder that multitudes of people should be swayed by a mighty impetus and consentaneous movement to attend to their eternal interests, the wonder ought to be that they should so long and so often neglect them. When we consider the relations of sinful dying men to a broken law, with its terrible penalties, to the cross of Jesus, with its manifestations of Divine love, and to the judgment seat, with its awards lasting through eternity, it is a cause for astonishment that men sit still, are careless as to their present state and impending doom, and do not as with one consent, like the people of Nineveh at Jonah's mission, humble themselves, repent of sins, and turn unto God, for the averting of His deserved wrath, and the ensuring of their tranquillity. The transactions of Redeeming love, as culminating in the tragic scene on Calvary, opening the way to a pardoning God and a glorious heaven, have attractions which ought to win at once the heart and the man made acquainted with them and coming under their power. The cross of Jesus is the great magnet for immortal souls, and the health-giving medicine for sin-stricken men, and should draw them more readily than the magnet does the iron filings, and as steadily as the tides follow the influence of the sun and moon. Yet men, who pride themselves on their knowledge and philosophy, object to sudden and wholesale conversions. The metropolitan press sneered at them when occurring in those days. Philosophic banter tried to ridicule them out of existence. Weatherwise predictions of the press said that the falling barometer, and its telegrams from different points of the compass, portended that gravest mischiefs were coming on. The wish, possibly, was father to the thought. But the prophets of the press were again at fault. No such mischiefs ensued. Did the Revival movement stop on account of these jeers and prognostications? It 'bated not one "jot of heart or hope," but "steered right onward." The barque of Methodism keeps on her voyage with prosperous gales.

"For day and night
Escort her o'er the deep,
And round her solitary flight
The stars their vigils keep.
Above, beyond, arc circling skies,
And heaven around her pathway lies."

This spiritual movement received a great accession of power through the labours of two remarkable men, each with his special gifts, and in his own methods of labour, under God's blessing, successful in turning many to righteousness. Mr. Matthew Burnett came to this colony in October or November, 1863. He began his work here in the Brighton Circuit. He proclaimed his mission to be to the masses. He sought, with the moral levers of personal sympathy and enthusiasm, the temperance reform, and the saving power of the Gospel, to reach the fallen, and uplift the degraded. He tried to bless especially the lower strata of society, and many converts were won from those classes. Some have fallen back through the power of ensnaring temptations and former habits; others remain as trophies of Divine grace, and many will be gems in the Redeemer's crown. His mission also took greatly with the poorer classes that were of respectable manner of life. A thin, spare man, of bilious temperament, yet of very hopeful spirit, he was unwearied in his efforts during a campaign to bring victory to the Lord's banners, and marshal numbers of recruits in the Lord's hosts. We cannot write in terms of unqualified praise of some of his methods of work. There were extravagancies in his personal actions; exaggerations, apparently unwitting, in his assertions and published statements of success; a laudation and bespattering with praise of all and sundry, big men and little men, who helped him in his labour, that did not commend themselves to persons of more sober thoughts and ways; but despite these drawbacks, he was the agent of the reform of hundreds of drunkards, and the conversion of a number of degraded sinners; and we, therefore, honour the man, and are glad for his mission. Brighton, Scarsdale, Clunes, Drysdale, Ballarat, and other Circuits were in quick succession the scenes of his unique labours; and later on he was employed in the Metropolitan Circuits, as, indeed, in most in the land. Matthew Burnett was a welding of egotism and enthusiasm, employed as a Protestant devotee, and a self-constituted dervish in the cause of religion. He was a forerunner of the Salvation Army, and introduced some of their tactics and strategy: flaming placards, monster meetings, torchlight processions, sensational methods, stirring, noisy exercises, having often more of sound than of sense, more of shouting than of grace. However, he indulged in no irreverent slang, but gave sound instruction, and now and again a powerful gospel sermon. These means together brought about like results with the Salvation Army, the bringing of all sorts of fish into the Gospel net. His movement was an erratic, comet-like orbit in our planetary system, going in and out among the regular and steady courses pursued by Circuit Ministers, and after years of labour he passed to other colonies, and is still under the Southern sky.

A man, still more marvellous in the power he wielded both over the educated and the illiterate masses, had preceded Mr. Burnett in his arrival. The Rev. William Taylor landed in Melbourne on June 16th, 1863. He had been a street Preacher in Baltimore, San Francisco, and other cities of America; a pastor also of a Bethel Church in San Francisco. In connection with the Bethel was a Seaman's Home, which had been burned down in one of the numerous fires which had taken place in that city. The loss by fire had involved Mr. Taylor in heavy pecuniary liabilities, for which he had made himself responsible; but as he had no means of his own, he bestirred himself to meet honestly the heavy sum owing by him. He wrote books in his peculiar vein and forcible style. They were readable, full of graphic incident, and of original or quaint views of men and things. By the sale of books, pushed by his personal influence, he made the effort to wipe off a debt of thousands of pounds, and succeeded. The 23,000 dollars were paid. He journeyed through the States of America, Great Britain, and Ireland, lecturing and preaching, with great success. He came to Victoria and began services which were marvellous in their results. His first Sunday in Melbourne was spent in Wesley Church, and thereafter a series of revival meetings was held. Mr. Draper has left this record about them:—"On each evening during the week a large congregation attended, and many came forward in the prayer-meetings which were held after preaching, requesting to be prayed for and taught to accept the Lord Jesus. Many found peace, and a deepening of the work of God was experienced in many of the Church members. On Sunday, June 28th, Mr. Taylor's labours were continued, and in the evening about forty-eight or fifty persons were in distress of soul, some fifteen of whom pro-

fessed to find peace with God through faith in Christ. . .
On Monday evening there were at least forty persons
around the altar of prayer. Several most interesting cases
of conversion occurred. On Tuesday evening the congregation was still larger, and very many were in distress, some
of whom obtained Divine consolation.

So the record travels on with similar entries over the
remaining days of the three weeks' services.

Meetings followed at Geelong, Ballarat, etc., with like
results ; and this earnest Minister went through the land
like a flaming torch-bearer and herald of salvation.

Mr. Taylor is tall, of dark complexion, of robust frame,
possessed of a resounding voice, with the intonations which
savour of America. In his preaching he deals out clear,
pointed, heart-searching truths, in a plain, nervous, vigorous
style. For clearness, force, and directness, few preachers
surpass him. No one goes to sleep under his sermons ;
attention is kept awake by clear statement in homely
words, by abundant illustrations quaintly told, by narration
of incidents mostly falling under his own observation, by
what he calls 'surprise power'—unexpected turns of thought
or oddities of expression, or a sudden change from the
secular to the sacred, from the serious to the odd and even
ludicrous, from the laughable to the pathetic, or any swift,
strong contrast that presents itself to him. He can reach
the fountain of tears, or excite risible ideas and organs, and
is rather partial to such practice. He is not as emotional
as most English revivalists, but keeps himself and his
movements well under control. A more reverential tone
in prayer would have suited English ears better, and they
could have dispensed with some of his familiarities in
description. But he showed, by his shrewdness, tact,
vigour, directness of aim, and his use of song, great aptitude
for evangelistic work, and God wonderfully owned his
labours in this land. He was received into the Ministry
of the Methodist Episcopal Church of America in 1843 by
the Baltimore Conference, and has spent years in the

Eastern and Western States, in Great Britain and in Australia. After his visit here, this indefatigable Minister went through Southern Africa, from Cape Town to Natal, winning many trophies for Christ amongst the Kaffirs, as well as among the colonists. He has planted Missionary Churches in various parts of India, in South America, (where Romanism so largely prevails) and has of late been constituted by the General Conference of the American Methodist Episcopal Church, Bishop for the Continent of Africa. He is the grandest Itinerant that Methodism or the world has yet known.

The Revival work proceeded in many places around Melbourne not visited by Mr. Taylor. Such was the spirit of religious enquiry and awakening that was abroad, that it made but little difference who was the preacher that conducted the service. Almost every one was blessed in his ministry of the word, to the conversions of sinners, and saw immediate fruit of his labours. Prahran, Moorabbin, and Williamstown, were places that Mr. Taylor did not visit; but there also extensive Revivals took place. In the latter town incidents occurred which illustrate the mental phenomena, the spiritual struggles, the petty persecutions, the spiritual uprising and life which take place in a Revival. A boatman had been a drinker, and occasional gambler. A fortnight before the special services he began, under a deep conviction of personal sin, to seek to the mercy of the Lord. He was the first to come forward the place of prayer when the invitation was given one Monday night. On the following night he was made happy in the conscious favour and love of God. When asked to give testimony of God's work, he fell on his knees in the sight of all present, and thanked God for His pardoning mercy. His prayer at the time was remarkable for simplicity, fervour, and even fluency, considering that it was the first public prayer that he had made. He afterwards endured much petty persecution. A young clerk was converted. His business took him daily to Melbourne.

In the railway carriage, a youth, urged on by older persons, struck him. The assailant was younger than himself, and the mean young men, who were urging on the offender, said to the clerk, as the blow was dealt without any provocation on his part, "You ought now to turn the other cheek." The young clerk felt, as he said, somewhat ashamed, whilst yet he contended with the feelings of indignation and resentment, but he was enabled to bear the provocation without returning it in the same coin. He had afterwards to bear some similar persecution, although less violent; but his faith was made stronger in the Lord by patient endurance of these aggressions. Another bank clerk, a gentleman in a responsible position, was converted in a Sabbath school prayer meeting, and became earnest and zealous for God. He was of a warm temperament. A tradesman, converted at the same meeting, was of the opposite disposition: very impassive in his feelings, and somewhat inert in his mental action, so that some expected that it would be some time before he would be in downright anxiety for God's salvation, and that, when he found it, he would not be very joyous over it. But as the Minister was explaining the way of saving faith to the children of the Sabbath school, this man apprehended the relation of Christ as a Saviour to him, and believed to the saving of his soul. He said afterwards that his joy of that afternoon, he could not before have conceived it possible for a man to possess.

The Minister had visited a lady of his congregation in the course of his pastoral duty. During prayer, a few children, playing outside of the house, were making a disturbing noise. After prayer she apologized, laying the blame upon her neighbour's children. A little time elapsed when she came to the Minister, and acknowledged how her conscience had troubled her that she had blamed the children of other people, when she believed some of her own were as noisy as her neighbours'. This showed the tenderness of the woman's conscience. Some would think so conscientious and tender-hearted a lady had no need of any saving change, but when the Revival began, her conscience pricked her for other offences, both against God and man, and she was early bowed amongst the seekers of mercy, and enabled to rejoice in the Lord. Then her husband was stirred to enquire for this experience of salvation. As the lady knelt by her husband at the 'penitent form' she spontaneously declared what God had done for her soul, and said she would not exchange the happiness of the past few days for a kingdom. She encouraged her husband to believe, and during the week he was also rejoicing in the possession of Divine love. The sister, and sister's husband were converts shortly afterwards. Captain H—, who had been of note on the goldfields, came to Church with a revolver in his pocket, believing that some kind of magic or mesmerism had caused the people to be led like like a flock of sheep in seeking religion, and resolved, as he said, that no one should touch or molest him, except at his peril He went away unharmed and having hurt no one, although the Minister spoke to him directly and personally about his soul's welfare; and Mr. H— afterwards said: "The meeting was quiet, and the Minister very civil." One enquirer, a lady, was at a particular meeting in great distress of soul, weeping before the Lord. The meeting was prolonged later than usual, in the expectation that she would find the blessing sought. Just before 11 o'clock her prayers were heard, and she burst forth in a doxology of praise in which those around gladly joined. Her acquaintance had little idea that she could sing, but sweetness, strength, music, and heart were in her voice as she sang, "Praise God from whom all blessings flow, etc." When she got home, her husband was ready to complain, because of the late hour, but she said little in reply, beyond a brief explanation of the cause of her delay. He had attended one or two of the special services, and was a regular hearer on the Sabbath. His presence at any Revival meeting had been partly from curiosity, partly for amusement; but now he came in a more serious frame of mind. He sought interviews with the Pastor, and in a short time was travelling heart and hand with his wife in the way to heaven.

Another wife brought her husband to the meetings. He had been a backslider, and in the whirl of those exciting business times, had gone grievously astray. But when this pious woman had brought him to the altar of prayer, she knelt by his side, and told the Lord about the grievousness of his sins, and her own anxiety to save him from ruin, for she had come 16,000 miles for the express purpose of leading him (if possible) back to Christ. The husband had restored to him the joy of salvation. Some received the peace of the Gospel at their work, some on journeying home from Church, one in a railway carriage, some in the quiet of their chamber, but a great number at the meetings in the house of God. About sixty-five or seventy adults in that town then began a religious life, besides a great number of young people in the Sabbath school. Persons, formerly neglectors of worship, and grossly immoral, backsliders, those of moral lives, and of respectable standing in Society, were all sharing in one common joy of experimental godliness. We are not asserting that all kept on steadily in the way of the Lord. Alas! some did not; but numbers are to be found this day as Lay officials in different parts of the colonies, others are respected Church members, one, Rev. W. Burridge, has become an active, devoted, and very acceptable Minister of the Wesleyan Church. Some sailors were converted who went away in their vessels to other parts. The Bethel flag at that time was hoisted over the Wesleyan Church and attracted many seamen to the services. Captain Hedstrom, now harbour master at Levuka, Fiji, was then brought to a saving knowledge of Christ. At a later date, in 1864, a Swedish ship, commanded by Captain Swenson was in port. He was already a pious man, but the Second Mate, and some of the sailors were brought into the enjoyment of heartfelt religion whilst attending the Wesleyan service, and the

Captain wrote afterwards to Mr. Blamires, acknowledging the good that had been done, that the work of conversion was going on amongst the seamen, and that the crew were. often singing hymns of praise to Jesus, as they were crossing. the Indian Ocean. The praises of God not only resounded over the ocean wave, but in many tabernacles of rejoicing on shore, for there was great joy in that town ; not only with the Pastor, his excellent wife, his fellow helpers, but amongst the children, also many of whom were converted to God. The shipmaster alluded to, sent the following letter to the Rev. Kerr Johnston, Seaman's Chaplain, at Sand-ridge :—" My crew was very much blessed during our stay in Hobson's Bay, particularly in the Wesleyan Chapel in Williamstown. But they have told me that they understood you best of all they heard in Australia, when you were talking to them in the cabin of the *Cecilia*. Oh ! it has been a pleasant voyage from Australia ! Sweet hymns have sounded over all the ship in the Indian Ocean, and fervent prayers have been sent up to our Heavenly Father by my dear Brethren among my crew. We are now loading rice for Europe, and I hope to see my dear wife and children next spring. May we all be united in Christ by faith, ready to enter the kingdom of glory, when our beloved Saviour comes or calls us to depart from this world. . . . Signed, Joseph Swenson, and dated from Indromago, Java, October 15th, 1864. (See *Wesleyan Chronicle* 1864, p. 208.)

Similar accounts of Revival work and spiritual success in other Circuits could be multiplied. The sowing and reaping came together in many places ; but in others a longer time elapsed between the reaping and the planting God gave the increase. The offerings of praise, for his servants rejoice together, were a chorus taken up by many voices, an ode common to the whole Church. It is not asserted that all the blossom of these Revivals has been followed by ripe fruit in every instance where the bud and bloom seemed so promising, but a glorious harvest has been gathered. Do critics of the movement aver that some fell away, that some kept not their vows and pledges, that a low state of piety followed in others, that worldliness crept in to alloy the pure gold of religion, that some deteriorating elements came to mar the work? We admit *that*, in some degree, as, alas! too true. But we ask, Does polished steel get no tarnish in a surrounding moist atmosphere? Does the stream get no earthy matters mixed with its volume from the adjacent banks of the river bed or tributary streams as it flows on farther from the fountain head toward the ocean? Yet we rejoice in the good quality of the steel, notwithstanding a little tarnish now and then. And the stream of water has many good qualities for refreshment of man, life of beast, and fertilizing of the soil, notwithstanding it is not so pure as at the source or spring. So, despite some drawback, the glorious result, on the whole, has been an immense gain in accessions to Messiah's kingdom, a steady advancement in the cause of Scriptural holiness, and a wider exemplification of practical piety. Methodism is wonderfully the better for these revivals. They have raised members to a higher standard of piety, and led them to a life of greater usefulness. Mr. Elijah Stranger may be quoted as a sample of this. About this time he, with a number of others, entered into the experience of entire sanctification, and the influence he has exerted, for years past in his Society classes, numbering about 150 youths of both sexes, and in the Sabbath school at Brunswick-street, where, perhaps, spiritual results have been more ample than in any other school in this colony, has been of the most gratifying character. He stands out as a prince in our Israel, (despite the drawbacks of a little narrowness of view), for his ministry to the sick, his success amongst the young, his mission labours amongst the lower classes in Collingwood, and the general fruitfulness of his devoted life. He gives his whole time as an unpaid agent to the cause of God in several departments of the work. In many circles his name is as ointment poured forth, and his record is on high, It has been affirmed that sixteen Ministers of the Gospel now in these colonies are fruits of Mr. Taylor's labours in his first visit. We are not able to state this positively. but we have understood that Messrs. D. O'Donnell, Thomas Adamson, B. Butchers, B.A., Moses Bullas, and others in the Wesleyan Ministry, date their conversion to Christ from his labour and that time. The Revival has had a blessed fruit in the younger generation of Wesleyan Ministers. Whilst other colonies have needed to send to the home country for a supply of young Ministers, Victorian Methodism has been able since that period to raise her own supply and furnish a few to other lands. She has many to guide the Churches of the sons whom she has brought forth These are for Ministerial effectiveness and varied gifts and earnest piety, comparable with any like number that Britain has sent to the Southern world. Of Victorian Ministers, now in the prime of their strength and days, men such as Messrs J. W. Tuckfield and Charles Lancaster are eminent for their simple-hearted and devoted piety; Thomas Adamson and Edmund S. Bickford for their energy and administrative ability; William H. Fitchett and B. Butchers, for their keen weapons in polemic warfare; Richard Fitcher and Alexander R. Edgar, for their popular soul-saving preaching; Messrs. T. Grove and David S. Lindsay as effective Superintendents, who have witnessed extensive Revivals. Messrs. Burridge, Ingamells, Ingham, J. H. Tuckfield, Knee, Cowperthwaite, are energetic, acceptable labourers in the vineyard, who work well in their respective Circuits; Messrs. A. Powell, J. P. M'Cann, E. C. De Garis, are younger men of popular talents as public speakers; and a host of others, Samuel Adamson, Marsland, Saloway, Robin, James Lowe, David S. Lowe, etc., are doing good service in Colonial Methodism and find a glad acceptance amongst the people. The majority of these commenced their Christian career about the times we are now passing in review. Tasmania has also furnished able men in Messrs. E. W. Nye, R. Brown, J. J. Brown, R. Philp, S. T. Withington, now labouring in Victoria, and in the Rev. G. T. Heyward, who has retired from active service because of delicate health.

The rapid strides of the Wesleyan Church, owing largely to Revivals which occurred in almost every Circuit, also to the ordinary operations of the Church, are shown by the increase of membership in these years. For 1858, (reported at the Conference in January of the succeeding year), that yearly increase was 743; 1859, 765; 1860. 722; 1861, 485; 1862, 100; 1863, 374; 1864, 1705. The membership had more than doubled in those seven plenteous years, mounting upwards from 3194 to 8088. For these successes, the Church, by her pastors and people, raises her anthems of praise—

> " O the goodness of God, employing a clod
> His tribute of glory to raise !
> His standard to bear, and with triumph declare
> His unspeakable riches of grace.
>
> O the fathomless love, that has deigned to approve
> And prosper the work of our hands !
> With our pastoral crook we went over the brook,
> And, behold, we are spread into bands.
>
> Who, we ask in amaze, hath begotten us these ?
> And inquire from what quarter they came,
> The full heart, it replies, they are born from the skies,
> And gives glory to God and the Lamb."

CHURCH INSTITUTIONS, MOVEMENTS, MEMORIALS (1863-85).

CHAPTER IX.

THE progress of the Church during these years of increase had led the Conference of 1863 to divide the One District of Victoria into Three, respectively entitled, "The Melbourne," "The Geelong and Ballarat," and the "Castlemaine and Sandhurst," Districts. The Districts were nearly equal in numerical strength, the first-named having 1893, the second, 2394, and the third, 1718 members. Geographical reasons, the ready means of oversight, and the convenience of assembly without lengthened travel, which had required this convenient first partition, led subsequently to the Ovens and Murray District, and the Gippsland District being formed out of the Melbourne District, and to the excision of the Western from the Geelong and Ballarat District. Such are the divisions of the colony at the present, for the Methodist province, called the District, which is an aggregate of contiguous Circuits, having their representative annual meetings of Ministers and Circuit Stewards, which prepares business for Conference in the more minute examination of Ministerial character, the qualification, and studies of probationers, fitness of candidates for the Ministry, and review of the spiritual and financial state of the Church. Such meetings are also used, though rarely, for some purposes of discipline.

The cause of Day and Sabbath School education had still engaged much of the attention and liberality of the Wesleyans. Their success was marked by the gratifying statements in the Registrar-General's report, 1861-2:—" Of the three principal Protestant denominations, the Church of England, the Presbyterian, and the Wesleyan, the last-named was found to have the largest number of children at the schools, all possessing the rudiments of instruction ; inasmuch as 88 Wesleyan children in 100 could read and write, against 82 Presbyterian children, and 77 children of members of the Church of England." The Denominational Board had not, however, encouraged, as it should, the active zeal of the Wesleyans by proportionate grants, so that Wesleyan efforts were somewhat crippled, and the Wesleyans hailed with joy the enactment of the Heales' *Common Schools Act*. This superseded the Denominational and National Boards, which had been competing, and merged them into one. This made more economical and uniform the system of public education. This Act was comparatively silent upon religious instruction, but it was understood that it should be given, and so in practice the Act was administered by all concerned. But when afterwards an act was brought in by the Attorney-General, subsequently Judge Stephen, which changed the voluntary, paid, and religious system, into one, compulsory, secular, and free, we fear that the religious denominations were not sufficiently alive to the one pernicious quality of the Act amid its many good provisions for popular education. They protested against the ban put upon the Bible in the Statute Book, in reference to State schools, but saw that in administration the Act might be so interpreted and carried out, as to allow of religious instruction at some time, either in or out of school hours. But the Act has usually been administered to bar or impede religious instruction. But not always. Much has depended on the bias of the Minister of Education for the day; Mr. Stephen, Mr. Mackay, and Mr. Ramsay, have rendered themselves notorious for their opposition to any kind of religious knowledge creeping in by any sanction of theirs, the latter Minister of Education being responsible for the excision of the name of Christ from the School books, and the small distinctive Christian teaching that had remained in them. Mr. Munro and Mr. Service have been more indulgent, and have permitted religious instruction by competent persons other than the teachers. The Wesleyans were somewhat deceived in hoping that the administration in respect to religious teaching would be as gracious as under the "Heales' Act," but they have never varied from the view that all sound education must have a religious basis. Hence their strong, tenacious, reiterated expression to the Legislature and to the public at large, that the present valuable Act needs immediate alteration in allowing or directing Bible instruction in School hours. Those who are deaf to the voice of the Churches now remember but little how much the cause of popular education, in cheap schools and by cheap books, is the child of religious enterprise. Wesley moved in these matters long before any one else in England. Church action did the most to spread and popularize schools in this land when commercial men were busy in looking after gold and gain, and politicians had as much as they could do in settling party questions, and in allaying political ferment and strife. The choicest minds of our Church look with alarm upon the present exclusion of the Bible and Christian teaching from State schools, as pregnant with serious educational and moral evils to the whole people. The Wesleyans have done their best in the middle class schools established by them, Wesley College and the Methodist Ladies College to leaven the whole of education, and of the every day life of the young, with the religious spirit, principles, and training. They have, nevertheless, done this in a way as to offend no reasonable religious prejudice. In that way, as well as in the ordinary curriculum of secular studies, these Colleges have been a great success. The foundation stone of Wesley College was laid on Wednesday, January 4th, 1865, by Governor Sir Charles Darling. The buildings are in the Italian style of architecture, and occupy the four sides of a quadrangle, the front being 126 feet in extent, and the sides 150 feet in depth. The area of ground occupied for school premises, is eight acres, facing the St. Kilda road, and reaching back to Hoddle-street. The first outlay was £5700 for building alone, towards which the Government had granted £2700. More expenditure was made for furniture and school fittings, and other buildings were required. The furniture, etc., cost over £2000, of which £1000 was given by the munificence of Mr. Walter Powell, on condition of a similar sum being raised in the colony. £1500 was thus raised, and Mr. Powell's liberal sum was secured. The College was opened in February, 1866, and its success has been assured from the first, and has more than answered the sanguine expectation of its promoters. Some of the foremost young men in professional and commercial life in this and adjacent colonies, have been educated there. Its honours gained at the University by the youths grounded in rudiments of learning, and in studies suitable to their age at the College, but afterwards passing through other courses of study at the University, have been equal to those of any similar institution. These successes have been owing largely to the several head masters, Dr. Corrigan, Professors Irving and Andrew, and the present accomplished Head Master, Mr. Way. But Rev. Dr. Waugh's name is most identified with the prosperity of Wesley College, as he was its first President, and continued to retain that position for eighteen years. His judicious management, and blended firmness and considerateness in treatment of the youths, have served largely to place Wesley College in the high position in public esteem which it holds. The domestic department could not have been presided over by a more judicious, winsome, and kindly lady than Mrs. Waugh. Dr. Waugh has rendered more important services to the youth of Victorian Methodism than any other Minister that could be named. The Students, who have in our Provisional Theological Institution been prepared for the Wesleyan Ministry, have for years been under his care, and testify to the efficiency of the intellectual drill, and soundness of theological knowledge which they obtained from their President. Dr. Waugh has been a firm defender of our doctrine and polity on the platform and in the press, a faithful servant of the Church during his long career, and now in retirement he has the well-earned esteem and reverential attachment of all who know him. His grey head is a crown of honour. His upright, stalwart frame is indicative of the unflinching fidelity of the man. His energy is abating, but his graces are ripening in the decline of life. A crown of glory from the Master's hands awaits him in the better world.

Another eminent Minister, who has been prominently before our readers, enchains attention now by the tragic character of his death, through the foundering of the *s.s. London*. Mr. Draper had fallen out of the Circuit ranks in 1865, and took a well-earned holiday in a visit to the home country. His brethren of the Clergy and Laity had bidden him farewell on his departure in a series of brotherly meetings, with gifts and prayers, expecting his return after the expiration of his trip to Europe. But it was not so to be. In the violent storm which overtook the ill-fated ship in the Bay of Biscay, he and others were engulfed beneath the wave. But the circumstances of his death and the nobly heroic part which Mrs. Draper and he played in the solemn position in which they were placed, have awakened the wondering admiration and praise of the civilized world. In that terrible conflict with the horrors of death, he was calm, self-possessed, and eager to proclaim the Gospel of a present salvation through Christ to the poor creatures around him. By the many memorial services held in the fatherland and in the colonies, the Christian world showed the esteem in which he was held. The Wesleyans have perpetuated his memory by a tablet in Wesley Church, a scholarship at Wesley College, and by a memorial volume which was issued by the Revs. J. C. Symons and Joseph Dare, D.D. It has also been kept green in the memory of Cornshmen by a Life Boat named after him, which is stationed at Penzance, and has already been useful in the rescue of many persons from a watery grave.

Another memorial of Mr. Draper is in a volume written by the Rev. John C. Symons, whose literary industry has been considerable. His has been the most active pen amongst us. Besides contributions to the serial press, he has issued controversial pamphlets, which are good for their able reasoning and logical force. One other pen may be mentioned beside his as a prolific one. It is that of the Rev. W. H. Fitchett, B.A. He has, from his entrance to the Wesleyan Ministry, wielded an able pen in the cause of truth and religion. It is keen and caustic in satire, vigorous and epigrammatic in argument, racy and graphic in description, at times poetic and imaginative in its treatment of nature's grandeur or beauty, and in all respects well-fitted by its taking style to enchain a reader's attention and interest. For its *verve*, point, incisiveness, it is a style like to that of good French writers, and for its masculine force and simple, but expressive, diction, it could vie with some of the best Anglo-Saxon authors. He is, as a prose writer, one of the foremost in Australian literature. Pity that so much of his strength and ability has been expended in ephemeral articles of the daily or weekly press, and that he has furnished nothing worthy of himself in a permanent form! Mr. Fitchett, as a Circuit Preacher and Administrator has been most loyal to Methodist doctrine and polity, and has reined in a mind, which, by reason of its imaginative scope and power, might be supposed to have great tendency to fancies and vagaries, new speculations, and experiments, by an exemplary fidelity to Wesleyan principles. His mind, whilst carrying strong sail, has good ballast, and we can wish him a prosperous voyage. His chivalrous enthusiasm and energy, that will not always take the counsel of more cautious minds, has done excellent service to the cause of education in the establishment of the Methodist Ladies' College at Hawthorn. He has been very sanguine about it from the start, and the first-class character of its training, and its increasing numbers and favour with the public are a grand certificate to the soundness of his views, and to the energy of his character and habits. No institution in this Southern world is more prosperous. 'Tis in its early youth, having only commenced in April, 1882; yet it gives promise of great usefulness, and of permanent success. Long life to it.

A name worthy of mention in connection with Methodist literature is that of the Rev. Benjamin Field, a Minister from the ranks of the British Conference, who came to reside in this colony for the benefit of his health. He was for a short season, the editor of the *Wesleyan Chronicle*, and has given to Methodism a most valuable contribution to its literature, his "Handbook of Wesleyan Theology." It is the best *vade mecum* that we know of, for young Local Preachers, Candidates, Students, and Ministers. Mr. Field was of a sweet spirit, very devout, an able preacher, with a rich unction attending his Ministry. His comparatively early death was greatly mourned by the Methodist community.

The Wesleyan Sunday School Union was inaugurated by a public meeting held in Hotham, on August 18th, 1873, and since that date has done good work in stimulating Bible studies amongst the young, and is gradually raising the standard of excellence in our Sabbath schools. The cessation of State aid to the Churches tried rather severely the financial resources of small and poor Circuits; some for a few years were greatly embarrassed, but a Circuit Relief Fund was formed which bore them through their difficulties to a more prosperous state, and on to better times. When State aid was abolished, the Wesleyan Home Mission was formed, mainly by the proposals of the Rev. John Watsford, and its management was entrusted to his care. In the older and wealthier Circuits his enthusiastic advocacy raised large sums of money, and in the newly-settled districts he travelled extensively, at great personal inconvenience and fatigue, with means of locomotion and accommodation very varied, but pioneering the Methodist cause, installing Methodist agents, encouraging local men and local efforts, and exercising a powerful Ministry, which has been singularly successful in the salvation of souls. The Northern Areas owe more in their religious provisions to good Father

Watsford than to any one besides. His labours and oversight, followed up by the devotion of young Ministers, Home Mission Agents, zealous Class Leaders, Local Preachers, School Workers, have made the Wesleyan Methodist the leading Church in those parts, and most influential in activity and numbers. Under his leadership Methodism has gone up and possessed most part of that fertile land. To God be all the praise!

Mr. Watsford is a strong man in physical energy, in intellectual force, and in religious and revival enthusiasm. Having depressing moods at times, constitutionally alternating between the sanguine and the melancholic, yet with a sound heart, a well modulated voice, capable of sonorous or of pathetic tones, with a physique and features that proclaim him every inch a man, he is an indefatigable worker, in labours more abundant, and in zeal, if not beyond measure, beyond most. He was the chief instrument of a remarkable visitation of grace and power at Surrey Hills, Sydney. At a memorable service which he conducted on November 14th, 1858, the sermon was with great power, hundreds remained to the after-prayer meeting, and it is computed that upwards of a hundred mourners were crying for mercy, and forty professed to receive assurance of pardon and peace that night. So in the Circuits in New South Wales, South Australia and Victoria, where he has been stationed, and in the places in the colonies and in England where he has preached, similar seals of a heaven-commissioned Ministry have been given, and hundreds from these lands converted through his instrumentality will meet him in heaven. He is a true son of Wesley; a Revivalist of the school of Bramwell, Smith, and John Hunt; a grand Missionary, for the early part of his Ministry was spent as a coadjutor of Hunt in Fiji; an ardent lover of every good cause, for he is warmly fervent and enthusiastically devoted in every movement that he favours or takes up; and is a Methodist Apostle and Bishop, if anyone be worthy of the position and name. He has the small spice of human infirmity to flavour his truly Christian worth, that he is not as tolerant as could be wished, of the opinions of other people who cannot see through his glasses, yet is he catholic-spirited, tender-hearted, charitable. He has been President of the Australian Conference; was elected first President of the General Conference of Australasian Methodism; and was the chief Represetative of this part of the world at the Œcumenical Council of Methodism held in London. Two of his sons are Wesleyan Ministers, like-minded with him, and are treading in their father's footsteps, and one devoted daughter, Mrs. Danks, is the wife of a Pioneer Missionary in New Britain. The name of Watsford is graven deeply on the Home and Foreign work of Christian enterprise in connection with Wesleyan Methodism in the Southern Hemisphere.

Exigencies of space deprive us of the pleasure of commenting worthily, however briefly, upon the devoted labours of Ministers who have appeared in later years upon the scene of Victorian Methodism, such as W. A Quick, John Cope, Spencer Williams, Robert C. Flockart, Henry Bath, who have been Presidents of Conference; Samuel Ironside, Nathaniel Bennett, William Brown, Alfred Rigg, Thomas Angwin, Jesse Carey, Richard Osborne Cook, Joseph White, who have been Superintendents of Circuits, and whose praise is in all the Churches; and upon junior Ministers that are worthy to stand side by side with their fathers in the Ministry, and to whom is committed the trust of perpetuating Methodism, and, under God, making it a greater power in the land; also Laymen who have rendered good service since the time of the first gold discoveries :—Messrs. W. Nettleship, John Danks, Callaghan, E. John, J. Wilton, T. Vasey, Leonard Robinson and others. We leave to those who become the future historians of the Church, the work to fill up where we have been lacking, in placing portraits in the historic gallery, and in sketching the later years of religious life in the first half-century of Victorian Methodism.

SUBURBAN METHODISM.

CHAPTER X.

THE Melbourne Circuit for a time embraced the whole colony, and such remote places as Portland and Port Fairy figured on the Circuit plan. At length these dim and distant extremities were cast off, and the Methodism of Melbourne was built up by the development of nearer interests, outlying positions which first received, and then radiated light and blessing to regions beyond, for most of them have since become Circuits and centres themselves. It is our purpose to trace the rise and course of what may be called SUBURBAN METHODISM. The first in chronological order is—

WILLIAMSTOWN—at that time the Port of Melbourne. The Rev. J. Orton calls it the Gravesend of the colony. It was more like a kind of *Appii Forum*, where those arriving or embarking at "The Settlement," as the district was first called, encountered each other. To be named after King William the Fourth indicates its antiquity, according to Colonial standards, for when it was first founded our Queen was then some steps from the throne. In 1838, Mr. Charles Stone, then an ardent and enterprising youth, arrived from Hobart Town, bringing "letters of commendation," and a sort of general commission from the Rev. J. Orton. It was proposed at first that he should join the Buntingdale Mission * but he at last settled as schoolmaster at Williamstown, occupying a lean-to room attached to the School building, in which Divine service was held, and he was, for a time, almost perpetual incumbent of the little cause. A Bethel flag waved over the spot, the liturgy of the Church of England was used, and doctors and captains of vessels were often found in the congregation. Mr. Stone describes the anxiety with which that rare event, the visit of a preacher from Melbourne was anticipated.

* NOTE.—See the story of this Mission in twelve papers in the *Methodist Spectator*, August 7th to December 31st, 1885.

The roughness of the way and the difficulty and delay of the Spottiswoode's Ferry, made the visit very uncertain, and after watching and waiting at a little look-out window, until the time was past, Mr. Stone had too often to supply the place. He was soon after married to Miss Hurlstone, and a Methodist home was established. This was one of the first marriages performed in the colony; the Rev. Mr. Grylls was the celebrant, there being no Wesleyan Minister. In 1840, the preaching was held in the open-air. At the first Quarterly Meeting held in Melbourne, on Jannary 28th, 1841, Williamstown is mentioned as greatly needing a new Chapel, and a Committee was appointed to secure one. The Rev. Mr. Orton and Mr. Witton visited the place together, and were grieved at the gross Sabbath-breaking and forgetfulness of God which they witnessed. In October 1841, the new Church was opened. The Rev. J. G. Millard then visiting Melbourne from Sydney in the steamer *Sea Horse* (Captain Ewing), heard the Rev. J. Orton at the opening service, and says that "a small steamer, the *Governor Arthur*, was chartered to convey the Melbourne friends to and from Williamstown, to participate in the inaugural services, and a good many availed themselves of the opportunity." In 1842 the name appears on the Melbourne plan with three services attached to it, viz:— 11, 2.30, and 6.30. In 1845 Mr. Stone removed to Brighton, and Mr. Witton to the Western District, and the Church was closed for some time. At length, Mrs. Captain Sutton, now Mrs. Mason, settled there and opened forthwith her house as the preacher's home. The Revs. Messrs. Sweetman, Lowe, Harcourt and various local brethren, after walking from Melbourne, to minister to "the little flock," often found rest and comfort there. Mrs. Sutton took a hearty and generous interest in maintaining Methodism in the place, and was for some years its mainstay and "nursing mother." In 1851, Williamstown disappeared from the Melbourne plan and became a separate Circuit. In 1854 the Rev. W. C. Currey was appointed to the Circuit by the General Superintendent, and a stone Church built. The writer was first welcomed by this Minister on his arrival from England in February, 1856, in the contingent then known as the "Nimrod men." He preached in the new Church, and found the old Church in the form of an attached skillion, constituting the Bachelor's quarters of the resident Minister. The next Ministers were the Revs. Messrs. Albiston, Dubourg, S. Knight, E. I. Watkin, and the President for the Jubilee year was its first married Minister; while the arrival of valued brethren as Messrs. Rupert Smith, M'Callum, Bunting, Burridge, Courtis, Murrell, etc., gave strength and weight to our Church. The present spacious Church and parsonage testify to the enterprising energy of the Rev. J. Harcourt, during whose superintendency they were erected. Those ancient and primitive places Albion and Maidstone, between Williamstown and Melbourne, were supplied by local preachers from town; but they are now comprised within the bounds of the new and promising Circuit of Footscray and Yarraville.

BRIGHTON comes next. It was then a scattered hamlet on the opposite side of the Bay, and communication between it and Williamstown was for awhile effected by a whaleboat, which set out in answer to a signal smoke raised on the shore; or else by trudging round on foot and crossing the Saltwater and Yarra in punts. Mr Charles Stone, then in his youthful prime, tells how, with his coat on his arm, and subdued with the sun's fervent heat, he has had to pick his way through the bush, which lay between the Yarra and Brighton. There was only one Circuit horse for the colony, and many competitors for that, Mr. Witton's celebrated "pony" being reserved for a few personal friends. In 1843 Messrs. Pemberton and Orr, members of the Melbourne Society, were wont to walk to Little Brighton to distribute tracts, and this opened the way for preaching and prayer-meetings. These were first held at the early home of the late Mr. G. Thomas, in a little slab hut, covered with thatch. A second service was held in the morning in the home of the late Mr. Thomas Walton, of Great Brighton, or Dendy's Survey, as it was then called. Mr. Walton was one of the members of the first class-meeting held in Melbourne, and his homely cottage at Brighton was dedicated to the worship of God by many a hearty prayer and faithful sermon from local brethren who "missioned" the place. The little room was often crowded, and the congregation sometimes diverted by sundry cooking and domestic operations which were carried on behind the preacher's back. In after years Mr. Walton was a familiar figure at all our services, and is remembered still as a sort of curiosity famous for the peculiar style of his public prayers, and other eccentric habits. He died about thirteen years since, leaving his cottage and allotment of land to the Wesleyan Church. The land on which the present Church and Parsonage stand, was also secured by Mr. Walton from the late Mr. Were, the agent for Mr. Dendy. The Home Government permitted at that time special surveys 4 x 2 miles in extent, and within six miles of the city. Mr. Dendy selected what has since proved the magnificent area on which Brighton stands, although he himself died not long since in comparative poverty. A small brick Church first marked this site, and afterwards became the Minister's study, the basis and beginning of various extensions which followed and constituted the old Parsonage. A strip of the reserve was also fenced off as a cemetery, and there some of "the rude forefathers of the hamlet sleep." Messrs. James Webb, Gifford, Baker, and others settled at Brighton, and in 1852 the Rev. William Byrnes was appointed to the Circuit, to be followed by the Revs. Messrs. Sweetman and Bickford. Little Brighton also profited by the arrival of Messrs. Hurlstone, Stone, J. Webb, Abbey, Head, Thomas, etc., who soon gave strength and shape to the infant cause. Classes were commenced, both at Little Brighton and East Brighton, under the care of Mr. Stone, whose fruit abides to the present day, and under the visits of such men as

Messrs. Marsden, Gallagher, and Hewitt, the word of the Lord grew and multiplied. Mr. Head soon removed to Gardiner's Creek (now the picturesque and prosperous township of Oakleigh) and opened his house for preaching. He was for a time the veritable "head" of the Church and sole representative of Methodism in that part, until joined by Messrs. Evans, and Beacom, etc. From these points the Word of the Lord "sounded out" to Moorabbin, Mulgrave, Kingston, Lightwood, and regions beyond, and good earnest work was done in these places at that time by Messrs. H. Baker, Lewis, Blencowe, Preston, Sykes, Cameron, and others, most of whom have fallen asleep. Our Church at Moorabbin is a fruitful vine, and has had a precious history. More than thirty years ago a few praying souls were wont to meet in the cottage, or in the bush, or at the stump of a tree, to greet each other in the Lord, exhort one another, and pray one for another. First a class meeting was started, then a Sunday school, next a small tenement was used for service, until the present holy and beautiful house of prayer arose, the joy of many hearts, and the scene of many blessings. True to the tradition of our fathers, and driven by the impulse which embodies itself in the ceaseless question: "What more can be done to promote the work of God?" we find an early minute in the Brighton Circuit book to the effect that a movement be made "to visit the outlying villages of Prahran and St. Kilda, and supply them with the ordinances of religion." Brighton was, for some years, a contingent of Melbourne, and governed by the Quarterly Meetings held in old Collins-street Church. The late Mr. Duffy, for some years sexton of that Church, was wont to recite some sharp passages-at-arms which took place at the Quarterly dinner on the temperance question, then just beginning to stir the conscience of the Church, and such instances of godly discipline and simplicity, as the following prevailed in those early days:—A Mr. W—, one of the earliest members of Society expelled for marrying a worldly and unconverted woman. A Local Preacher was "overtaken in a fault," and such was the zeal to purge this scandal, and "put away that wicked person," that the Circuit plan which had just been issued, was called in that his name might be struck off the same. Another brother was suspended for going to the New South Wales' goldfields, without having made proper provision for the support of his wife and family. "And I don't think," observes the narrator, "that he applied for compensation when restored." The present comfortable position of the Circuit in financial respects is largely due to the generous bequest of the late Mr. Carey, of about £2000, which has helped to discharge most of the trust debts and to sustain three Ministers on the ground. A contrast this to the panic and impoverishment entailed by the first rush to the diggings, when the senior Circuit Steward, in his dismay, proposed to repudiate the appointment of a Minister to the Circuit. For some years Brighton was the only Circuit South of Melbourne, and comprised, as a poetical brother used to phrase it, "the region from the Australian Alps to the South pole, and from the eastern main to the setting sun." Gippsland was then *a terra incognita*, although in 1847, according to the *Gleaner*, the Rev. F. Tuckfield was about to visit it with a view to establish religious ordinances. Meanwhile at Keysborough, near Dandenong, a staunch and worthy Irish Methodist, "Father Keys," as he was long and fondly called, had settled, and for many years the old root, and now the branches to the third and fourth generation flourish large and fair, the strength and stay of our cause in that part. The hospitality and true Irish welcome of the dear old couple, the first of that name, is still lovingly remembered. One Minister tells how the hostess used to ply him with good things, until he was fairly beaten, and in no mood for afternoon preaching, and the writer recalls the memory of those grand Circuit luncheons, a combination of Lovefeast and Quarterly Meeting,—genuine feasts of tabernacles, held in booths of bowery bushes,—and how the company beamed, and the tables teemed, and the knives and forks worked their way! But better than these things were the scenes of revival and "times of refreshing" with which this part was blessed under the labours of Mr. M. Burnett and others. The work at Berwick, Hastings, The Clyde, etc., was opened up in due course, Messrs. Ritchie, Searle, Patterson, etc., being the prominent agents in the same. Mr. Sykes, senior, one of the earliest East Brighton converts, became an earnest Local Preacher, and did good pioneer work around Dandenong and in parts of Gippsland, and so the old mother Circuit is now " spread into bands."

BRUNSWICK, COBURG, AND PLACES TO THE NORTH OF MELBOURNE.—Before the year 1841, occasional preaching had been held in this part in the houses of Captain Buck (Captain of the first "John Wesley"), and Mr. Thos. Jennings (late undertaker, of Queen-street, Melbourne). Merri Creek and Moonee Ponds are found on the first MS. Circuit plan. The latter place was soon dropped owing, as Mr. Stone informs us, to the neglect of the place by the Preacher appointed, and has only in the last year or two recovered from the "heavy blow and great discouragement" it received thirty years before. Mr. Stone remembers preaching there in those days in the men's hut of a Mr. M'Crae, a squatter, the men were very rude and restless, and the Preacher felt at the time, " I have laboured in vain and spent my strength for nought," but sixteen years after he was accosted by a man in Collins-street who recognised him with gladness and gratitude as the Preacher who had told him in the woolshed the way of life. MERRI CREEK—this was the vague designation of a district now more definitely known as Brunswick, and that name first appears on the Melbourne Circuit plan, November, 1841. Pentridge followed in August, 1842, with an afternoon service, held in the houses of Messrs. Sidebottom Harding, Kendall, etc. In March, 1850, after the name Pentridge, is added "Jeffery's Farm," and on the next plan, " Jeffery's " eleven o'clock, and " Christie's " three o'clock, appear as separate appointments taken by the same Preacher.

"Jeffery's Barn," at Irishtown, now Preston, and "Christie's Farm," on the Darebin Creek, near Janefield, are still fondly remembered by some surviving Preachers of that day, as the farthest outposts in that direction. The Revs. J. Harcourt and S. Waterhouse often visited these suburbs. There was also preaching at "Meagher's Barn," Greensborough, and at Mr. Fletcher's, at the lower Darebin Creek, now known as the district of Alphington. In 1855, PENTRIDGE was separated from Melbourne West, and Brunswick with a good brick Chapel, Schoolroom, and Schoolmaster's iron house, reverted to Melbourne East. The Rev. Barnabas Walker was the first Minister appointed to Pentridge, and this was his first Circuit. He had a good deal of ardour and enterprise, and sought to prospect and possess the land for Christ. To this end he undertook long journeys, and followed the people that were scattered abroad. In one direction he went as far as the old Caledonian diggings, near Queenstown, and traversed the region occupied now by the villages and townships of Eltham, Research, Kangaroo Ground, Queenstown, Kingstown, Christmas Hill, Panton's Hill, Yarra Flats, Healesville, Marysville, Lilydale, etc. There were no made roads in those days, the bush was very thick, and Mr. Walker often lost his way. Mr. Rodda, senior, returning from the Caledonian diggings settled down at Research, between Eltham and Kangaroo Ground. Preaching was commenced at LITTLE ELTHAM, and held for some months in the slab hut of Mr. Honeyball, late Postmaster, then a site of land was secured and a small brick Church built, since sold to the Rechabites, to be followed by the present handsome structure. Mr. Rodda, senior, a grand-nephew of one of John Wesley's own Preachers, was the father of our Church at ELTHAM, and Messrs. Rosier, Harding, Ford, Foley, and Harmer, etc., were among its earliest friends. Mr. Rodda still survives, a saintly and venerable man waiting for his change. He leads a peaceful and sequestered life in a home hallowed by meditation and prayer. Though unable for some years to leave his own ground, yet he is a most interesting and instructive character, whom it is a privilege to know. Well read in Methodist lore, he will recite its stirring facts and incidents to you whilst his grand old progenitor, "Mr. Richard Rodda, Ætatis, 74" (an enlarged photo., taken from the old *Methodist Magazine*, in ample and graceful wig, like to that which John Wesley wears in our old Hymn-books), looks down upon us from two or three points, as though to confirm it all. Listening to him the sun dial of one's life has seemed reversed for the space of two or three generations, while the simple, tender, and lofty piety which fed and feasted daily on the Word of God and Wesley's Hymns has made our sojourn with him like a bit of the intermediate state, "quite on the verge of heaven." Mr. Rodda's daughter was the wife of the Rev. B. S. Walker, late Anglican Minister, and he has three sons Ministers of that Communion. Eltham is the farthest Methodist outpost in this direction, while the region beyond, although prospected thirty years ago by this pioneer brother, is to this day a Methodist wilderness. Warrandyte (Anderson's Creek) had also occasional services and two Local Preachers resided there, but it also is now derelict so far as Methodist service is concerned. On one of these occasions the Rev. B. S. Walker stopped at the house of Mr. Robert King, Yan Yean. He held service there that night but was at a loss for a precentor, when one offered to whistle the tune, saying he could sing songs but not hymns. The service, however, was not in vain, for Mr. King offered forthwith a site of land for a Wesleyan Church. The present Wesleyan Church at Yan Yean was soon opened for Divine worship, and Mr. King's house became a warm and welcome preacher's home. The first Local Preacher's Meeting was held at Pentridge on April 3rd, 1855, Rev. B. S. Walker in the chair, and Messrs. F. Thomas, Cooper, D. Brown, Lucas, and Dredge were present. These are all now passed away. The Circuit then comprised Pentridge, Thomastown, Irishtown, Mickleham, Phillipstown, Rocky Waterholes, Back Creek, Tullamarine, Plenty, Doutta Galla, Box Forest, Greensborough, etc., and they were even then reaching out from time to time to such places as Epping, Campbellfield, Kilmore, Keelbundoora, Upper Plenty, Merriang, and other sundry farms and stations. The Ministers who succeeded the Rev. B. S. Walker were the Revs. W. C. Currey, H. Waddington, W. G. R. Stephinson, R. Hart, and J. Pemell. None of these are in the active work in this colony. The ranks of the Local Preachers were increased by the addition of the names of B. and S. Johnson, Kendall, Hall, Thompson, Standing, M'Clure, Fletcher, Kyle, Grimshaw, R. Sidebottom, Wilson, Abbey, Bull, etc. The Quarterly and Local Preachers' Meetings were held in turn at Pentridge, Irishtown, and Thomastown. Long *walks*, often eight to ten miles, from such distances as Greensborough, Yan Yean, Thomastown, etc., were taken by the brethren, in order to reach the Quarterly Meeting. Mr. Kendall is to be remembered, among other services rendered to our Church, for the way in which he secured the site of land at Coburg, on which our present valuable Church premises stand. PENTRIDGE struggled on for awhile as a separate Circuit, until it was re-absorbed in the Brunswick-street Circuit, and at length under the name of Coburg, attached to the present Brunswick Circuit. On March 30th, 1858, it was resolved "that Merriang, Mickleham, and Rocky Waterholes be dropt in favour of Mr. Mewton." The Rev. J. Mewton had just been appointed with a colleague to KILMORE, which was then made a Circuit town. It was a somewhat bold start—two men on untried ground, a population somewhat alien to Methodist influence (for the late Sir John O'Shanassy was then king of Kilmore)—and no Home Mission Fund behind them! But Mr. Mewton was equal to the occasion, with the lavish energy which characterized him, he cut out a large programme of work, and, to use a racing term, "made the running" for those that followed. The writer, who succeeded him, well remembers the change from the halcyon content and bliss of a Circuit in Tasmania to this debt-distracted scene, how, on his arrival, he had to face at the local bank, bills for £40, £50, and £90, being sums required to start and develop the Circuit, and how, frantic with this terror, he raced hither and thither, wherever he could get on the track of a pound note, haunted by imaginary goblins, worse than those which followed Tam O'Shanter's mare. The Circuit too was one of magnificent outlines and distances, being some eighty miles long, and comprising what is now four Circuits; and there were other peculiar trials and discomforts, but they need not be named among "brethren of the common lot." Kil*more* (which in those days was a stage after Kil*many*) is now reduced and feeble, but whether those former days were better than these, who shall say? Few Circuits have seen more vicissitudes. MERRIANG, once the very eye of the Circuit, is gone, MICKLEHAM is shut up, ROCKY WATER-HOLES—described as the busy thriving township of DONNYBROOK, with its large through-traffic to the diggings, its two rival hostelries, "The Happy Home," and the "Real Happy Home,"—is now a desolation; while our stone Church, after being turned into a potato store, is now a heap of ruins, the withering breath of time and change has swept over it, or we might rather say, the railway train has swept past it, "and it is gone, and the place thereof shall know it no more." The very site, we are told, if not the habitation of owls and dragons, is as undistinguishable as that of Tyre itself. But there were brave and good men connected with the Circuit, whose names deserve to be enshrined and preserved in loving remembrance, to wit Messrs. M. Thompson, Waite, Hawke, Foster, Wright (still surviving), Adams, T. B. Young, Lobb, Kyle, and others. Coming back to the places which skirt the Plenty-road, we find what is now the

PRESTON AND HEIDELBERG CIRCUIT.—Father Jeffery, the oldest inhabitant of Preston, remembers when no house existed on that side of Melbourne, but all that one sees from the top of Rucker's Hill, was a virgin wilderness. Mr.

Jeffery came in 1840, and was soon followed by Messrs. R. King, Woods, and other pilgrim fathers. With a true Irish welcome he opened his house for preaching. "Jeffery's Farm" figures on the earliest Melbourne plans, and was a favourite appointment with the preachers of those days, as we have heard Father Hewitt and others testify. The service was held in the "Barn," a large slab building, not always very snug and wind-tight. On one occasion Mr. Butters was so troubled with the draught, that he preached with his hat on, a similar experience to that of the Rev. Mr. Sweetman at Brighton. At that time the roads or tracks were very rough, and Mr. Jeffery was wont to meet the Melbourne preachers with his bullock dray at the foot of Rucker's Hill. About 1850 Mr. Jeffery gave a valuable site of land, in what he still loves to call "Irishtown," resenting the name Preston as a modern innovation and impertinence. The present Sabbath school, or at least two-thirds of it was erected on this land and then enlarged, until in 1863 the present stone Church was built from designs prepared by the late Rev. F. E. Stephenson, the first Superintendent of the Circuit. PRESTON Church and Circuit was a favourite resort for young preachers and "new chums." We can count four of our ex-presidents who began their commission here, while some ten Local Preachers found the work of this Circuit good training ground for the Christian ministry. HEIDELBERG was first known as "the Forest" (see Mr. Orton's MMS Circuit plan). The locality indicated by that name lay, says Mr. Stone, on the other (the Templestowe) side of the Yarra, which was then occupied by the huts of splitters, who supplied Melbourne with firewood. The Local Preachers were wont to take out tracts and hold service in some hut or in the open air. The access to this region must have been at that time, either by punt or through Richmond and Kew. About ten years after, preaching was commenced in Hick's paddock, Bulleen, first in Pullen's "Barn," then in the Denominational school built there, and the Rev. J. C. Symons and J. Harcourt, with Messrs.

Michael, Cleverdon, Coleman, Alexander, and Chivers, first missioned the place. The late Messrs. Burnley, of Richmond, offered two acres of land in the township of Doncaster, but it was declined in favour of a site offered at Woodhouse Grove, while Doncaster proper became, and still remains, a strong hold of the Christian disciples. A grant of land (N.S.W.) at Heidelberg, was secured as early as 1851, and preaching commenced by the Rev. J. C. Symons and others, first in the open air, then in the Presbyterian Church kindly lent, next in the house of Mr. Hobson, and then under the shade of the trees in our Church reserve, until in 1859 the present Church was built, and for some years well filled, until our people dispersed for fresh fields and pastures new, and only a few old standard-bearers as Messrs. Williams, Robinson, Pascoe, etc., are left to stand by our cause and wait for brighter days. At ALPHINGTON a small Church of hard-wood stood on the hill opposite Rockbeare. It was then supplied by the Baptists, afterwards purchased and undertaken by the Wesleyans. Then the site of land on which the Church now stands, was given by Mrs. Hordern or Mr. Beaver, and Messrs. Fletcher, Webb, Bloys, Wimble, Wymond, Bogle, Adams, and P.W. Smith were identified with the outset of Methodism in this place. The old Church of hard-wood was removed to the present Church ground, and for awhile used as a stable, and at last the remains of it were (in 1884) sold for £1, at the time that a new porch to the present Church was being erected at a cost of £80, an illustration this of the old and new dispensations. SOUTH PRESTON.—After preaching for a while at Wilson's (Wilson's Farm), the Rev. R. Hart purchased the Church built by Mr. John Moon Bryant, (called by Mr. Ramsay, M.L.A., the Blacking Box), for £400, and many a good sermon has been preached, and many a pulpit fledgling first tried to fly there. The present Church was built in 1881. THOMASTOWN is an old preaching place, named after Mr. and Mrs. J. Thomas, who sleep with other " rude forefathers of the hamlet," in the little

graveyard at the back of the State school. Preaching was first held in a thatched house of Mr. Francis Thomas, then a weather-board Church was built for £700, and then the present bright and comely brick Church. Early friends :—Messrs. Thomas, Cooper, Perry, Abbey, Standing, Bishop, Sanson, B. and S. Johnson, Bower, etc.
BUNDOORA.—In 1848 a Class was met at Mr. A. Hurlstone's mill on the Plenty River, between Janefield and Greensborough, and Mr. Grimshaw, senior, walked three miles along the Plenty river to lead it. The "Old Mill," in the form of a picturesque ruin, still stands, a favourite resort of visitors and picnickers. There was preaching at Greensborough and Darebin Creek alternately, until Mr. Horatio Cooper offered Bundoora, and it was thought that a central Church at that place would meet the wants of the whole district; but finding that the Thomastown friends were intent on having a Church on their own account, this was abandoned, and the use of Mr. Cooper's schoolroom was gladly accepted. Mrs. Cooper, sister-in-law of Mr. Witton, survives in the cheerful piety of a gay-green old age, a generous mother in our Israel, and one of the oldest inhabitants of the colony, having arrived in "Glenelg," or "The Settlement," as it was first called, on January 1st, 1837.
GREENSBOROUGH.—Preaching was first held in "Meagher's Barn;" then in Mr. A. Grimshaw's house; then the old Church was built on the brow of the hill, opposite the Cemetery, and part of it may be seen in the late Mr. Britnell's stable, now standing, until at last the present pretty Church was erected. In the early days, Revs. Messrs. Butters, J. C. Symons, S. Waterhouse, J. Harcourt, B. S. Walker, Waddington, Currey, etc., preached here, and Mr. Grimshaw and his family, who had removed further into the bush, thought little of walking eight or ten miles to the means of grace. Messrs. Britnell, Hobson, and others took up the work, and Mr. William Fletcher (brother of Mr. P. P. Fletcher, now of New South Wales) was an an active agent in the founding of our

cause. The Church, which began under the auspices of such Methodist names as those of Grimshaw and Fletcher, soon grew. Similar records of Methodist evolution and development might be given of YAN YEAN, LINTON, WOOLLERT and EAST LINTON. WHITTLESEA.—Our Church here had an interesting origin. Mrs. F—, in early days the good hostess of the Alphington Hotel, found salvation in connection with our cause in that village, and took a lively interest in the erection of the Church, consecrating the spot by many prayers as the building was going up. The Circuit was blessed with rich revivals of religion, and, as the child of a revival, Mrs. F— took this spirit with her when she and her family removed to Castle Hill, near the Yan Yean Reservoir. She pined for the lost means of grace, and eagerly asked of a boundary rider if there were no Christians in those parts. The man stared in blank dismay, as though to ask what sort of animals those might be. Mrs. F— next secured a room in the Yan Yean Reservoir Hotel, where weekly prayer-meetings were held, as many as sixty or eighty of all creeds and classes attended, and reformed lives and happy deaths attest that those labours were not in vain. Then followed the visits of the Revs. Messrs. Stubbs, Royce, and Tuckfield, and the local efforts of Messrs. Cunningham, Horsley ("the honest miller"), Lockwood, Freeman, etc. A brick Church was soon erected and paid for, and Mrs. F— has lived to see nearly all her large family active and ardent members of the same.

PRAHRAN, ST. KILDA, SOUTH MELBOURNE, ETC., ETC.— These places could hardly be called suburbs in the days (1851) of which we write. They were rather straggling outlying villages. EMERALD HILL wore its virgin green with scarcely a dot or spot of building upon it. It had been known as Canvas Town, and before that as Brickfields, a collection of huts and tents on the flat across the Yarra, and near the punt which preceded Princes' Bridge. Newtown (now Collingwood) is described by the Rev. N. Turner in 1847, as "a growing town about a mile from Melbourne." It is pleasant to trace the start and spread of Methodism in these places. PRAHRAN.—While the Brighton Circuit was proposing to prospect and invade the little villages of Prahran and St. Kilda, a good brother from Tasmania had settled in the former place, and was casting about for opportunities of doing good. This was John Smith, one of a tribe of that name who have been famous in many ways. He was one of the Rev. J. A. Manton's young band who had introduced Methodism at Perth, began the preaching at Longford in a barn, at Westbury in a Court-house, and at Launceston in a private room. He opened his cottage in the bush (a site now found between Union and Raleigh-streets), for prayer and preaching. Messrs. Archibald Somerville (a warm-hearted Irishman, now in New Zealand) and Frank Brown, were the first to hold forth in this place. Mr. Smith further built, largely at his own expense, the first little "Chapel" at Mount Erica, which grew and prospered, and whereof the present handsome Church premises are the outcome. Mr. Smith also "prospected" in conjunction with Mr. Kingham, what was then known as Owensville, and Sunday school and preaching were held there for twelve months; but under the new name of Caulfield it has long been a Methodist blank. Then came another from "the other side," "Tommy Turner," a remarkable man. In his unconverted state he was a member of the Ring, and used his double knuckles when occasion required with compound interest. Under the Ministry of the Rev. Messrs. Eggleston, N. Turner, and Butters, he found mercy and soon became an earnest worker for God. He opened his house for preaching, and then put up what is still lovingly remembered as "The Raggetty Tent," near where the Windsor station now stands. Messrs. Bailey, Moorhead, and Green, still living, have worshipped in that tent. Mr. Bailey also stood by Tommy Turner as his faithful henchman, when they held open-air service under a peppermint tree where Green-street now runs. A Mr. John Turnbull, of Richmond, is said to have been the first who preached there; he was a fine Christian man, "who laboured hard for two years and then through much tribulation, entered the kingdom." Cottage prayer meetings were also held in Mr. Green's house. Then Mr. and Mrs. Moorhouse (warm Irish Methodists) taking a child to the Rev. W. Butters to be baptized, that faithful watchman spoke to them of a site for a Church at Prahran, when Mr. Moorhouse, turning to his wife, said, "What do you say wife?" and they agreed there and then to give the corner of Margaret-street and Commercial-road, on which was erected the first iron Church. A more eligible site of land was soon after obtained from the Government at the corner of Punt-road and Commercial-road, and the "iron pot" was removed thither, Mr. Moorhouse giving a handsome donation and had the land back again. Mr. Moorhouse also gave, some few years after, a worthy son to our Ministry, who was called, before he had finished his student's course, to the rest and service of the Church above. The new iron-pot Church was opened about the year 1853. One of the sermons was preached by the then Mr. B. Cocker, since then the Rev. Dr. Cocker, Professor of Ann Arbor College, Michigan. At the tea-meeting which followed, Mr. John Bromley, who had just arrived by the first trip of the good ship *Great Britain* was present. The advent of this good brother of ominous name created a little commotion. He had acted as Chaplain on the voyage out, and on his arrival was confounded with the Rev. James Bromley, a prominent leader of the Methodist agitation of 1851, and it was presumed that he had come to these shores on a similar mission. The *Argus* thus reported this imagined disturber of the peace, but a more loyal Methodist or kindly brother one could hardly meet, the only resemblance between the two was that they were both first-rate preachers. The writer preached in this famous iron-pot Church the first Sabbath after his arrival in 1856, and had a melting season, owing to the intense heat of the day. But it was a converting furnace in a better sense than this, and the scene of many blessings. After the present Church in Punt-road was built it was used as a "Common" and Sabbath school, then demolished and brought to the hammer in 1877, when the present school premises were built. The elaborate and expensive pulpit apparatus of the old iron-pot may be seen in the Wesleyan Church, Alphington. The Rev. Dr. Waugh, then a single man, was the first resident Minister of the Circuit, and its spreading growth and strength in later times owes much to the wise and faithful Ministry of its early pastors, as well as to the simple and primitive labours of the pioneers before noted. In the quiet days before the uproar and distraction of the diggings began, Mr. Turnbull, who had begun prayer meetings at Richmond and Prahran, was engaged with a fellow-workman (Robert Glenfield?) in felling and sawing timber in the neighbourhood, and was desired to start a cottage prayer meeting at ST. KILDA. This they did in a cottage near the present railway terminus, carrying the forms to and fro on their shoulders, until October, 1851, when the rush to the diggings seemed for awhile to arrest and upset everything else. The first preaching was held under the verandah at the residence of the Hon. F. E. Beaver, Alma-road, and Mr. Stevens his next neighbour, and then in Mr. Stanford's parlour, the house in which Mr. Bell, father-in-law of the late Mr. Walter Powell, lived and died. Mr. Bromley remembers preaching there in those days. The first Class meeting was held in Acland-street, and the late Mr. Henry Jennings, solicitor, was its Leader. He too had opened his house for preaching, and Mr. Bailey often carried the forms to and fro between "The Raggetty Tent" and Mr. Jennings'. Mr. Bailey remembers too that the services were somewhat stiff and solemn, inasmuch as the hymns were "said" instead of "sung." Mr. T. J. Crouch, afterwards the popular precentor, had not then arrived. Mr. Jennings was also at that time the treasurer of the Children's Fund, while Mr. Galagher was treasurer for the old Preachers' Fund, and

Mr. Beaver for the Kingswood and Woodhouse Grove schools. A second Class was started at Mr. Watchorn's, corner of Argyle and High-streets, and Mr. J. Smith was its Leader for about eighteen months. Then a small weather-board building, playfully called "the pepper box," was put up, a part of which is now used as the Sunday school. The present Church was erected in the days of the Rev. Mr. Bickford (?), and opened by the Rev Dr. Jobson. Messrs. W. Powell, Gardiner, Stevens, Beaver, Burgess, Frazer, J. Smith, Hurst, and Peterson were some of the early pioneers. The Rev. S. Knight and R. M. Hunter, of South Australia, and Floyd, Anglican Vicar of Fiji, were among the men of note, who began their career in this Circuit. SOUTH MELBOURNE, formerly Emerald Hill and Brickfields. —Mr. John Bromley remembers preaching here in a tent (1853), which, however, was soon capsized and laid low. He (Mr. Bromley) had brought the claims of Emerald Hill before the Quarterly Meeting just held, and himself with Messrs. Powell and Cooke were appointed a Committee to make arrangements for a Church. In concert with Mr. Bee, a small weather-board Church was built, and in a fortnight was found insufficient to contain the congregation. A transept was added, and at length the present noble structure erected; the old premises being utilized for Sunday school purposes. Mr. J. Bromley, who had commenced the cause, preached the last sermon in the old weather-board building, the congregation removing to the Mechanics' Institution, until the new Church was ready. The Circuit has grown since that day, having a fine Church and prosperous cause in the centre, and out-stations clustering around. RICHMOND.—In 1848-50 Mr. John Turnbull with the hearty help of Mr. John Bailey, now of South Yarra, held cottage prayer meetings, and founded a small Sunday school and Library, until a small brick building was erected in Brougham-street, off Church-street, and going down to the Richmond Flat. One who came over from Prahran to this place in 1848, describes the people as "very social and homely, the Church crowded, and the services delightful: it seemed like one prolonged revival." Mr. Watchorn also remarks that "though we seldom had the itinerant Ministers in Little Richmond, yet the Master was there, for His Spirit often descended with power. Once, while singing, an extraordinary influence was felt, and Mr. Frank Brown, the preacher, exclaimed, "If here we feel like this, what must it be to be there!" Mr. Blackledge, then "a terror to evil doers," used to play the flute, and remembers Messrs. Dredge, and Parker preaching there. Messrs. Blencowe, Baldwin, Wellard, Galagher, Horton, Hewitt, and O'Brien preached there in after days, and notably a warm-hearted Irishman, named Archibald Somerville. Two Classes were formed, led by Mr. O. Parnham, senior, and Mr. N. Guthridge. Mr. R. Guthridge was the superintendent of the Sunday school. The writer in 1866 saw the remains of this old Brougham-street Chapel a dilapidated ruin, a shelter and refuge for the goats of the neighbourhood. The present Church was undertaken with great enthusiasm. Mr. Horsfall who was present on the occasion, speaks of the first tea meeting held on its behalf, when some £1500 were promised. Mr. Henry Miller gave the land on which the Church now stands, and was one of the first trustees and seatholders. The following are some of the names prominently identified with the early days of the present Richmond Church. Messrs. Hurst, Andrew, Fielding, Burnley, Stirling, Bosisto, Winter, Hyde, Shaw, Britten, Bedggood, etc. At that time (1866) there were Churches at Baker-street, Hoddle-street, Charles-street, and service at Simpson's-road (Mr Puckey's school), and Rose-street, all of which have since disappeared or been superseded. CREMORNE.—The present pleasant Church quarters are the outcome of hope deferred and weary waiting, When the writer first knew the place there was but a small weatherboard building, unattractive, and insufficient for both Church and School. The neighbourhood was low, and we had to fight to keep the public houses at a decent distance from our Church. The Sabbath school was doing good, and as it was a sort of School-Chapel, its anniversary was generally popular. Mr. J. T. Harcourt or Mr. Bosisto was commonly in the chair, and took a great interest in the place. Mr. and Mrs. Hewitt, Messrs. Moad, and Parker clave to the cause from the first. Mr. and Mrs. Hewitt were godly and devoted Yorkshire Methodists, Class Leaders, and Sabbath school Teachers, almost up to the end of their long and happy lives, and until all the powers of language and memory failed. Like Simeon and Anna of old they departed not from the temple, but served God night and day, and often wondered whether they should see a more beautiful and becoming Sanctuary rise on the spot. They had "long patience" for it, and when at last it came to pass, they were ready to say, "Lord, now lettest thou thy servant depart in peace; for mine eyes have seen thy salvation." Father Hewitt, in his palmy days, was a power for good. There was great heart and life in his preaching. "He could give," says Mr Watchorn, "a long sermon in the orthodox short time." Who that heard him will forget his pleading prayers and the heartfelt glow with which he would give out his favourite hymn, "Jesus, the name high over all." He believed, and therefore spake. For sixty years with unsparing zeal, he preached the death by which we live, until the weary wheels of life stood still."

HAWTHORN.—The Rev. J. C. Symons first preached here on a stump, and then the Local Preachers followed. A little brick Church was built at Red Gum Flat (Upper Hawthorn); and in 1865 the splendid site of two acres at Lower Hawthorn was fenced in, and a neat weather-board Church built upon it. Some slight conflict between the claims of Upper and Lower Hawthorn, culminated in the disposal of both these properties, and the erection of the present Church, which in turn, has become too small for the wants of the locality. The Church and ground at Lower Hawthorn were disposed of for what would now be deemed a very inadequate sum, and the Church turned into a Flock

Manufactory. A site has been secured again at high cost for another Church in that thriving and populous district. Messrs. Copeland, Vasey, Pease, Johnson, Brookes, Powell, were among the early ones. BURWOOD, (formerly Ballyshannasy, and before that Damper's Creek and WOODHOUSE GROVE, are old stations with very pleasant associations, and many worthy names are entwined in their history.

GEELONG AND BALLARAT DISTRICT.

CHAPTER XI.

GEELONG.—Mr. Tuckfield preached the first sermon in this place on July 28th, 1838, from the text Psalm lxxxiv., verse 11. He not only visited the natives in the district and prepared to commence his mission to them, but gathered the white people together, first in Dr. Thompson's parlour, and then in a barn or end of the store on the banks of the Barwon, belonging to a company, for whom Mr. David Fisher was manager. On the first or second occasion of this kind, it is stated by Mrs. Caldwell, then Mrs. Hurst, that Miss Newcombe found salvation in Christ, and became henceforth a valued and devoted servant of Christ. Mr. Hurst settled at Geelong in February, 1839, and began at once to conduct Divine service and care for the many natives living there, until the Van Dieman's Land District Meeting in October, 1839, directed him to join Mr. Tuckfield at Buntingdale, and the two Missionaries gave themselves mainly to the native work. They, however, supplied Melbourne and Geelong alternately, each one staying eight days (two Sundays) every two months, while the intervening Sundays were occupied by Local Preachers. The Rev. Mr. Skevington also, who sojourned sometime at Buntingdale, helped the cause both at Geelong and Melbourne. He was a saintly man and popular preacher. His

I

sturdy principle once forbad him to kill a sheep on the
Sabbath, even though it was to provide a dinner for
Governor Latrobe and suite, who had unexpectedly arrived
at Buntingdale on that day. He fell dead in the pulpit, the
first of more than a dozen of our Colonial Ministers, whose
"life and work" have been closed by a sudden and tragic end.
On May 5th, 1839, the Rev. J. Orton, then on his second
visit to Port Phillip, preached at Fisher's store—Miss
Newcombe leading the singing. In 1840 Mr. James Smith
arrived at Geelong, and commenced the first Class meeting,
consisting of six or eight members. In 1841 Mr. James
Sanderson followed, and shortly after the Rev. F. Tuckfield
"announced" that on a specified Wednesday a second
Class would be commenced, under the care of Mr. Sanderson, much to the astonishment of that dear brother.
This class prospered and grew, until Mr. Sanderson had to
leave for Western Port, and Miss Newcombe was appointed
the Leader. After twelve months Mr. Sanderson returned
and resumed work in Geelong. He commenced a new Class at
Mr. Hindhaugh's, Ashby, and for seventeen years this devoted
brother met two or three classes every week, and preached
generally three times on the Sabbath. Mr. James Smith
was equally active and useful, and on these two brethren,
associated with the Missionaries from Buntingdale, the
burden of the work at that time lay, and by them the
foundations of our Church were laid. The only change was
an occasional visit of a Local Preacher, or the Rev. S.
Wilkinson from Melbourne, at an expense of two guineas,
the steamer fare. God's blessing was upon the infant cause,
and the societies and congregations greatly increased. The
next step was the erection of a Church. This is the Rev.
B. Hurst's account of it :—"The friends of Geelong were
now desirous of building a Chapel, and a subscription-list
was opened for the purpose, and considerable sums were
promised. But as mechanics were scarce, and materials
and labour high, it was deemed a matter of prudence not to
commence the Chapel at present. But as the wants of the

congregation were urgent, Mr. Wilkinson requested me to relieve them of the difficulty, by providing them with a temporary place of worship. This I consented to do, on condition of their paying me a moderate interest on the outlay, and which was to be deducted from the £50 which I had promised towards the new Chapel. I now purchased a two-storey weatherboard store, which was offered for sale, and which was to be removed from the land on which it stood. I then had to purchase land to put it on. This being accomplished we commenced preparations for removing it. We took out the doors and windows and braced the windows as firmly as possible. By leverage we raised it so as to be able to put two wooden axle trees under it. We borrowed four wheels, and on Saturday, 12th February, 1842, we hooked two teams of bullocks to it, and drew it to the land I had purchased, about 150 yards off. The whole of the next week was spent in fitting it up for Divine worship. We cut away about two-thirds of the upper floor leaving the other third for a gallery to which we ascended by a step-ladder placed in the front. On February 20th, 1842, I had the honour and pleasure of opening it for divine worship, and as a Wesleyan Chapel and Schoolroom, it was used for about four years." The building above referred to was purchased from Mr. Williams, and the spot of land to which it was removed was in Yarra-street, the new Church stood at that time "alone among the trees of the forest in a highly romantic spot." A tribe of natives, "numbering 170 souls, had pitched their camp close to the Chapel and passed their time either in playing at war or amusing themselves with "boisterous fun and games" (Sanderson). This sufficed to remind them that they were in a heathen land and to provoke and engage their Missionary zeal and sympathy. The Rev. S. Wilkinson, in the Jubilee number of the *Spectator*, May 22nd, 1886; gives a graphic and humourou sketch of this two-storey Church. At the Jubilee meeting of the Geelong Circuit, one was present who had worshipped in this odd place, while another aged lady was "presented" who had heard Orton's first sermon on Batman's Hill. Another survivor of Mr. Orton's small congregation, Mr. Reid, was present at the Bairnsdale Jubilee services. The Church and congregation at Yarra-street so grew and multiplied, that it was resolved to secure some one to take charge of them. The leading men called a meeting and gave themselves to prayer for Divine direction. They could not obtain a regular Minister, and as the Church was not erected on Government ground, no State aid could be obtained. The Melbourne March Quarterly Meeting deputed two of their number, Messrs. Witton and Thorpe, to visit Geelong to ascertain what pecuniary aid the people would render. The sum of £106 (another account says £70) per annum was promised, and Mr. Dredge, "a most acceptable Local Preacher, who had just resigned his office of Assistant-Protector of Aborigines," was engaged as hired Local Preacher, and opened his commission there in June, 1842, Dr. Thompson kindly providing him with a cottage, rent free. The narrative before us (Sanderson's) is glowing and enthusiastic in its admiration of this excellent man. It speaks of his mighty genius, great abilities, deep sympathies, great self-possession, and untiring attention. He possessed great power in prayer, and was mighty in the Scriptures: his preaching being of the expository style, duly noting the context and explaining the whole in language plain and simple, so that all the people understood him, "the clear development of some fine train of thought winding through close and convincing reasoning, and warming into earnest appeal, his thoughts multiplying towards the close of the sermon." His praise was in all the Churches, the cause began to spread, and many other places were opening up for the preaching of the Gospel. First among these was Ashby, where Mr. Hindhaugh opened his house for preaching, and the Class, before mentioned, was meeting, "which survives unto this day (1871), and meets in Hope-street." (See a pleasant sketch in the *Spectator* for 1884, page 283, of the subsequent history of Ashby Church and cause from

1857.) Mr. James Smith undertook the care of this place, meeting the Class alternately with the other leader (Mr. Sanderson), as well as his own Class in the Chapel on Sabbath morning. At New Town, land was given by Mr. James Austin, of Barwon Park and a cause commenced. Mr. Dredge laboured with great acceptance for more than two years, when an insidious disease obliged him to remove to Melbourne, and then return to England. He died, however, shortly before the ship reached his native shores. He was buried on the land, and as a token of the esteem in which he was held, Dr. Bunting, who had selected him for the position of Aboriginal Protector, conducted the service. The Chronicler dwells lovingly on Mr. Dredge's farewell sermon from "Work out your own salvation with fear and trembling, etc.," and describes the farewell tea meeting held on the following night, when Mr. James Smith, for himself and others, presented Mr. Dredge with a purse of sovereigns, in token of the high esteem in which he was held, and their grief at parting. Mr. Dredge, in acknowledging their gift, makes especial reference to those "elect ladies" who had laboured with him in the vineyard of the Lord, and to whose kindness he was so greatly indebted. Thus early did one of the distinguishing glories of Geelong Methodism, viz., the loyalty and devotion of Christian womanhood, assert itself. Of that meeting the narrative rather boldly asserts, "that no meeting since held has equalled it in the love they displayed for one another, and for the great Redeemer's cause." The first Missionary Meeting in Geelong was held during Mr. Dredge's ministry, March 1842. The Chapel was filled to overflowing, the chair being occupied by F. Fenwick, Esq., P.M. A deputation from Melbourne was present, and addresses delivered by F. Champain, Esq., Messrs, J. Smith, Dredge, etc. Glowing reference is made to the rich influence that attended that meeting, and the eloquent speech of the Rev. A. Love, who, while discoursing on the results of this salvation, appeared to be "caught up to the third heaven." Next came the movement to erect a new Church on the two acres of land given by the Government, and occupied by the present Yarra-street Church. The foundation-stone was laid by Dr. Thomson, several Ministers were present, addresses delivered, and a "collector appointed." Then a most crowded tea meeting was held in the old Chapel, "the first public tea meeting held in Geelong." Dr. Thomson presided at the public meeting, and the narrator gives his speech at length, consisting of a pleasing exposition and application of Jacob's dream. Then followed speeches from Rev. F. Tuckfield, Mr. James Smith, and Captain Forsythe (a good Local Preacher, and whose crew, being all members of Society, were present in their naval uniform). The lively and popular Rev. A. Love created some diversion, by complaining of the morning slumbers and the prolonged toilets of too many, which made them late for worship, and suggested that a bell should be placed at Mr. J. Smith's, Kardinia-street, to ring them up on a Sunday morning, indicating a respectable tradesman present, who would provide the bell. Captain Forsythe, however, claimed this pleasure. Mr. Dredge then followed with the collection-speech, quoting Dr. Newton with happy effect. After the laying of the foundation-stones, a lull of some months followed owing to the declining health of Mr. Dredge. Mr. Thompson, a sort of supply (though not from the President's list of reserve) came to help him, and gave "great satisfaction to the people." Indeed, the historian says, these pioneer preachers reminded him of the simplicity and devotion of the Apostles of early Methodism. Mr. Dredge was succeeded by the Rev. William Lowe, 1846, "whose Ministry was made a blessing to many who will be the crown of his rejoicing in the day of the Lord Jesus." (Hurst.) Then came Revs. W. Cox Currey (1847), F. Tuckfield (1848), when Geelong was detached from Mel- and constituted a separate Circuit, F. Lewis (1850), W. Lightbody (assisting or supplying for Mr. Lewis, 1852), R.

Hart (1853). The years from 1853 come within the memory of many still living and need not be amplified. Interesting incidents and illustrations of this period are given in the Rev. T. Williams' "Memoirs of Mr. James Wood." In those years came the varied and grateful ministries of the Revs. Messrs. J. Harding, Symons, Hill, Dare, Daniel, and others, under which the Circuit prospered and grew. Mr. Harding had something of the ardour and spirit of a pioneer Bishop of the Far West, and has since found fine scope for these gifts, and done good service in New Zealand and Queensland. There was just at that time a danger of contracting debts in reckless fashion, and of our developing some Colonial edition of Valentine Ward, a name identified in Methodist tradition with the debts and difficulties of our work in Scotland. But the peril had the effect of inspiring Geelong Methodists with a wholesome dread of debt, and of provoking those heroic efforts which have been made from time to time to encounter it, until the Circuit has attained a state of financial relief and repose which looks in the eyes of others almost Elysian. Mr. Harding, if not like Nimrod, a mighty hunter before the Lord, had the nobler fame of an ardent appetite for Chapel building, a line in which he has had some worthy, though remote successors. SHENTON HOUSE, in Geelong, for many years past the scene of a flourishing Sunday school, will ever be associated with Mr. Harding's name and work. Under date of June 1st, 1855, he says :—" My esteemed predecessor, the Rev. F. Lewis, with his helper, Mr. Hart, completed our principal Church in Yarra-street, at a cost of £3000, of which a floating debt of £850 has lately been cancelled by our liberal people of Geelong. At SOUTH GEELONG, a brick Chapel has been erected and paid for at a cost of £1400. At CHILWELL one has also been built at a cost of £2,200, with a debt of £850. A brick Chapel is also completed at TUCKFIELD to a considerable degree through the liberality of Miss Newcombe. A stone Chapel is also in course of erection at CERES, amidst the cornfields of the

Barrabool Hills, which will cost £500, and at HIGHTON a neat little brick Chapel was opened the other day. These, besides five other Chapels of wood, have been erected during the past year, while five Day schools have been established. So that the Geelong Circuit now comprises twelve places of worship and eight Day schools affording accommodation for 2,300 souls, and daily instruction given (gratuitously when necessary) to 510 children, with at least an equal number of Sabbath schools, which are conducted with as much zeal and ability as similar institutions at home." The Rev. J. C. Symons with his wonted energy seems to have paid special attention to Sunday school work, and he and his colleague gave lectures to teachers, held a preparation Class, and formed a Sabbath school Quarterly Union, in which young native talent was developed, and wise counsel taken as to the best methods of teaching. This was long before the Sabbath school branch of our work had become so prominent and popular as the Wesleyan Sabbath school *Union* and *Magazine* have made it. Geelong has long been famous for its State and Grammar schools, and thus early and wisely did our Church begin its career of Sabbath schools, the finished result of which is found in the excellent pattern schools of Yarra-street, Newtown, and Chilwell. A Methodist visiting Geelong will hardly fail to visit the Yarra-street school, whose enthusiastic Superintendent, Mr. G. Hitchcock, may well be proud of its perfect organization and excellent results, while in one particular form of fruitfulness, the Chilwell school seems beyond all others—the following Ministers having graduated there:—Revs. Messrs. Minns, Moore, Maddern, Ingamells, Adams, Lowe, Osborn, Hillard, Johns, Fitchett, etc. (See a most interesting sketch of the Yarra-street Sunday school, past and present, in the *Spectator*, October 3rd, 1884, p. 246, which we would gladly transfer to these pages, if space permitted). The Circuit was further blessed with the solid and edifying Ministries of Messrs. Binks, Wells, Eggleston, Bickford,

Cope, Watkin, and Bath, with their equally worthy colleagues, while among its faithful Laymen of earlier days :— Messrs. Towle, Rix, Howell, Hunt, Balding, Mowbray, Peters, Gaylard, Ham, Hitchcock, Thacker, Wyatt, Ducker, N. J. and W. H. Brown and others deserve honourable mention. "Grandfather Lowe" is a name which "blossoms in the dust," and whose memory is fragrant in many hearts and homes. Geelong has also been rich in "elect ladies" of noble Christian worth, as Mrs. Wood, and Miss Nanette Quinan among the departed, whose characters have been beautifully delineated by the graphic pen of the Rev. T. Williams, in his "Memoirs of Mr. James Wood," while among the living, the "unfeigned faith" of the fond and pious ancestry suggested by the name, "Grandfather Lowe," is preserved and prolonged in the abundant philanthropy and Christian devotion of the estimable wife of the superintendent of Yarra-street Sabbath school and others that might be named. Other notable features of Geelong Methodism are its Missionary spirit, and especially its attachment to its Ministers. The aggressive spirit of our Church overflowed in various directions. COLAC was visited by the Rev. Mr. Hill in 1858. Mr. Hill preached at Mr. Dennis' in the morning, and at the Presbyterian Church in the afternoon and evening of the day. Though in theory, attached to the Geelong Circuit and visited by its Ministers, the spiritual wants of the place, so far as our Church could supply them, were met by the appointment of Mr. Hiskens, of Collingwood, as Home Missionary. Mr. Hiskens laboured there with diligence and acceptance for many years, preaching in Mr. Dennis' "Barn," the Manse, and in the township, until he lived to see two substantial Churches of brick and stone erected, and the place occupied as a "fully-accredited" Circuit. The first brick Church was erected on the five acres of ground on which the handsome new parsonage, the gift of Alexander Dennis, Esq., now stands ; it was afterwards removed and embodied in the present Sunday school which stands at the rear of the new Church built in Main-street during the ministry of the Rev. T. Grove. Mention should be made of the generous help and services of Messrs. Butcher, Talbot, and especially of Mr. Dennis, a right hearty Methodist of the old school, one of the early pioneers of that part, whose hospitable home was a favourite resort and rest for the Buntingdale Missionaries, and after them for Messrs. Harding, Dare, Field, and many others,—whose hand and heart were given in loving service and generous benefactions to that Zion which he preferred "above his chief joy"—and who survives in a green old age to magnify the grace of God, and rejoice in hope of his glory. Mention is made to those early days of Christian labours at Swan Lake, Lethbridge, Kensington, Indented Heads, Tuckfield (now Drysdale). The latter place must be ever associated with the names of those "elect" and estimable ladies :—Miss Newcombe and Miss Drysdale, who for many years resided there, and were ready for every good work.

BALLARAT.—A somewhat nebulous haze lies over the outset of Methodism in Ballarat, so far as it is now possible to determine the exact spot where our Church started, or the agent and instrument who first introduced it. Through this mist there are seen flickering sundry "sparks of grace" in various directions, which presently kindled and combined into one steady and aspiring flame. In other words amid the fortuitous concourse of human atoms which came together at the outbreak of the diggings, there was also the good seed of the kingdom which in a kindly soil, forthwith began to germinate and grow. Various detachments of Methodists had hastened thither from Melbourne and elsewhere, and three parties known to the writer claim to have been the first, or among the first, to hold some kind of Methodist service on the diggings. Mr. Mathew Waite, Mr. Thorpe and "Father" Hewitt, of Richmond, since gone to their reward, at once formed little bands, and held prayer meetings in their tents. Mr. Waite sketched out a rough plan of work for the few Methodists then in the field, while Messrs. Bailey and Hewitt have told the writer that they were present at the first Love Feast held under a tree. In the Rev. T. Williams' "Life of Mr. Wood, of Geelong," is a graphic sketch of such tent worship as was frequent in the first days of digging life at Ballarat, Mount Alexander, and elsewhere. Messrs. Hunt and Wood had joined the tent party, which now numbered five. Not only did they take in turn to conduct family worship, night and morning, but at noon and "crib time," two of their number would read in turn a portion of the Scriptures, and offer earnest prayer. Instead of the usual cry of Smoke O! was the more grateful dessert of Prayer O! This proved a bond of strength and help, and blessing "than gold and pearls more precious far!" But the most definite and authentic narrative is that supplied by the venerable Father Sanderson, the true pioneer preacher of Ballarat Methodism, who has just passed away at the ripe age of eighty-seven years. The narrative which is as follows, was taken from Mr. Sanderson's lips by the Rev. G. Daniel and published in the *Spectator* :—

EARLY DAYS OF METHODISM IN BALLARAT.

The first Methodist sermon preached in Ballarat was delivered by Mr. James Sanderson, of Geelong, on Sabbath, 29th September, 1851, at eleven a.m., from 1. Cor. vi. 19, 20. After the preaching a subscription-list was opened for the purpose of purchasing a tent in which to worship God. The first donation (£1) was given by a young man, Edward Jones, from Hobart. Nuggets and gold dust from their match-boxes were freely given by the diggers. This was the first collection in aid of a place of worship made on the goldfields of Ballarat.

At the above service it was announced that the members of society would meet at two o'clock that afternoon. A small tent was filled by them long before the hour, and many were unable to get in.

A Class, consisting of the following persons, was at once formed :—James Sanderson (leader), Edmund Mathews,

Amos Downing, Thomas Morgan, James Bradley, Mathew Waite, John Rees, William Foster, James Tonner, and several others. While the Class-meeting was being held, a gentleman, attracted by the singing, rode up to the tent, and inquired of those outside what was the nature of the service. He was told that it was a Methodist Class meeting. The gentleman replied, "I am the Rev. Mr. Hastie, of Buninyong. As I shall be preaching at the commissioner's tent shortly, I will wait half an hour for them to come and sing for me." A good number went. This concluded the first Sabbath services observed at Ballarat.

On the next Sabbath, 6th October, sermons were preached by the Rev. Frederick Lewis, of Geelong—in the morning on the flat below where the present Christ Church, Lydiard-street, stands, and in the afternoon at the foot of Black Hill. Large numbers attended both sermons.

On the 13th October I was to have preached, but through indisposition was unable, and Mr. Hewitt, of Sydney, conducted the service. "His text was, "The Lord shut him in." The sermon was one of the most suitable I have heard preached on the goldfields. On the 20th October the Rev. Mr. Moody, of Geelong, preached in the afternoon. As I was meeting my Class I did not hear the sermon.

On the 27th October we held a fellowship meeting very near the spot on which the Freehold Bank (Mr. James Oddie's) now stands. There were some fine trees on this spot, which gave a good shade, and when we had cleared away the fallen timber there was ample space for the large company. The singing was good. Many gave their experiences, gracious influences were felt, and the whole service afforded not only immediate spiritual benefit, but the most blessed memories.

Owing to the inclement weather, there was no service on November 3rd. During the following week we were busy preparing to erect the tent. I sat up the whole of one night helping to get it in order for the following Sabbath.

On the 10th November I preached in the new tent, at two p.m., from Isaiah xii. 2—"Behold, God is my salvation." In applying the subject, I observed that it was a personal matter—"*my* salvation" and the Good Spirit applied the truth to the heart of a Mr. Davis, from Geelong. As he was returning from the service with his sons he said to them—"You go on; I must return to the tent." He came in and told us of the distress of his soul. I and another prayed with him, and continued pleading for about three hours, when at sundown, he was enabled to say —"God is *my* salvation; I will trust Him, and not be afraid." This was the first conversion known to have occurred in connection with our services in this district. Mr. Davis had from his boyhood been a member of an Independent Church in London, but had never felt the Spirit's witness and power as at that service. A short time after this he met with an accident which proved fatal. His son sent me an account of his death, which was triumphant. And so our friend went soon to heaven, "being the firstfruits" of Ballarat Methodism "unto God and the Lamb."

Mr. Howell qualifying a little Mr. Sanderson's statement, speaks of a small prayer meeting and class meeting held in Mr. M. Waite's tent, and of Mr. R. Wilson, of Geelong, and of himself retiring with Bible and Hymn book into the bush, and getting at times as far as Buninyong, for want of regular services, and in order to get away from the dissipation and Sabbath-breaking which prevailed. It is possible that both these statements, from different points of view, are substantially correct. The diggings were so shifting and widespread, and such multitudinous confusion prevailed, that it would be well nigh impossible to get a clear and comprehensive view of what was going on, and probably simultaneous efforts arose in various directions. A short lull next follows, occasioned by the superior attractions of the Forest Creek diggings, which left

Ballarat almost deserted. . The tide, however, soon turned, and the next incident in the history of our Church, recorded in the first page of the " First Minute Book of the Ballarat Circuit," as follows :—" List of subscriptions and donations towards the purchase of a tent, to be erected on the Ballarat diggings, for the purpose of public worship in connection with the Wesleyan Methodist Church ; also, for the establishment of a Sunday school and of a Day school, if found practicable. March, 1853." Thirty-four subscribers contributed £39 13s. Only two names of the first members of Society are found in the list, indicative of the shifting character of a population " with no certain dwelling place." Some eight or ten names are found in this primitive and honourable list, or may be traced in their descendants, who are still true to their first love, though now worshipping in a temple instead of a tent. A meeting of the subscribers was held on April 7th, 1853, when it was agreed " that in case of a majority of them removing from the Ballarat diggings, they shall be entitled to carry the tent with them ; unless in the event of the arrival of a Minister, and the formation of a regular Society here, when the tent shall be considered the property of such Society, in trust for the purposes for which it was purchased." This was a wise precaution, as subsequent events showed, for, after all, this joint-stock-moveable-tent, like a certain moveable feast controversy of ecclesiastical history, created debate and difficulty. The " little flock" did not wait for "the arrival of a Minister," but vindicated the character which Methodism has borne from the days of Thomas Maxwell, its first Local Preacher, as a child of providential emergencies, by beginning to work and organize. The tent was removed from Winter's Flat, Ballarat East, to Wesley Hill, near Pennyweight, and at a meeting of the Society held therein on May 26th, Mr. Hill presiding, various Sunday and week day services were appointed, consisting of prayer meetings and preachings, Sunday school and Bible class. The Society classes were held, one in Mrs. Morrow's tent on Sunday morning, one in

"The Chapel" on Tuesday evening, and one in Mr. Reynolds' tent on Wednesday evening. Two leaders (viz., Messrs. Thompson, Hill, M'Cutchan, and Lowe) were appointed to each Class, except the female Class. Mr. Thompson was an able Local Preacher, and surprised his Presbyterian hearers by his extemporaneous eloquence. Mr. M'Cutchan is now a respected Minister of the Presbyterian Church, the others remain, or are represented among us to this day. Mr. Matthews was Chapel Steward; Mr. M'Cutchan, Sabbath school superintendent; Mr. Wearne, secretary; and Messrs. Harding and Matthews, visitors. Mrs. White was permitted to begin a Day school in the tent, under certain conditions. This was the germ of that series of Day schools, which, under the complex denominational system, for many years prevailed. The Lydiard-street Sabbath school is justly esteemed one of the glories of Ballarat Methodism, and this record of its start is valuable. Even before this, a Wesleyan Sabbath school, numbering from twenty-five to thirty children existed, according to another witness. Mr. Parry, from Tasmania, was its superintendent, and Mrs. Robert Smith (then Miss Carkeet or Cargeeg) was its first teacher At the time of the Eureka stockade, Mr. Robert Smith was building, what is called in the narrative before us, "the first substantial ecclesiastical edifice on Ballarat." It stood on the site of the late Wesleyan school, at the corner of Lydiard and Dana-street. It was built of sandstone from the Black hill, and when, through the subsidence of the adjacent ground, the building had to be taken down, the stone in the old building, on which had been graved the words, "Wesleyan school, 1855," was replaced in its old position in the new house, and it may be seen, says the narrator, "by the moderns," at least, until recently. Meanwhile, the Rev. F. Lewis had visited the place from Geelong, and the Melbourne District Meeting of 1852, resolved to send a Minister "to the Eureka or Ballarat diggings," of which the estimated population was 7000. The next event is a tea meeting, with Mr.

Rippon in the chair, and Messrs Hill, M'Cutchan, Lowe, Mewton, and Parry for speakers. The sum of £11 5s. was collected for preaching tents for Cornish Town and Canadian Gully. Then follow the appointment of Mr. Joseph Doane as Sabbath school superintendent, the formation " of the district of Ballarat into a regular Wesleyan Circuit," and the appointment of the Rev. T. B. Vipont as its Minister, who arrived on September 3rd, 1853. The first regular meeting of the officers of the Circuit was held in the tent at Wesley Hill on September 13th, and thirteen were present, including the new names of Messrs. Hodge, Crombie, Lilley, etc. The Local Preachers present, severally and unanimously declared their adhesion to the grand cardinal doctrines of Christianity, as held by the Wesleyan Methodist Church, and their determination to continue to maintain and preach those doctrines under all circumstances and at all times." Changes were made in times and places, new preaching stations were to be occupied at Winter's Flat, Buninyong, Eureka, and Ballarat township, and new recruits were sought for "our plan" in the persons of Messrs. Smith, Currey, Harris, and Eustace. Number of members, eighty ; and estimated expenditure, £600 per annum. Monthly collection, as well as weekly contributions are urged. It is reported that a site for "Church and house" in the township of Ballarat has been chosen, and a small committee is to canvass for the same, while Messrs. Lilley and Doane are appointed the first Circuit stewards, and a collection is authorized "in all our Chapels for the purchase of bells." The Mr. G. Lilley here mentioned figures most honourably in the outset of Methodism in Melbourne and Portland Bay as well. He was an auctioneer from Launceston, who had large trading connections with Port Phillip. In 1827 this name with two others is found in the list of agents for the Tonga and Fiji Missions. They were engaged as artisans and agriculturalists. Mr. Lilley soon left and returned to the colonies, and is believed to be identical with the Mr. Lilley of this narrative. From the

Circuit Minutes which follow it appears that early in 1854, Mr. Vipont was succeeded by the Rev. Theo. Taylor, and a Circuit meeting was held at Cornish Town on March 13th, 1854, under his presidency. Difficulties arose about the Connexional funds, which were subsequently settled by the concession of "two Ministerial collections per quarter," and various Committees were nominated for the erection of Chapels at Cornish Town, Golden Point, Eureka, and the site of Mr. Taylor's tent. The "tent" dispensation, which had served its generation, was to pass away, and be succeeded by the more substantial order of "slab" or "pine" buildings. One tent was sold for £5, another which had cost £100, realized £10, while the old tent at Gravel-pits, "which in its history of twenty months had cost £500, was blown to tatters, and the ruins sold for £6." In 1853, the receipts were £102 5s. 5d. per quarter, and the expenditure, £200 14s. 11d., whereof £111 4s. 11d. was for horse-hire and travelling expenses. No wonder the question arose, "Shall we buy and keep a horse for the preachers?" The expansion of the work was rapid, new places appear on the plan as Portuguese Flat, Spring Hill, Canadian, Warrenheip, Dowling Forest, Leigh, Sebastopol, Cobbler's Gully, Creswick Creek, Gravel-pits, Magpie, Clayton's Hill and new names are found associated with the work, as Messrs. Hoiles, Little, Nankivell, James, Morgan, Gripe, Jeffery, Polkinghorne, Huddart, Cooper, and Francis; while among the earliest Circuit Stewards are the names of Messrs. Doane, Oddie, Raw, Tregaskis, and Benney. At the first Quarterly Meeting, the Rev. T. Taylor's claim for quarterage is only £9, although the allowance for "washing" is raised to £5, and for "postage" to £3 per quarter. The income, however, grew; a large surplus was handed to the Minister every quarter on Mission House account, and it was soon proposed to raise the Minister's salary, "as he is on the eve of marriage," to £400 per annum. The receipts were much swollen by marriage and funeral fees, which reached in October, 1859, as much £213 10s. 2d. per quarter. When

K

they dropped to £114 16s. 6d., a debt accrued, the authorities grew concerned, a special effort, for which the services of the Rev. D. J. Draper were secured, was made, and then a prompt appeal was made to the Contingent Fund for a grant, "because of the failure of marriage fees." There are points too of spiritual interest and progress. Our rules are to be circulated, and our people urged "to observe them as far as possible," protracted Sunday Class meetings are complained of, Mr. Benney is to preach a special sermon before the Quarterly Meeting, and Ministers are asked to preach on entire sanctification. Saturday night and Sunday morning prayer meetings were enjoyed, and mention is made of two interesting conversions on the Quarterly Fast Day. Weekly payments in the Class are urged, together with mid-day simultaneous prayer for each other. Mr. Thomas James is engaged to assist Mr. Taylor, and then recommended as a candidate for the Ministry. The Quarterly Meetings of those days were large and popular gatherings, as many as sixty being sometimes present, whose "table mercies" would absorb nearly £10 of the revenue. Mention is made of the interesting and "argumentative" character of these meetings. Mr. Taylor was enterprising and devoted in a high degree, as well as "a wise master-builder," and he laid the foundations of our Church broad and strong. The sword was, however, too sharp for the scabbard, and the spirit so ardent, that it well-nigh consumed the frail tabernacle in which it dwelt. Ballarat was his first and almost his last Circuit in the colony. He left it the wreck and shadow of his former self, and after a few months in the Brighton Circuit soon passed away. What the unsparing labours of the Local Brethren who opened up many of the places on the plan must have been, can never be fully told. But their witness is with God, and their record is on high. The Rev. Isaac Harding thus characterizes Mr. Taylor's labours in a letter to the committee. "I have recently visited Ballarat with its 60,000 souls located within sixty miles of the centre where the township stands, and where there is one street nearly as crowded with people and vehicles as a principal street in London. Our valuable Minister at Ballarat, the Rev. Theo. Taylor, has had no ordinary difficulties, and no easy duties to cope with; and he has done his duties well, having under his charge more souls than all the other Protestant denominations together, and Christendom is indebted to him for having baptized, married, buried, and preached the Gospel to all sects and parties whatever:" A similar tribute and meed of praise was already due to the Revs. J. C. Symons and J. Chapman who had been the first accredited and recognized Ministers at Forest Creek and Bendigo, and under the auspices of the Methodist Church, erected the first place of worship, established the first Tract Society, and commenced the first Sunday schools on the goldfields. It was no easy thing to find a Minister to succeed Mr. Taylor, and to take up and carry on the work as he has done. But the appointment of the Rev. Mr. Bickford in 1857 was suitable and opportune. He was a true "father in God," a strength and stay to our Church, a "guide, philosopher, and friend" to many. His ministry was an era of consolidation, and yet of extension and enterprise, for Smythe's, Steiglitz, and other places were soon embraced in his charge. It was a season too of revival and increase, and under the Ministry of Mr. Bickford and his lively and popular colleague, the Rev. Charles Lane, many were added to the Lord. CRESWICK was at this time detached from Ballarat, and with Mount Bolton, Belfast, One-Mile Hill, and Lake Learmonth constituted a Circuit of itself under the care of the Rev. J. W. Crisp, who also had the honour of preaching the first sermon at Clunes. Much was done also in the establishment of Day schools; but the greatest undertaking of that time was the erection of the old Lydiard-street Church, since sold to the School of Mines. The only previous building of any account, "the stone Schoolhouse, cost £2400, held 500 people, and was filled from the first." The foundation-stone of this

Church was laid by Sir Henry Barkly. For the tea meeting which followed, butter had cost 6s. per lb.; milk, 3s. 6d. per quart; bread, 5s. for a 4lb. loaf; and currants, 2s. 6d. per lb.; and the intellectual fare was, no doubt, equally rare and precious. Mr. Tonkin was engaged as hired Local Preacher, until the Rev. William Weston was secured as junior Minister. The Rev. J. G. Millard then succeeded to the superintendency, and carried on the work in the spirit of his predecessor. In his time the organ in Lydiard-street Church was erected, and opened by a musical "function" of considerable merit, and its anniversary was celebrated for some years with an imposing programme of first-class music. This was the foundation of what is said to be the best choir in Ballarat, and which flourishes, "large and fair" at the present day, under the leadership of Mr. Eyres. The Rev. Dr. Waugh, who succeeded Mr. Millard, found the elements of social and religious life assuming a more settled form, and contributed by his luminous teaching and high personal influence to this result. He infused life and strength into the Young Men's Bible and Improvement class, and did much to develop and train those who have since made their mark in Church or State, to wit, Messrs. Campbell, O'Donnell, Fitchett, Tuckfield, Little, etc. These services were duly acknowledged in the profuse valedictory testimonials which were a strong fashion of those days. The amount of official letter writing devolving upon a Minister at that time, was something serious. Dr. Waugh was correspondent for more than twenty Day schools, a service to the State none the less generous, because gratuitous. A similar record might be given of the Ministers who followed, Messrs Binks, Watsford, T. and S. Williams, Daniel, Dare, and other venerated names. In Mr. Binks' day, the colony was divided into Districts, and Ballarat with Geelong, formed the joint head of a separate District. In Mr. Watsford's day, the Ballarat Circuit was divided and Barkly-street made the head of the second Circuit. In Mr. Cope's day the present new Church was projected and the enterprise prosperously begun. In 1875, the Conference was held at Ballarat, under the presidency of the Rev. J. C. Symons. The political strife and faction which were disquieting the country, had a reflex influence on the Church, and some wild and revolutionary theories were broached. But the healing grace of the Holy Spirit, which was shed on many of the Conference assemblies, made them scenes of unwonted emotion and blessing, and preserved our Zion in peace. The Local Preachers' Association has met many times in Ballarat, which may almost be regarded as the metropolis of the craft, and where the order has long been represented by such worthy names as Russell, Bell, Morgan, M. Hosking, Hodge, Ham, James, Letcher, Tregaskis, Polkinghorne, and many others. The Lydiard street Sabbath school has had a noble history under such chiefs as Messrs. Doane, Proctor, Campbell, Wills, Curtis, Coltman, and has proved the Alma Mater of various young Ministers as Rev. Messrs. Persley, Cox, etc. The rise and growth of such Churches as Barkly-street, Neill-street, Pleasant-street, Rubicon-street, and others, is worth telling, did space permit. The last-named may suffice as a sample of the rest. At a recent anniversary it was said that "the shell of the new building was erected and opened July 7th, 1867, the money for the same being kindly advanced by the trustees of Lydiard-street Church; the pulpit, lamps, Bible and Hymn-book being given from the old Church at Pleasant-street. The Church was soon found to be too small, and within one year an addition equal to the original was made. From that time the Church so prospered that further additions to the building were necessary. One of our Ministers received the whole of his religious training in this school, two other Ministers, one Home Missionary, eight Local Preachers, and seven State school teachers, partially so. The amount of spiritual good done is incalculable." We have seen how the work branched out in various directions around Ballarat. CRESWICK'S CREEK was, for a time, the best outlying part of the Ballarat Circuit, boasting of a "slab" Church, which cost £650, but it and its neighbour, CLUNES, have long been strong and substantial Circuits, embracing within their borders as genuine and hearty Methodism as can be found. The growth and development of our Church in these places is that of " a tree whose seed is in itself." The blessing of God, which maketh rich, has made that seed to prosper and grow. We may glorify Him in the human instruments which have been used in this work, such as Messrs. Jebb, Gardner, Raw, Preston, Reed, Cooper, Richardson, etc., together with the faithful Ministers who have from time to time had charge of these Circuits. BALLAN, in another direction, was supplied for some years by Mr. Hampshire, from Geelong, one of our earliest Home Missionaries, and the first to establish Protestant service in this place (1858-70), while STEIGLITZ was first missioned by Mr. Bannister, a local brother, who used to gather and conduct his Sunday school in the open bush, and afterwards procured and adapted for Church purposes, a weather-board building which was drawn up from Geelong on a bullock dray. Mr. Osborne's home, Emly Park, became also a centre of Methodist work and influence, and is connected with some precious episodes in the "Life of the late Mr. J. Wood, of Geelong.* These places are now embraced in the recent and thriving EGERTON CIRCUIT. At MELTON, between Ballarat and Melbourne, Methodism was introduced by the Rev. W. L. Blamires in 1862, ably seconded by the late Mrs. Westlake (afterwards Mrs. Spargo), Mr. J. James, the active and indefatigable Rev. Ebenezer Taylor, and such workers as Messrs. Corr, Atkinson, Ferris, Mawson, and John Dare. In 1867 the foundation-stone of the present Church was laid by the Rev. Dr. Waugh. Melton and Toolern have benefitted by the generous help of the family of M. J. Browne, Esq., of White Hills station, Diggers Rest, and are now comprised in the Sunbury

---

* See Memoir by Rev. Thomas Williams.

Circuit. The SCARSDALE AND LINTON CIRCUIT began with "Brown's" and "Smythe's" two rich rushes, found on the stations of squatters bearing those names. They were first "missioned" or "prospected" from Ballarat during the Ministry of the Rev. J. Bickford, and then with a group of other places formed into a Circuit with the Rev. Messrs. E. Taylor and W. C. Currey for its first Ministers. The Circuit has a somewhat unique and interesting history. Some of our best Ministers have graduated here. Under the devoted labours of the Rev. William Woodall and Mr. Matthew Burnett, a large ingathering of souls, and striking conversions, equal to any we read of in the olden time, took place. Many of these have joined the Church triumphant, others are found in the Circuit still, or in various directions have been honoured of God in turning many to righteousness. Among these may be mentioned Brother B—, first a sailor, then a publican, one of a gang, all the rest of whom came to a violent end, or had to suffer for their crimes. His conversion was very wonderful, and for many years he has been a devoted Home Missionary, in another colony. Brother R—, now a very successful Minister of another branch of Methodism. Though he had "been among the pots," yet his were as " the wings of a dove covered with silver, and her feathers with yellow gold." He was meet to be set among the princes of our Israel, for as a prince had he power with God and prevailed, and his little tent was to him and to many the gate of heaven. Who that heard his prayers and preaching could ever forget them ! Brother C—, once a "child of the devil, and enemy of all righteousness," now a chosen vessel, who takes a sweet savour of Christ with him wherever he goes, one of the most faithful, prayerful and useful of men who is always about his Master's business. The first preaching place was a tent at " Browns," shifted three different times as the diggings changed, then superseded by a weather-board School-Church, which was afterwards burnt down, then rebuilt, and ultimately sold and transported to do duty in another part. After this followed tent preaching at Gemini, Black Hill, Golden Lake, etc. The tide of golden prosperity was soon at its flood, and Churches, fast and free, almost heedless of cost, or debt, were erected, but a reverse and decline set in, and the debts became grievous and intolerable. Thus one soweth and another reapeth. For some years the Circuit took two Ministers, now with the utmost difficulty it maintains one. In the days of Revs. E. S. Bickford and J. B. Smith, almost "heroic" measures were adopted, and by the issue of debentures, bazaar, and undaunted importunity, the parsonage debt was paid and the Circuit saved from utter collapse. The Loan Fund had "long patience," and as it was, many Churches have been closed, sold, or removed, to wit those of Browns, Brownsvale, Black hill, Gemini, Piggoreet, Rokewood (not even the name it bore, the Jubilee Church, could save it), and Skipton, the last, strange to say sold to the Roman Catholic Church. Still the Circuit is fondly regarded by many as their spiritual birthplace and home, and Italians, Monkey Gully, and Happy Valley are potent names to charm with. Among the early friends and workers were Messrs. Raddenberry, Benney, S. Matthews, Peart, Bird, Fox, Felstead, M'Murdie, Johnson, Jennings, Dunstan, etc.

CASTLEMAINE AND SANDHURST DISTRICT.

CHAPTER XII.

CASTLEMAINE CIRCUIT.—This is a mining centre, and dates as one of the earliest goldfields Circuits. Gold changed the quiet vale of Forest Creek into a honeycombed hive of mining industry. The pastures of the roaming sheep and the bounding kangaroo were transformed first into the encampment of the nomad diggers. then into the towns and settlements of busy miners. The story anent Pactolus' stream, whose sands were gold, was realized in modern times in this quiet little stream, and in the other and adjacent tributaries of the Loddon river. The former beds, and the present ones, of these creeks gave forth the rich treasures that had been buried through the centuries. We may say, that the Divine wisdom, forecasting the events of the after-time, had laid up these coffers, and rivulets of gold, so as thereafter to induce human settlement, and the spread of population over the land. Yet it was the timely enterprise of a few prospectors, and the *auri fames* which seized the breasts of the many-tongued peoples of several continents, that brought together the motley crowd which in the months of August and September, 1851, began the Mount Alexander diggings. Vultures do not scent the carcase more keenly, bees do not cluster around honey more thickly, than did human crowds, from far and near, search out and settle in quest of gold. Here it was at their feet. In shallow surface-diggings, ounces, yea, pounds weight of the precious treasure could be obtained by the persevering exertions of a few days or weeks. With the likelihood of this swift way to competency or wealth before them, almost the whole manhood of the colonies swarmed upon the goldfields, to be followed by shoals of the active, stalwart sons of Europe and America. Who can tell what fortunes were gained, and what were squandered? It took little time to extract one, and as little to spend it. Human life was put into feverish activity; and human foibles and faults were immensely intensified and exaggerated. The scum of the earth and the choicest were gathered here. The best and worst were brought into contact, and somewhat commingled. With some men, as lightly come, so freely wasted, was the gold in riotous living, drinking, or extravagances. Some were lightened of their treasure by midnight marauders, or by bushrangers in the Black Forest, a dense piece of "bush" half-way between Mount Alexander and Melbourne. Others proceeded to new goldfields, when cost of travel and living, with "shicer holes" in their speculative digging, made away with a good portion of their first prizes

The small minority saved thriftily, and used wisely their portion of the precious finds. Meanwhile, society was in a state of flux. It was seething with excitement and disturbance of the old order and ways. It was in a condition little favourable to morals and religion. It needed the care of the Evangelist or Minister, and the leaven of the godly, but presented no very promising field for their influence and work. What was done for these diggers by Methodist agency, we now narrate.

We presume that the Rev. William Butters paid a visit to this goldfield in the course of the year, 1851. We know that he did so again in February, 1852. Visits were made by Bishop Perry of the Anglican Church, and other Ministers. Mr. Watchhorn, of Prahran, heard Rev. Samuel Waterhouse preach in December, 1851, his pulpit being a wheelbarrow. A prayer meeting followed the service, at which the people knelt on the grass. Mr. Hill (S.A.), Mr. Martin, Mr. Brian Abbey were Local Preachers, who with others, took their part at this date in open-air preaching. Mr. Martin led a Society Class in a shepherd's hut. A minute of the Melbourne Quarterly Meeting of December 31st, 1851, estimated that 20,000 persons were at that time on the goldfields, and 4000 adherents of the Wesleyan Church. That meeting deemed it advisable to send a Minister to Mount Alexander, and suggested that the Rev. Mr. Harcourt should be sent. Mr. Harcourt paid a visit or two accordingly; but the paucity of Ministers in Melbourne, the great work there to be done, and the removal of one Minister at this juncture from the colony, prevented his settlement on the goldfield. Meanwhile, one agency, largely suited to such a time of emergency, had occupied the ground. Supplying what was lacking in others, and supplementing the occasional services of Ministers, that most valuable body of men, the Local Preachers, gathered from Victoria, South Australia, Tasmania, and other parts, had instituted Sabbath services, and maintained them with more or less of regularity. They stood up in the rough garb of diggers, under the shade of a gum-tree, or upon a fallen log, and with lusty song, gathering a number of people around, preached to them the Gospel of Christ. Brave hearts, desirous to stem the tide of ungodliness, tender spirits yearning over the souls of their redeemed fellow-men, were alive to the importance of Gospel preaching and religious ordinances. A "jealous, just concern" for the honour and worship of God fired the breast of these men, and moved them to lift up the standard of the Cross, in the hope to succour the religious life of disciples, threatened by so many temptations, and to rescue others from the moral snares and perils by which they were surrounded. In few places and times besides, had there been more fearful illustrations of the words of Scripture :—"They that will be rich fall into temptation and a snare, and into many foolish and hurtful lusts, which drown men in destruction and perdition." These true-hearted men, referred to above, sought to lead their fellows to the waters of life, so that the feverish thirst for gold might be abated, or to remind them of their relationship to God, the cross, and eternity, so that amid the engrossing things of earth, some right care might be given to the things of heaven. The public of that time and this day owes a great debt to these devoted men. These events led up to the appointment of a resident Minister which, however, did not take place before March, 1852. The Rev. J. C. Symons was the first Minister of the Gospel settled upon this goldfield. His ministry began there on the first Sunday in March, and his first services were held in the neighborhood of Pennyweight Flat and Old Post Office Hill (now Chewton). In the middle of the month Mr. Symons was joined by Mr. Joshua Chapman, a probationer for the Ministry. He arrived at Forest Creek on the 19th, and on the 22nd preached his first sermon, taking for his text that trumpet note of alarm contained in Romans, chapter i., verse 18. The service was held in the open-air, near to the then burial-ground ; the weather was showery, but the bulk of the congregation remained to the close. Prayer meetings were also at that time held in the open-air in the evening. A lantern would be placed on the ground and the people stand in a circle around whilst the meeting lasted. Mr. Langsford, of South Australia, is mentioned as zealous in turn with the Ministers, in conducting such meetings. Probably, that company of praying people would remember concerning their Divine Master, that—

"Cold dews and midnight air,
    Witnessed the fervour of his prayer,"

and in their spirit hold fellowship with Him, and in their act, in an humble measure, copy Him. Class meetings also were held; but, in some respects, in an extemporized manner and time. The tickets of membership have been written on the bottom of a rusty frying-pan, as the only flat surface available, save the ground. Meetings were held in an empty tent, used as a kind of store-room, and situate at or near Old Post Office Hill. A tin dish or an old chemist's mortar was used as a Baptismal font, on the rare occasion when the rite of baptism was administered. The accommodation for the Ministers was of the rough and ready kind, incident to those early days. They put up their first tent near Pennyweight Flat; furnished it with rude stretchers, constructed by themselves, and in the provision of other articles of necessity, attended more to the useful than to the ornamental. The cooking was done by themselves; their diet was chiefly of mutton and damper; they were their own hewers of wood and drawers of water; and yet were better off than other worthy followers of their Lord, "who had no certain dwelling-place," some of whom also "wandered about in sheepskins and goatskins; being destitute, afflicted, and tormented." Heb. xi., verse 37. Yet the successors of these pioneers on the goldfields, now so snug and comfortable, may do honour to those worthy men who had the discomforts and inconveniences of this primitive life. It must have been trying to the health, as we glean from Mr. Symons' own report that he was, by a severe illness, laid aside from work for about a month. This was in April. The bulk of service, both religious and secular, must then have fallen to the junior Minister. They could not then have taken turn about in fetching water and cooking damper, and circumstances made it good for the younger that he should bear the yoke in his youth. It was apostolic or Pauline, that "these hands have ministered unto my necessities, and to them that were with me." The ordinary Church meetings too must be kept up by him at Forest Creek, whilst in the following month of May, he made his first flying visit to the Bendigo goldfield, and preached there. Yet, with returning health, Mr. Symons was able, as well as willing, to put his shoulder to the work. Manual labour was required in many ways. With the toil of his own hands, he put up the first structure used for public worship at Wesley Hill, and built of slabs, with bark and canvas roof. We presume that he was assisted by his colleague, and by some slight and occasional help of Church adherents. The Ministers stuck manfully by their work, despite inducements to leave it, which would have been strong in their influence if a money value had been their standard of judgment or duty. For diggers around them were in a short time realizing fabulous amounts, and provisions were almost at famine prices. At secular work a high rate of wages or returns could be readily gained, whilst their remuneration was a mere pittance. One member of the Church offered Mr. Chapman the high wage of £1 per hour, to rock the cradle (the digger's cradle.) But this was declined in order to attend to his own proper work, even though the stipend was at the first at the rate of £36 per annum for the younger man, though afterwards increased. Prices were so high that six ounces of gold were paid for a bag of flour (200lb.), and 4s. per week must be paid for washing linen, if done by other hands than his own. No mercenary consideration swayed them. They had little temptation to continue in the Ministry for a morsel of bread. We appreciate their self-denying adherence to their proper vocation and work. We wonder whether a stray nugget came into their hands, as 'tis said came into the hands of the Rev. Robert Young, gifts from his admirers and friends. His fathers in the Ministry exhorted Mr. Chapman to give attendance to reading, but through dearness of cartage, they kept his books for a long while in Melbourne. His superintendent used playfully to assert that Mr. Chapman studied when asleep. The heat, din, and excitement were not favourable to study; that was a work for the quieter and more settled time, which duly arrived. At a somewhat later period, the horse was stabled under the same roof with the bedroom of the Minister—a canvas partition dividing the sleeping place of each—which led one night to Mr. Chapman's waking up by feeling a tug at his shirt, the horse's nose having pushed through the dividing canvas, while with his mouth he was tasting the quality of the blue shirt of his master. Oats were dear in those days. 'Twas said that blue shirts supplied food for horses and milk for dairymen; that the milk sold by the latter was so blue, because the cows fed on discarded diggers' shirts.

As the population was uncertain and migratory, the "preachers' plans" were issued weekly, and afterwards from month to month. This is a copy of the first weekly plan, which is in the handwriting of Mr. Chapman :—

SUNDAY, MAY 2ND, 1852.
ADELAIDE GULLY.—Morning, Chapman.
COMMISSIONER'S (CAMP ?).—Afternoon, Do., half-past 2.
MISSION TENT.—Langsford or Grassley.
OLD POST OFFICE.—Hill or Pearce.
ADELAIDE GULLY.—Afternoon, Orchard or Williamson.
SHEPHERD'S HUT.—Gurr, Yandell, Green, Broad.
COMMISSIONER'S.—Morning, 11 a.m., Boundy.
BARKER'S CREEK.—Bone or Broadbent.
CAMPBELL'S CREEK.—Collins.

Langsford and Bone have since done yeoman's service in our Church work in South Australia. Mr. Yandell died recently in Castlemaine, after much energetic labour spent in the Master's cause. Mr. Collins was an effective speaker, had been in the movement of the Reformers, so called, in England, and was afterwards a Minister of the Free Church of England, Ballarat.

Mr. Symons in his report, dated July 10th, 1852, makes mention "of the prompt and valuable assistance rendered by the Local Preachers' . . . who have been constantly ready to do all in their power to maintain religious services, and to strengthen their Ministers." The same report adds:— "The congregations generally have been very gratifying, both as respects numbers and attention. I have frequently addressed from four to five hundred persons, who have listened with the most devout attention to the Word of Life. It must not, however, from this statement be supposed that anything like the number of persons attend Divine service who might and who ought to do. In many parts of the goldfields the population is enormous, and certainly a very small proportion attend the preaching of God's word."

So the infant Church grew in strength, until a first home and centre was provided for it in the rough slab Church, built at Wesley Hill. That building held about fifty persons. It was opened on Sunday, July 4th, 1852, by preaching services in the morning and evening, attended by a crowd of hearers, and by a Lovefeast and Sacramental service in the afternoon, at which seventy members were present. These had renewed to them the religious fervour and blessing which had been granted to them in other and more beautiful houses of prayer in former times, so that all felt it good to be there. The amount of £17 collected which, with the previous subscriptions, met the cost of the building. The first Sunday school was started on July 11th, and there were seventeen in attendance in the morning, and twenty in the afternoon. Mr. Vickery, who was engaged in buying gold for Mr. Alexander MacArthur, of Sydney, was the first superintendent. This was at

Wesley Hill, which was the centre of Methodist operation for a long time.

In his report of July 10th Mr. Symons further states that one gratifying case of conversion had come to his knowledge, that the expenses of the Mission had been nearly met by the allowance from the Government and by £93 collected on the spot, and that 70,000 persons were estimated to be on the goldfields, which by this time had embraced Barker's Creek, Campbell's Creek, and Fryer's Creek in this neighbourhood. We presume, however, that in this estimate of numbers he includes the Ballarat, Bendigo, and other goldfields, besides those of Mount Alexander.

The District Meeting held in Melbourne, September 22nd, was attended by Messrs. Symons and Chapman, who reported on the state of the Church and Christian work on this goldfield. 150 was the return of membership on the goldfields. Mr. Symons was appointed to Collingwood, and Messrs. Currey and Chapman were the appointments for Mount Alexander. One source of information, however, states that Mr. Currey came to Forest Creek about the middle of August. He continued in charge of the Circuit, widening its area, planting the Church in Castlemaine, and stretching out operations to the Fryer's Creek Districts, until the arrival of the Rev. W. P. Wells in 1854. No more suitable person than Mr. Wells could have been sent to this Circuit in this formative period of its history. He was exact, orderly, methodical; active and energetic; and attended to matters, great and small, that had connection with the establishment and progress of the work. His pulpit efforts, too, were of an instructive and painstaking character. His was beaten oil that he carried into the sanctuary by which the flame of the Divine life in many hearts was constantly fed. He had to endure the hardships and fatigue of pioneer work, but the community around him was gradually adopting more durable habitations, and more settled habits of life. After the first excitement was over the comforts and methods of civilization to which most beforetime had been accustomed were reasserting themselves or regained. The style of working to secure the gold changed also from the cradle to the puddling period, and passed into the stamping one. Rocking, rounding, pounding, marked the several stages and epochs of gold digging and mining. The cradle, the first primitive implement for separating the gold from the wash dirt, was easily worked, readily shifted, and favoured migration from one goldfield to another; but the puddling-machine which meant more outlay of time, labour, and means to construct and use, was employed mostly to put through the process of washing again the dirt which had been imperfectly manipulated before, and could, when once erected, furnish men employment for months or years; whilst, when the matrix of the gold deposits was found in the quartz reef, that soon necessitated the erection of stamping batteries, to which European miners had been accustomed in the Northern Hemisphere. That gave longer work, induced settlement of a permanent kind, and brought the miner to cluster his family around him, build a substantial house, form his acreage of garden, and make one home of the many that constituted the "diggings" township or hamlet. Quartz mining became in the after years the permanent form of the gold industry in these Northern goldfields of Victoria.

Mr. Wells witnessed largely this transition at Forest, Fryer's, Campbell's, and Barker's Creeks, and other places embraced in his wide Circuit. For that Circuit spread out mostly to the west and south, to distances of twelve, twenty, and even fifty miles, as we narrate when taking up the story of the Maldon, Maryborough, Talbot, and Amherst, and Avoca Circuits. New rushes had occurred in these directions, and the Evangelist must look after the migratory population. So encouragement was given to volunteer labourers pioneering the Gospel amongst these human swarms, correspondence was kept up with official and other Laymen, occasional visits were made to distant places, and Churches planted in these new fields.

L

Meanwhile, Castlemaine had been surveyed as a central township. It was the site for the Government offices and authorities, and was found most suitable for a prosperous town. To that place Mr. Currey had turned his attention, securing the valuable area on which our Church premises are built. He pitched his tent there, which long remained as a relic of former times. But when Mr. Wells came, Castlemaine was fixed, both as the residence for the Minister and as the head of the Circuit. Yet, for a considerable time, Methodism remained puny and dwarfish in its representation in this town. Other Churches had a local habitation, and buildings of good size, and as Ministers constantly occupied their pulpits, those circumstances competed more prosperously for public support, than did a small Church at which the Circuit Minister could only occasionally attend. The town grew in size and, in the early mining and coaching days, was the centre and pivot of a large district in the middle of the colony; but Methodism did not keep pace with the growth of the place. When the Rev. Mr. Draper paid it a visit in August, 1855, he readily saw that to give our Church a fair stand, and open a sure prospect of success, a better building was essential than the first slab structure that had been raised. Preaching at Castlemaine in the evening of Sunday, August 26th, Mr. Draper recorded in his diary these terse but significant comments: —" Congregation not so good as was expected. Poor chapel; sacrament after; about twenty-five communicants. The cause here must wither if better accommodation be not provided." The two Ministers consulted together about a new Church, and plans were prepared for a building to cost about £1200, which, after an immense amount of trouble in contriving the ways and means was subsequently erected (in stone), and forms a portion of the present Barkers-street Church. Mr. Draper preached also at Wesley Hill Church, but stormy weather came on, which prevented his intended journey farther on to Chewton (Old Post Office Hill). The rough weather continued through Friday and Saturday, so Mr. Draper wrote on Saturday 25th:—"A wet and stormy night. Much disturbed in my tent. Canvas walls and roof not suited to my ideas of comfort. Great storm in the afternoon." He had, however, pleasant social intercourse with Mr. John Boots, who had been one of the first Methodists in South Australia, as they conversed together about old times and friends. John Boots was a man of sterling worth and of deserved renown. Tall, upright, with soldier-like bearing, he was staunch and true, firm as a granite rock in the cause of the great Master. He had given himself to self-improvement, and was a creditable Greek scholar. His sermons were acceptable, and he remained a pillar of the Church here and at Maldon to the end of his days. Mr. Draper visited Fryer's Creek, then in its prime as a goldfield. Four places were occupied as Churches on the Creek, two being only tents and other two of weatherboard; those at Spring Gully, Fryer's Town, and Vaughan, were afterwards replaced by more substantial structures, and at Chapel Hill, in 1856, a new Church was built of stone. The names of the places nigh to Chapel Hill were indicative of the character of the first people and the rowdy scenes that had been enacted on the outbreak of the rush. One was Chok 'em Flat, another Murderer's Flat, another Deadman's Flat, within the radius of a mile. The names given by diggers were generally more graphic than euphonious. These places had a queer history. Gold had been found in large quantities, but wholesale robberies and not infrequent murders had been committed. It is related that a notorious desperado, with his gang, did, in broad daylight, or at dusk, descend the holes where diggers were at work, and stick them up, robbing them of their gold. Their prowling and marauding at night, plundering tents, and maltreating or shooting men, were terrible. The civic authorities could do but little to protect life and property amid the gambling and the orgies that lucky but low-minded men carried on. Other men, it is true, went down the holes or shafts; University graduates, professional men, doctors, and lawyers descended them by the ladders, or in the buckets, and used pick, shovel, and other implements, showing a new version of High Life below stairs. At nightfall the bivouac of tents had lights within them, shining dimly through the canvas like an array of Chinese lanterns, and had fires nigh to them, blazing away something like in the "black country" in England. Dogs were howling and barking. Firearms were discharged by the honest ones to indicate defence and defiance; but by the dishonest too, as preparation for, or performance of violent misdeeds. Yet either by the clutches of the law, or by other means, the Creek was gradually cleared of most of these ruffians and lawless men. A number of men had from the first been there, who were on the side of right, order, honesty, and religion. These after a while acquired the ascendancy, and when the writer came there in 1858, except for sly grog shops, it was an orderly community that would compare well with most in the land. Here and there, the writer met with queer characters. One asserted that religious people had no business there, delving after the filthy lucre, and he maintained that the rough were always the lucky ones, which held true only in part. Another would on most Sunday mornings fire off his revolver, just as the people were collecting for Church, and despite remonstrance, would, outside his hut, clean his pistol or do other work. One Sunday morning the revolver exploded and beat in a portion of his skull, and he had to be carried to his bed. When he was somewhat recovered, a lady said to him, "Ah! my man, the Lord had to hit you pretty hard to bring you to your senses." The man was sobered in mind by this accident, for he replied, "You are right, so He had." He indulged in no more bravado to show his disregard of the Sabbath, and to annoy worshippers of the Lord, and became a comparatively steady man. A digger, a member of the Church, who had no wife to look after him, came to Church one Sabbath, with one side of his face duly shaved, and the other side unshaved, causing intense merriment to the juveniles in the congregation. An elder, who ventured to draw the brother's attention to the fact, received the reply from him, "Oh! I am so absent-minded!" The comedy and tragedy of life were being enacted in rough and ready fashion in those days.

By this time, the Circuit had extended to Tarrengower (Maldon), and was become so important and extensive that an additional Minister was appointed by the Conference of 1856. The Rev. John Mewton became the colleague of Mr. Wells, and was resident for two years at Fryer's Creek. He was indefatigable in his labours, and under the conjoint administrations of the two Ministers, the Circuit made steady progress. The number of members reported at the Conference of 1856, was 304 (inclusive of Avoca), and at that of 1858 (Avoca excluded), 335. In 1856, 781 children were in the schools.

The cause of education had been well looked after, so that in almost every place where we had a good building as a Church, we had opened Week day and Sabbath schools. Day schools, under Wesleyan auspices, and in connection with the Denominational Board, were started at Castlemaine, Wesley Hill, Chewton, Vaughan, Spring Gully, and other places, and the Superintendent gave much valuable time and care to their oversight and to promote their efficiency. They educated a good proportion of the rising youth of the District. The Sabbath school work was taken up with zest and intelligence by many willing workers, and the foundations of the flourishing schools of the present time were then laid. No religious body did more for the secular and religious instruction of the young than Methodism in all parts of the goldfields.

Mr. Wells' successor in the superintendency was the Rev. Thomas Raston, who was as diligent in this, as he had been in his former Circuit. He was at times subject to mental depression, and would occasionally take the gloomy view; but the clouds soon passed away. Usually he worked away with a pace like to that at which he walked, and that is saying not a little. Though low in stature and small in body, he had a large stride, and a swift gait, so that his junior colleagues, who were tall men themselves, had to put their best foot forward, in order to keep up with him. His sermons were instructive and impressive, given with a loud voice and somewhat deliberate manner. His bodily presence was not imposing and majestic, so that people who at first measured him by his stature and appearance, were pleasingly surprised when they had heard one sermon from him. They had not anticipated that so much sound, and sense too, could come from so small a man.

" And still the wonder grew,
That one small head should carry all he knew."

The retort of James Jeffrey, when a huge burly speaker at a meeting in Maldon, disparaged Mr. Raston because of his small stature, was a smart and effective one. Said the first speaker, " Why one could almost put your little superintendent in his pocket." Jeffrey, who followed, said, " Mr. Chairman, the former speaker said he could almost put Mr. Raston into his pocket. One thing I am sure of—if he got our little superintendent in there, he would have a great deal more brains in his pocket than ever he had in his head." It was like an electric shock; there was a moment's dead silence, then a burst of deafening applause. Mr. Raston's life had been full of incident in the time of his Missionary career. He had served a term amidst the deadly influences of the climate of Sierra Leone, Western Africa, called because of these, the White Man's Grave. On one of his voyages thither, he was wrecked on the coast of Ireland, and we have heard him tell with great glee, that as he had lost everything in the wreck, save some old clothing in which he stood upright, his appearance was anything but respectable and prepossessing. Naturally, he made his way to the nearest Wesleyan Minister and told his tale of shipwreck, and appealed for house harbour, or a loan of money for a time. But he was eyed with suspicion, and catechised and cross-examined as though by an opposing barrister when he was in the witness-box. He saw the

Minister take down from the bookshelf the Minutes of Conference to test his story by the entries in the Minutes. He began to get a little testy himself, and tried to bewilder his questioner a little; but presently, as the story became clear to the Minister, and was in agreement with the records of the Minutes, and the news in the public paper, there was a warmth of greeting and entertainment, so characteristic of Irish hospitality. He had again been wrecked; this time on his voyage to Australia, and on the coast of Brazil. Amid his perils by flood and field, he had lost two wives, not together, but in succession, yet in his third he was more fortunate, for she stuck to him through long years of married life. He had for his colleague the Rev. John Mewton, who was also an immense walker and diligent worker. His voice was loud and monotonous in his then pulpit efforts, so that he was more effective in open-air services than at those in the small Churches. Yet some of his sermons, like the one on "Escape for thy life," were like gunpowder blasts to awaken careless sinners. Maldon at this time was worked as a distinct Circuit, the Rev. H. Chester being the first Minister resident there. Mr. Raston's colleague for the year 1858 was the Rev. W. L. Blamires, then in his first year in the Ministry. He has remembrance of first services (on his entry into Circuit work here in April 1858) which were to him of a somewhat novel, and not inspiring, character. He preached at the Sunday school anniversary at Spring Gully. He walked with Messrs. Yandell and Glenny over the ranges through Eureka to Spring Gully. At the morning session were about twelve adults and forty or fifty children. Some of the children recited during the service. One piece was a dialogue between a drunkard and a publican; another, lines attributed to Alexander Selkirk, commencing, "I am Monarch of all I survey." This selection of pieces, moral in their tone, but decidedly secular, the smallness of the congregation, despite his first appearance amongst them, and the coldness of the whole service, was like a wet blanket on any ardour he possessed. Afternoon service came, when the Church was filled with a congregation, composed largely of adults, and probably 200 were present. The service was conducted by an attractive Local Preacher, Mr. E. B. Burns, who next year entered the Ministry ; and such a contrast between morning and afternoon attendance, was an enigma to the young Minister that he could not solve, the more especially as he soon gleaned that the incorrect intelligence had been circulated (for unreliable news spread before the days of telegrams) that he was a Cornishman. Evening came, and service was conducted again by Mr. Blamires, when the Church was "full inside and out," as an Irishman might say. Numbers were outside that could not obtain admittance. The explanation was that the diggers loved hot dinners on Sundays above all days; the wives and daughters stayed at home to cook, and the men then in numerical preponderance, looked on, helped as might be, cleaned up around, but did not clean themselves, so as to be ready for Church until the hot dinner had been well despatched. After that they were ready in droves for any attractive service, where there was rousing preaching, lively singing, or children reciting. Times and manners changed.

The men whose names were then (1857-60) on the Castlemaine Circuit plan, included several who have become of note in the Methodist and Southern world. Some went subsequently to the South Seas. Mr. Langham went in 1858 to Fiji, and his long continued labours have been invaluable in that Mission field. Mr. Shirley W. Baker went to Tonga as a Missionary, and has since become noted as the Premier, and it is said, the virtual ruler of that fair island kingdom. Mr. Wilkinson lived on the Parsonage land at Castlemaine, and was willing, but somewhat feeble, as a Local Preacher. Since that time he has been heard of as secretary to some native chieftain in Fiji, as Planter, and as Commissioner for Native Affairs. Mr. E B. Burns, then living at Chewton, was next year taken into the Ministry. He had popular gifts, and spent several years of useful labour in Victoria and South Australia. Rev. Richard Osborne Cook, who has had Circuits in Tasmania and Victoria, was a Local Preacher, earnest and laborious. He entered the Ministry in 1859; was rendered useful in his first Circuits in the Southern island, and has fulfilled acceptably his terms of service in Circuits in this colony. Mr. Annear was at that time placed on the plan, and from the first showed a few eccentricities of manner, conjoined with force and fluency of speaking, which have made his pulpit efforts much prized by many congregations. If he has not shone in administrative ability, he has done so in sensible, vigorous, sometimes quaint, speaking power. He will be recognized by many as the "Paul" whose contributions to our periodical literature have been so uniformly excellent and readable. At Spring Gully were then in the Sunday school the two brothers, David and William Lindsay, since very useful Ministers in Victoria and Fiji. At Castlemaine, the Rev. James Graham was then commencing to preach, so that Castlemaine Circuit at this period was somewhat rich in men of competent ability for the preaching work, and was a school for rising young prophets, who afterwards were effective in other parts. Besides, good men and true were found at most of the preaching places standing by the cause as Leaders, Stewards, and Local Preachers. Yandell, Adams, and Robinson at Castlemaine, were active men; although, for various reasons, they afterwards left the ranks. Clowes, Cleave, and Crow were the names of prominent Wesleyans of that day; Barkla, Andrew, Stribley, Bennetts (T. and P.), Collins (a devoted man), Pearce, Roden, and Rowley, were very valuable at Campbell's Creek. Here was the congregation as to strength of numbers, and fervour of piety, standing first in the Circuit. Several interesting Revivals occurred there, winter after winter, so that the membership was greatly augmented. One, later on, in Mr. Dubourg's pastorate, was very notable for its power and permanence. Chewton had Ebbott, Russell, Ellis (afterwards at Eldorado, Ovens District), and Baker (since a Home Missionary and rendered very useful in the Northern plains), and others at its head. The Archbolds were young men in the school. Wesley Hill had Bell, Bouridy, John Dare, Jenkin, and others. On Fryer's Creek were—at Spring Gully—Dawe, Hutchings, Gill, Tregellas, afterwards Hicks, Angwin, and Wilkinson. Fryer's Town was very weak. Redhouse, Nettleship, Peake, and White were the principal supporters there. At Chapel Hill were T. Williams, Ebbott, Attenborough, M'Neilance, Smith (a good Local Preacher), as leading men, and Dr. Mercer's family were warm supporters. Here was the first stone Church on the Creek, and for a time, the more numerous Society, but subsequently it dwindled to a small one, as removals took place and the diggings were worked out. Curious recollections linger around the spot, some about a brother who often led the singing, but who could not read. But whilst he sang he had his eyes fixed on the Hymn book, probably the most intent on reading in appearance of the whole congregation; and another brother, who had a partiality for big words and expressed them in strange connections and confused order. He has been heard to beseech God to save those souls "that would run paralysed through eternity" (parallel with eternity). It was there good father Russell, of Chewton, a coloured man, praying for the Minister about to leave and for the members of his family, asked that they might "turn many to righteousness," and continue to "shine as the stars for ever and ever." Russell was a loveable man, good, genial, always in a happy mood, ready for work at any moment, and was of the first band of Local Preachers to unfurl the King's banner on this goldfield, and that stood in his lot as a faithful Methodist Local Preacher to the end of his days. At Vaughan, situate at the junction of Fryer's Creek with the Loddon river, lived Mr. Joshua Chapman, formerly Minister, then schoolmaster, but still an untiring preacher, Williams,

Tenby, Ratcliff, upright as a poplar, the symbol of integrity and method, indefatigable in his work, and others of lesser note. The congregation was fervid and noisy when a good season of devotion came, and they felt at liberty. The writer has grateful recollection of revival services, when Hocking, who has been since a faithful Methodist at Long Gully, and several others were brought to God.

Other conversions took place during these years, of men who have been earnest and prominent in the Methodist cause. Hines at Fryer's Town, Thimbleby at Castlemaine, Jonathan Best at Campbell's Creek, and since resident in Tasmania, John and Philip Ebbott, afterwards working in the Sandhurst Circuit, and Etchells, son of a Wesleyan Minister, and active as a Local Preacher. At the lower part of Campbell's Creek was a united and earnest society, worshipping in a small weather-board Church at Donkey Gully. Mr. Waterworth was its Leader, who was a pioneer in these parts from the year 1852, and who remains to this day at Guildford, near by, almost a patriarch of the Church. He has been very reliable and staunch as a servant of Christ and His cause. Branching out from the societies at Vaughan and Donkey Gully, was the cause at Strathloddon, begun first with open-air preaching, then sheltering the worshippers in a neat structure of wood, but the cause has since become defunct. A small population exists there at this present time. So with Guildford, where for a time the work flourished, and a neat Church was put up, but which has since been sold. But Jacob Odgers, a worker in these Churches, and Leader of Classes, deserves honourable mention here. Another branch was at Tarilta: that was a lively though small society for a while. A weather-board Church was put up and opened by Mr. Blamires, with the assistance of local friends, and two Classes were formed, but this Church also was given up at a later time, because of the removal of population. Yet this place yielded one gem to the Methodist Church. Here Mr. Donnes was converted, who became the first

Home Missionary in Victoria, and was, a year or so prior to his death, in the status of a Minister. Some account of him follows at an after page. *(See also Ovens and Murray District.)*

The work of the Minister had by this time fallen much into the ordinary groove. But it was toilsome and fatiguing to the physical frame. The Rev. Mr. Raston could not ride, and during his superintendency no horse was kept by the Circuit. An occasional loan of one from a friend, was the variation in the way of locomotion from the long and monotonous walking. Mr. Raston could walk fifteen to eighteen miles in a day. Mr. Mewton was a smart pedestrian, but his constant travels and exposure appeared to some to be undermining his fine constitution. Mr. Blamires frequently walked sixteen miles on the Sabbath day, summer as well as winter, besides holding three preaching services with class and prayer meetings added. These physical toils, with other things, told adversely upon the health. Mr. Raston was seriously ill in the summer of 1857-8, and had Mr. Angwin as his supply. Mr. Blamires was laid aside by colonial fever, during some weeks of the summer 1858-9, and Mr. E. B. Burns took the junior Minister's work, until, by the care of friends, especially that of the late Mrs. Powell (afterwards Etchells) who entertained him most hospitably at her farm at Muckleford, the sick Minister's strength was recruited, and his active duties were resumed.

The remembrance of those fatigues is better than the feeling of them, yet the experience, in its novelty and variety, left behind some flavour and savour like to what is cherished by those who have had remarkable adventures by "flood and field." These Ministers of the early times do not now "shoulder the crutch, and show how fields were won"; they cannot compare with the catalogue of Apostolic sufferings. "In journeyings often, in perils of waters, in perils of robbers, in cold and nakedness, etc.," but they may relate by tongue and pen, not for vaunting of self, but to stimulate others to fortitude of spirit and action, some of the brave hardihood they showed, and severity of labours through which they passed. Even now, the recital of past toils is like the sound of a bugle to the old warhorse, revives the old spirit, and makes them ready for renewed struggles. But, ah! they are soon reminded they have not their former strength. Their day is nearly past, and they must leave to younger brethren to face the foe, carry on the struggle, and win the victories that are to come. They did not effect as much as they had meant to do in that golden day, but the day came and went, some blessed service was done in it, and they can now cheerfully hope that the young men succeeding, and taking up the work, will do better than their fathers in the gospel have done. May they grapple bravely with the difficulties, endure hardness as good soldiers of the Cross, and show far better outcome and results. To God be all the praise! " Neither is he that planteth anything, neither he that watereth ; but God that giveth the increase."

Not alone bodily fatigue, but the conditions of living told injuriously upon the health of professional men, and upon the greater proportion of the miners also. The water was often unwholesome. It was good when rain could be caught and kept in buckets or tanks, but was bad in the summer, as frequently the supply was only the drainage water from the diggings. The Minister at Chapel Hill had to be thankful for water drawn up from a deserted hole, and when brought to the top, looking of the colour and consistency of pea soup, then by ashes, lime, or alum cast into it, after some hours the water was cleared and became fit for drinking or for cooking. The diet was of little variety. Few vegetables, save in the form of pickles, could be had ; fresh vegetables were very dear. The man who brought the first dray-loads of fresh cabbages into Ballarat, made £60, by retailing them at 2s. 6d. and 3s. per head. Newly turned earth on a farm is reckoned healthy, but the newly turned earth with the stagnant water on the diggings was decidedly unhealthy. Many diggers by these prejudicial sanitary conditions, and by overwork, were laid low by sickness and a kind of fever termed colonial, overtaking them, proved often fatal—fatal, in many instances, not through the virulence or deadly nature of the attack at the first, but through want of good nursing. The writer has seen a good many diggers thus prostrate, with only their brother diggers to attend to them. Hard diet, occasional meals, inexperienced care were not the best things to pull them through; these rather aggravated the disease, and caused them to succumb. Good women nurses were very scarce. Frequently, the Minister was called for in the night as well as day time to visit a sick or dying man. Travelling by night on the diggings was often dangerous and always disagreeable. The digger coming for the Minister would equip himself with his primitive lantern, a clear bottle, with the end cut deftly off, and a tallow candle stuck into the neck. By this light he would guide himself, and on his return, the Minister also, as he threaded the network of deep and shallow holes on every hand, or took the range or hilly ground in preference, if such was near, even though the distance might be a little farther. Mr. Blamires used for such expeditions, and for return journeys from week night services at distant places, a small bull's eye lantern, useful both for seeing the path amongst "shicer" holes and deserted diggings, and also for defence against prowling dogs. The pastor's work was as successful amongst the sick and dying, as amongst any class, although it needed all his faith in the sufficiency of Christ's grace, and the universality of His atonement for human sin, to hold out the proffer of life to some dying reprobates. Nevertheless, the thought that he was doing something for a pious praying mother at home, animated him to do his best for the scapegrace son dying in a strange land. Moreover, the man, young or old, was the blood-bought property of Jesus, and was embraced in the promise of pardon, although the prime of life had been given to

Mammon, and the poor dregs of life were all that was left to give to God. The instruction had to be as simple, and the attention as prompt in the tent or diggings Hospital, as with the Chaplain to the dying on battle-field, or in soldier's camp.

Other part of Ministerial duty was to attend at the tea meeting, with its social enlivenment, and engage in its after speaking and singing. This was about the only recreation for the steady part of the diggings' population, and served to counteract in others, in some degree, the attractions of the dram shop and the dancing and gambling saloons. They became somewhat stale to the Minister who had to attend so many of them. Mr. Blamires had three nights in succession taken up with them, in his first week in the Castlemaine Circuit, and found them to recur in his own denomination, with occasional help to other Churches, on the average of one meeting a fortnight. Nevertheless, the vocal and instrumental music of open-air service, and of anniversary tea meetings, to say nothing of the mental and material food then given, were some counterpoise to the rollicking songs, banjo and tambourines, hurdy gurdies and concertinas, by which other places of entertainment catered for the public, with the far from laudable purpose to entice them to drinking, dice, cardplaying, and other ways of dissipation. At the tea meeting the mental food was not strong meat, and the music was not classical; but the provision, with its due mixing up of sandwiches and saffron cake, tarts and cream, was sound and palatable; the singing was lusty, hearty, congregational, and when given by children very sweet and attractive; and the speeches, conversational, humourous, with a few grains of wholesome instruction mixed in plenty of chaff, fun and anecdote, if not very refined, served as a pleasant entertainment, and often attracted persons to the gatherings, who would not have ventured inside Wesleyan places of worship. James Jeffrey was a very popular man on the platform, and few tea meetings took place but his services were sought after, and they were often secured. The mirth was a medicine, the explosive laughter was a good tonic, after the wearisome drudgery and monotony of the digger's toil, and the singing was a potent charm wherewith to allure earthbound men to nobler thoughts and a higher life.

In the years 1858-60 the Church had made good progress, so that the members had increased from 335 to 455 (inclusive of 58 at Maldon) and the Churches from 10 to 18. The Circuit had, from its commencement, a preaching station at Mr. E. Parker's at Mount Franklin, but latterly it had been extending its area in that neighbourhood, now embracing Churches at Franklinford, Yandoit, Spring Creek (Hepburn), which will be noted in the account of the Daylesford Circuit. At this period, a monthly visit was paid by the Ministers, in turn, to those outlying places.

At Franklinford was the Protectorate school for the Aborigines, some of whom were steady in work, and the younger of them could read, write, and work elementary sums. Usually some of them attended the religious service, and understood fairly the sermons preached in the English tongue.

The Circuit was subsequently favoured with the Ministry of the Revs. John Harcourt and John Catterall, during which time it continued to prosper, and returned 415 members at the Conference of 1863. The Revs. William Hill and Edwin I. Watkin succeeded them; and the Conference could not have sent at that time truer yokefellows and more efficient Ministers to forward the interests of the Church in this important goldfield Mr. Hill's intelligent and forceful exposition of the Word took hold of the more educated persons in the community, and some were led to unite with the Church. Mr. Watkin, vigorous, genial, unassuming, indefatigable, suited all classes, and his Ministry was blessed to very many. At this period came about Mr. Donnes' conversion, which was all the more notable, because of his race and creed, and because of the fruitfulness of his religious life after conversion. His father was a Greek, and a member of the Greek Catholic Church. His mother was a Roman Catholic, and so also was his stepmother, and his training as a child was in that Church. He was induced to enter the Wesleyan Church, on the occasion of an anniversary, and there he heard truths which set him thinking about his spiritual state. He was awakened to a sense of his sin and danger under a sermon by the Rev. John Harcourt, and some time after this, under the ministry of the Rev. E. I. Watkin, was led to Christ. He met with opposition from his family and friends at the first, but continued as a disciple of Christ, and began to work for Him. His effort led a brother to believe in the same Saviour and rejoice in His salvation. He became a Sabbath school Teacher and Local Preacher, was the first Layman employed as a Home Missionary by the Wesleyan Conference, after its Society for Home Missions was formed; and eventually entered the Ministry of this Church in 1883. After a life of devoted service and much usefulness, he finished his course on earth at Yackandandah, in April 1884, and has left a name fragrant with pious memories in the places where he laboured.

The Campbell's Creek society had grown, and the necessities of an increasing congregation demanded a new Church, which was accordingly erected and opened in October, 1863. This Church became the scene of a notable revival, in the years 1866-7, under the ministry of the Rev. Edward King and Rev. Charles Dubourg, the resident Minister. The good work spread to most places of the Circuit. The harvestmen, clerical and lay, rejoiced to gather in the sheaves. The membership, which was 506 at the Conference of 1886, reached 554 in 1869, notwithstanding a considerable depression of mining interests, and departure of numbers of persons to other parts occasioned thereby. This period seems to have been the acme of the spiritual prosperity of this Circuit. Strong and flourishing as it had been up to this time, it became henceforth subject to varied fluctuations. The mining activity has declined,

M

and the town and district have passed through the experiences which many of the older towns in the colony have known, and have witnessed the departure, in droves, both of stalwart men, and of the rising and enterprising youth of the neighbourhood. Nevertheless, the Circuit has had eminent Ministers as Superintendents :—Revs. Thomas James, Henry Bath, George Daniel, Thomas Williams, Peter R. C. Ussher and others, with active young men as juniors as—Revs. Ralph Brown and John H. Tuckfield. In this year of grace, 1886, under the ministry of the Rev. James Lowe, it numbers—13 Churches, 362 members, 1041 Sabbath scholars, and some 1500 adherents, and is still a strong and commanding Circuit. The names of Roden, Waterworth, Crow, Etchells, Ebbott, etc., dating from early times in their connection with the Circuit, are still found in the list of the active official Laymen. We have been glad to recount in this chapter the rise and establishment of a work of God, which has had interesting phases of religious life, and may be regarded as a fair type of the Methodist activity, and pioneering and progressive work on the goldfields of Victoria. Methodists have no hesitation in calling this planting of Churches and spread of religion a work of God for

"Be He nowhere else,
God is in all that liberates and lifts,
In all that humbles, sweetens, and consoles."

MALDON, MARYBOROUGH, AND ADJACENT CIRCUITS.

CHAPTER XIII.

THE station at Maldon was at first an integral part of the Castlemaine Circuit. The diggings and the township are on the slope at the foot of Mount Tarrengower. A more pleasant site for a town could scarcely be found than on the side of this mountain. The present town is close to some of the diggings, but is not so much intermingled with forsaken shafts and diggings, as are many other towns on the goldfields. It is compact and sightly. Some rich finds of gold were made here in 1853, first at Long Gully, then at Growler's Gully. Discoveries at the Beehive, Western, Eaglehawk, Nuggetty, Pegleg, Parkins', and Welshman's Reefs rapidly followed. A considerable population located here in the year above named, and in subsequent years. Among the first Methodists were Messrs M. Morgan, Noble, Crockett, Clarkson, then shortly afterwards came Messrs. John Boots, James Warnock, Richard and H. Tregaskis, and James Jeffrey. As usual on the goldfields, the Local Preachers had a good part in beginning the cause, and the several stages of Chapel erections were passed through, first of canvas, then on to that of brick. The preaching was from stump or log at the first; then a tent, or three tents together were used as a preaching place. The site was near that of the present Church. It is related that the first collection for this canvas Church was mostly in half-crown pieces (no threepenny bits in use then). One person outside stuffed a one pound note through a slit in the tent, which note was added to the collection. A new Church was erected in 1856, and the congregation had become sufficiently important by the year 1858 that a Minister, the Rev. H. Chester, was stationed, and in the next year a new Circuit formed. The outlying places embraced therein were a small structure at Eaglehawk, and a preaching appointment at Mr. Crockett's farm at Sandy Creek. The Eaglehawk congregation may be considered as one with that at Maldon for the purposes of our writing. The two congregations were closely identified. Mr. Crockett had a family of stalwart sons and daughters, who were of one mind in religion, and formed the Church in his house. Mr. Boots was a pillar in the Church. He was a devout, studious, respected, and reliable man. Every one held him in high esteem, and the congregations to which he ministered as a

Local Preacher, heard him with pleasure and profit, as he spoke to them the words of life. He had considerable changes in his earthly lot, and knew some sore afflictions in person and family in his later years, but he wavered not in his fidelity to Christ and his attachment to the Church of his choice. He had not much humour or quaintness, as had Jeffrey, not such push and enterprise as had many who had been long in the colonies, but he was as true as steel, firm as a rock. His name is intimately connected with the story of Methodism in South Australia, where he was one of the pioneers, and in Victoria, where he spent the latter portion of his useful life. Certainly he carved his name on Maldon Church and its interests, and there his name will be long held in memorial. Mr. James Warnock came to Maldon as a young man, an emigrant from Ireland, and was one of the many intelligent and foremost men which that fair Isle has furnished to Australian Methodism. As the chief founder and builder of a large business, held by Messrs. Warnock Brothers, he was closely associated with the social, commercial, and mining prosperity of Maldon. He was free, with his shrewd business ability and liberal gifts, to promote the interests of the Methodist Church. Not alone in Maldon, but in connection with General Church Committees, the District Meetings, and the Conference he has given ungrudgingly his time, and brought the influence of his social position, his wide acquaintance with men and business, and his considerable powers of thought and speech, to forward the peace, establishment and increase of Victorian Methodism. He is the foremost Layman in the Castlemaine and Sandhurst District, and was representative of Australian Methodism at the Æcumenical Conference of our Church held in London in the year 1881.

The Rev. H. Chester was an active, merry, brotherly Wesleyan Minister. When he began a sermon he hastened through at top speed, crowding in as much material as would suffice ordinary preachers for three occasions. Some of his sermons were well worth listening to. He had a "great gun," a sermon on the text, "Man dieth and wasteth away, etc." He preached it at his first service in many Churches, and we are shrewdly positive that he did so on his first Sabbath in Maldon. He could enjoy a good laugh, and could raise a laugh by his home thrusts or witty remarks. Passing by the Melbourne Gaol in Russell-street, in company with two Ministers, one of them, who had recently been visiting a prisoner confined there, asked of Mr. Chester, "Have you, at any time, been in the gaol?" "No," was the reply, "but I have been six years on the roads." (In old times convicts were employed to make main roads, and Wesleyan Ministers, as itinerant, are constantly travelling over the roads.) His ministry at Maldon was one of acceptance and usefulness.

It was at Maldon in 1858 that the writer first became acquainted with "Jimmy Jeffrey." The former had walked from Vaughan to Maldon, some fifteen miles, to hear the Rev. Mr. Dare preach a sermon. It was given in the afternoon of a day when the tea and public meeting was held in the evening. Mr. Dare could electrify an audience when he liked to address himself thereto by a suitable speech. His effort at this meeting told immensely upon the sympathies of the people, but when Jeffrey spoke also, it was at once seen by the writer, that he could play cadences and touch chords in the hearts of the people that, in his own quaint, original way, would evoke their enthusiasm, even as did the magnificent orator. A short, sturdy man, with dark hair and features, small eyes having a curious twinkle in them at times, with a demeanour in the pulpit and on the platform, quiet and modest, there was not much in the first glance at him, to indicate the fund of humour that was in him. Nor did the humour come out on all occasions. There were times when he was fettered in public speaking, and had (what he called himself) a "straight jacket on." But, usually, his homely talk, his quaint repartee, his Cornish brogue, his unexpected turns of remark, his pertinent illustrations, conjoined with his acknowledged piety, made him a great power with the congregations gathered in the mining districts. Tales of his quaintness, humour, force, linger with a sweet perfume about the goldfields.

He had a cut at stormy-weather Christians in the reply he gave to a Minister, when the ship, by which he and others emigrated to South Australia, came into port. It was a custom then for a Wesleyan Minister to go on board a newly-arrived immigrant ship to search for any of the Wesleyan flock who were passengers. The Minister on this occasion addressed himself to the chief officer of the vessel, and told him his errand. He was directed by the officer to go to a short, thick set man, who was on deck, who could give him all the information he wanted. This was our friend Jeffrey. The Minister spoke to him, "I have been told by the chief officer, that you could furnish me with particulars I want to know. I am a Wesleyan Minister. Are there Wesleyans in your ship, or are there any praying people amongst the passengers? The reply was, "Oh, yes, we have plenty of praying people on board"—(then a pause and comical side glance at the Minister)—when "there is a storm."

He did not spare in his sermons milk and water Christians, nor that class of sinners which is like the blacksmith's dog, that can stand fire when the hot sparks are falling all around. It is related that he was preaching in a Church in the Ballarat neighbourhood, when the weather was oppressively hot. Said Jeffrey, in the course of his sermon, "You boys (pointing to the auditory) think it fairish hot in Chapel to-day, but this is a mere nothing to the heat of the devil's kitchen, where, if ye don't repent and be converted, ye'll burn for ever and ever." This outburst of plain speaking caused a titter of laughter, something to the preacher's annoyance. He stopped, turned round in the pulpit, took off his coat, and wiped the perspiration from his face with his handkerchief, then he placed another hot shot amongst his hearers, when he added, "Ye laughed just now when I told you of the heat of a certain 'old villain's' kitchen. But, believe me, if the dear "Maister" but comes to any of your bedsides to-night, and takes you by the hair of the head, and shakes you over the burning pit, that will soon bring you to your senses and take all the giggling out of you."

On the other hand, the writer heard him appeal to his congregation on this wise. "You diggers mark out a claim, and put down your pegs near to a mount, say that it is Mount Alexander, or Mount Tarrengower, or the Wombat Hill, and you go to work in the hope of finding the gold, and some of you come on a rich patch, and others sink 'shicer' holes; 'tis terribly uncertain about finding the gold; but I'll lay you on to the best place. Here, you diggers, come mark out a claim by Mount Calvary; put down your pegs and you'll not find it uncertain work; there is the real gold to be got here, and no 'shicer' holes, not one, and no license fee; come and take salvation without money and without price, the gift of Jesu's love. The good Lord laid down the gold where many of you have been finding it, and the same dear Lord, out of His boundless love in giving His Son to die, has brought heavenly riches within the reach of every man of you, but you'll have to be smart in getting it, or the devil's police 'll have you in the lock-up." The troopers of that time were not at all in favour with the diggers, and Jeffrey availed himself of any local prejudices in his allusions, as he did when the squatters in the neighhourhood of Daisy Hill had been impounding the diggers' horses, which, when hobbled and turned out, the diggers thought should have free commons on anybody's run, without let or hindrance, seeing the squatters had so good a market for their sheep where there was a crowd of diggers. The text was, "Now they desire a better *country*, that is, an heavenly." Said the preacher, "You thought in the old country, when you could scarcely get bread for yourselves and family with very hard work, that you would like to go to Australia. You heard of it as a fine land for the poor man; plenty of wages or plenty of gold. Some weeks of the same labour as at home, would just keep body and soul together, would here give you a start for farming, or make your fortune by the gold. You desired that better country of which you had heard, and you were at some pains to get there. You paid your passage money and you braved the discomforts of the voyage and the perils of the sea to get here; and some of you have not found it up to expectation. But I tell you, if you'll be at pains to get to the heavenly land you'll find it indeed a better country, and beyond expectation. All healthy people, all holy spirits; no terrible pain; no tempting devil; nothing to disturb; no people to annoy; there'll be no *squatters* there," which was certainly a new way of saying, "there'll be no trouble there," but which took immensely with his digger congregation.

He was great at illustration. A favourite text was Psalm xl., verses 1-3. "He brought me up also out of an horrible pit, etc." He pictured before his mining hearers a wet sinking claim, where, as he said, the drives were unsafe, and the ground liable at any minute to fall in or be flooded. "There," said he, "is the man on top, one hand on the rope and the other on the windlass, ready, at a minute's notice, to draw up. The bucket is below; the schist and water is coming in, and will soon fill the drives. The word has been passed up, so that the man at the windlass is aware of the danger. He dreads a catastrophe, and shouts down the shaft—'Below there! jump in the bucket quick for your life.' But what do you think, boys," said Jimmy, "the stupid fellow of a man, instead of at once attending to the warning, runs here and there to gather up the picks and gads. 'Below there!' again the top man cries, 'jump into the bucket for your life, or it will be too late.' This time," said Jimmy, "the fool runs up another drive to get his old oilskin coat, and allows the shovels, picks, and gads to be drawn up in the bucket instead of himself." He then vividly described the horror of the top man when he found no man in the bucket. He lowers again, but it is too late; all is over; the drives are full and water rising in the shaft. "Poor fellow," says Jimmy, as he wipes the big tears away—" Poor fellow; he tried to save his old oilskin coat at the cost of his life. What a fool he was! Mates, don't 'e think so? But, although I know you will all say, '*A big fool, indeed!*' yet you boys 'up along there' are guilty of like folly. You are down deep in the mine of sin. Salvation's bucket is let down to you from the great 'top-man,' Jesus Christ, by the gospel rope. The dear 'Maister' cries to you to jump in and be saved; but you are saying, "No hurry, Maister; I must run for the picks and gads, and gather up my old, almost worn-out duds, and then I'll get in salvation's bucket, and be hauled aloft and be saved.' Poor fools," echoed Jimmy —poor fools! if you let slip your only chance of escape and be lost, ye will have no one to blame but yourselves. Ye will commit self-murder by allowing your working tools to go aloft, while you, yourselves, are flooded to death in the dark, deep mine. The good Lord save you all!" Another version gives Jeffrey as getting a man into the bucket and then crying out, "Wind him up, Lord! Wind him up, Lord!"

After Maldon, he was in Ballarat, then from 1871, at Bendigo; and his last place of sojourn was at Moonta mines in South Australia, where he died.

It is related of him that in this latter mining district, after the first Mrs. Jeffrey died, he paid his addresses to a buxom widow, with a view to renew his home comforts by marriage with her. On a dark night he had been to visit her, and on returning, he fell into a rather deep hole. It was so deep that he could not get out by himself, and was necessitated to call long and lustily, before help came to him. At length two miners heard him, found out who he was, and speedily brought him up to the surface. On enquiring, "Well 'Jimmy,' however did you get there?"

Oh! was the reply, I had been to Mrs. So and So's, and after some chat I thought it was time to return home, and you know, I can't see so well as I could, and so stumbled into this here pit; and when down there I thought, 'What a big fool you are at your time of life to go courting, and stop out late at night, and the Lord has made you suffer for it,' and I promised the Lord if he would get me out of that hole that I would never go courting again." Jeffrey kept his promise, for he got married immediately, and his second wife survived him.

James Jeffrey was born in Illogan parish, Cornwall, on Christmas day, 1817, and died in Moonta, South Australia in 1880. His last words were, as though referring to his landing on the heavenly shore from some emigrant ship, "'Tis packed up in a small parcel. I'm in sight of land. I'll soon be home." Then he slept in Jesus. One who visited him, when his sun was fast setting, declared, " I knew Jimmy Jeffrey from the time of his conversion. He was always the same, full of faith and joy; and as he lived, so he died." He was to the miners of this Southern world as those worthies of Methodist renown— Sammy Hick, in his simple-hearted, straightforward zeal; as Billy Dawson, in his graphic descriptive powers; and as Peter Cartwright, in his bizarre humour, and lion-hearted courage. Had Methodism a Westminster Abbey, she might well put him there, for she owes him a great debt, and his name and memory she will not willingly let die.

The Rev. W Woodall succeeded Mr. Chester as the resident Minister at Maldon, and gave himself with his usual fervour to the ministry of "the Word" and promoting social prayer meetings as a means to vital godliness. The result was a good work of grace, and many accessions to the Church of Christ. The returns given at the District Meeting, 1860, showed 69 members, and 82 on trial. The Rev. George B. Richards was appointed in 1861. A Christian gentleman, handsome in his personal appearance, and having the refined manners which might be expected from his education at Oxford, he could sympathise with the poor, and do service to the lowly; in which he found an admirable help-meet in his most excellent wife. Some thought him a valetudinarian, and too much given to the care of his health, but only those who suffer from chronic bodily ailments, know what prudence and care are required from such persons in order to preserve any health and life. Lengthened days are his best justification of his own procedure in regard to himself, and valuable service, that he could not have rendered with the vehemence and passionate energy which unthinking persons demanded, and which would have spent quickly his vital powers, has been given to the Church by more quiet methods, over an extended series of years. He was sound and instructive as a preacher, and esteemed for his courtesy and kindness as a pastor. The Rev. John Catterall came next, being transferred from Castlemaine to Maldon, by the Conference of 1862. He had good business habits, and considerable energy, which fitted him for the undertaking he at once commenced—the building of a new Church. The project was started in January, 1883, when the munificent donation of £150 from Messrs. Warnock Brothers headed the subscription-list. This had increased in a fortnight afterwards to a sum over £500. The structure is the present Wesleyan Church, which still speaks to the credit of the architects and promoters of its work by its neat appearance and its fine accommodation. It is a building, 60 feet by 35 feet, and was dedicated to the worship of God at the end of this year by services conducted by esteemed and popular Ministers.

Meanwhile, in this year of grace, so memorable for the extensive revivals of religion throughout Victoria, a great ingathering of persons to the fold of Christ had taken place, and many converts had experienced a saving change in their hearts. The Minister wrote, "There has not been much visible excitement, but the power of the Lord has been present to wound and to heal." The Holy Spirit's power had accompanied the preached word, and the varied agencies and services in use had been so blessed that it was computed that over fifty persons had received the end of their faith, the conscious salvation of the Lord Jesus, and were added to the Church." That local Church of old and new members, " walking in the fear of the Lord, and in the comfort of the Holy Ghost" was multiplied.

The Church has maintained a good hold of the people of Maldon, the Methodists having the most numerous congregation of the sections of the Church of Christ represented in the town. Smaller Churches have been located in several hamlets and districts adjacent. The district looks lovely in spring, with its green pastures, smiling fields of corn, pleasing contour of hills bounding the valleys and the plain. The majesty of Tarrengower towers above the whole, and Maldon is a gem of a town situate on its slope, much as a gold brooch is set on a matron's bosom. The place has a thrifty well-to-do community, and the pastor is favoured who in a quiet round of duties, preaches the word in this neat and commodious Church, and watches over the spiritual welfare of this simple-hearted and united brotherhood of people.

MARYBOROUGH, TALBOT, AND AVOCA.—The diggings at Avoca started about May, 1854. Mr. John Meaden was one of the multitude who came to the rush in search of gold. He started Methodist services, and gathered together some of the God-fearing people. Mr. Joseph Jennison, arriving from Adelaide, was soon at Mr. Meaden's side, assisting him. These and other Local Preachers maintained the services, encouraged by an occasional visit of the Rev. W. P. Wells. At the second visit of their pastor, a canvas tent, near the police court, was opened as the appointed preaching place. With the fluctuations of those early times, Avoca was sometimes almost deserted, and at other times it was a flourishing Methodist centre. The Rev. Mr. Dyson came as resident Minister in 1855.

Alma, near Maryborough, was one of the "rushes" where, so far as we can glean, the Methodist standard was early lifted up. James Jeffrey, who was general evangelist by his own appointment, to many goldfields, came here from New Zealand about three weeks after the first "rush" took place. This might be in 1854 or beginning of 1855. His tact and manner of managing a crowd were well illustrated on the occasion of his first service. He had asked his old fellow-workers on arrival, "Have you established preaching ?" "No." "How is that ?" "There are too many rowdies." "If you will help me, I will try." On Sunday the Methodists assembled, and by singing brought the multitude around them. After the opening exercises were over, Jeffrey mounted on a stump, and looked round on the upturned faces of his new audience. The levities of some and the movements of others indicated that a critical moment was reached, but the man was equal to the difficulty. Addressing those on the outskirts of the assembly, he said, "My dear friends" (then casting his eyes on the knot of professing Christians round him) "these Methodists here ought to be ashamed of themselves. They have been three weeks here among you, and never given you the benefit of one public service. (A laugh, and "hear, hear.") But they intend now to mend their ways; and if you will listen, I will try to preach." He had won the crowd to his side. He preached undisturbed, and for many Sabbaths afterwards public services were held, and worship offered to the Triune God. He had a great fund of humour, and was only excelled in his management of an out-door audience by the Rev. William Taylor, who did so much pioneer work in San Francisco and other parts of California. People ask, "What were his sermons like ? How could an uneducated miner hold a promiscuous audience ?" "I wondered until I heard him," said one. "I had heard English preachers of most Churches, from the Anglican Bishop downwards. I felt when he entered the pulpit the old, 'dost thou teach us' prejudice. But his manifest intelligence soon dispelled this; and as he went on in his well-arranged discourse, I lost the mastery of myself, and in vain tried to laugh inwardly and to cry inwardly at his sarcasm and pathos, the laugh would out, the tears would come." So this master in our Israel with his comrades, stood up for King Jesus amidst and against the overflowing ungodliness of the place   Men of all creeds and classes were there. Persons, some of learning and culture, having academic degrees, with others ranging down to convicts and criminals, all in feverish excitement, seeking gold. The law enforced a Sabbath of cessation from mining, but on that day trees were felled, clothes washed, and trade, more or less, openly carried on. Some were gambling, some drinking, the irreligious made it a day of revel, and not infrequently, a set fight took place. But the pious few stood up for God against the workers of iniquity. "They that feared the Lord spake often one to another," in fellowship of piety; they that were soldiers of King Jesus, clustered together in phalanx of indomitable steadfastness.

Presently, a Wesleyan Minister came to their help; the Rev. W. P. Wells paid them a visit, then speedily the Rev. Martin Dyson was stationed amongst them. On April 16th, 1855, Mr. Dyson passed his examinations before the Chairman of the District and other Ministers, and received his license as a Minister of the Gospel. Then he was sent to serve the migratory populations at Maryborough, Talbot, and Avoca. Those places with others, ranging from Beaufort on the south-west, to Dunolly and the Loddon on the north-east, were considered the junior Minister's branch of the Castlemaine Circuit. Travel was rough, the roads were execrable, being only bush tracks, some leading over the plains to the east of Carisbrook, which by reason of the number and badness of crab-holes, were locally called the Bay of Biscay. A journey on the coach by that route, was one of hard endurance or torture, when a man had occasion to travel that way. The young man, however, did most of his travel on foot. Now and then a friend would lend a horse, but not often. Long distances were measured and traversed by walking exercise. On October 12th he walked twenty-five miles home to his tent at Alma, and, on arriving there footsore and weary, found that some one had cut open his tent, and taken away everything but his books. On the following Sunday, some friend gave him a sovereign. Mr. H. Clarkson and others came also with their liberal help, but his loss was only partly met, and the thief was never discovered. Yet the true-hearted young Minister held on to his work, meeting Classes, conducting service, preaching sermons, visiting sick diggers in their prostration, and carrying the Gospel to some in their dying moments. A new difficulty confronted him. Most of the population left Alma, thousands went to Fiery Creek, so it was thought prudent to remove his tent and pitch it at Avoca, which was done in the end of October 1855. By this time preaching had been established in tents at Alma, Avoca, Daisy Hill or Amherst, Back Creek or Talbot, and Maryborough. Services were held regularly in them on the Sunday, and at times in the open-air. A tent was also set up at Fiery Creek in the midst of 20,000 diggers. Mr. Dyson says :—" There was an abundance of open and shameless sin committed with impunity, but we were not molested in our work. On no occasion was I insulted by a digger, or interrupted in public worship." The accommodation for worshippers was of a primitive style. The seats were commonly of roughly shaped or sawn timber, secured to legs made of saplings or odd lengths of wood driven into the ground. The tents were not always of good construction, and sometimes were torn to pieces. At Daisy Hill the roof of one which rested on a wooden frame, was blown off, but on the next morning (Sunday), service was held within the walls, minus the roof. A violent squall nearly brought the canvas Church at Maryborough to the ground. That at Alma was much damaged by a storm. The preacher, in order to reach distant places, often left his home at Avoca at five o'clock in the morning of Sunday, and walked to his appointments. The accommodation for him at different stopping places was rough also. The friends were kind, but their means were scanty. When he remained over the night at Maryborough, he had special hospitality, and provision for his entertainment above the average, through the kindness of Mr. and Mrs. Matthew Williams. At their canvas home, his sleeping place was in the storeroom, on the heights of well filled sacks. Then he thought himself "in clover." In other places, rough canvas stretchers were at his service. These were placed behind barricades and partitions, made of piles of cases in rough and ready stores. At other times he slept on counters or on the ground, wrapped in rugs or blankets. Happily, as he himself says, "I could sleep anywhere, and my work was delightful everywhere." He threw his whole heart into the work, but, nevertheless, met with considerable discouragement. If the accommodation was hard, and the roads were rough, it was immensely rougher in his spiritual enterprise. It was hard to sing the song of Zion amidst, at times, almost demoniac revelry; it was hard to breast, much more to turn the tide setting in, with so swift and overbearing a current, towards gambling, drinking, debauchery, perdition; it was hard to persuade men, grovelling in earth, bound to it as galley slaves to the oar, by the eager quest for gold, to strike for spiritual liberty, or lift up themselves for one good look at Heaven. There came a moment when he hung his harp upon the willow. The young man's heart fainted within him; but only for a time. Dismayed at the mass of evil, feeling his personal insufficiency to cope with its giant forms he, in a fit of mental depression, handed in his resignation to the Rev. Mr. Wells. This was about the time for holding the Quarterly Meeting (September) at Castlemaine. That resignation was not accepted. Judicious counsel by Mr. Wells, and the kindly action of the Superintendent, with all the officials of the Quarterly Meeting, saved Mr. Dyson from a perilous error in his judgment and course of action. The young Minister was heartened again. He returned to his duty with a renewed commission, and battled against distressing personal temptation, and surrounding wickedness of others, manfully and bravely, so the temptation to leave his post ultimately and finally left him, and he had the after joys of spiritual victories and successful labours. Mr. Dyson has since had an honourable and useful Ministerial career in the islands of the South Sea, and in the colony of Victoria. He writes concerning that time of mental depression:—"The kindly sympathy of dear old Father Boots, who is so well known and honoured in Methodism, has left a most fragrant memory in connection with my visits to Castlemaine. He was the first who turned my attention to the study of the Greek New Testament, and gave me an old copy which he had himself used. This had probably an influence in creating the desire for a knowledge of the foreign tongues which was afterwards gratified in my becoming tolerably well acquainted with the languages of the Samoan and Tongan groups of islands, where I laboured many years as a Missionary." St. John's encomium upon Gaius is well deserved by Brother Dyson—" Beloved, thou doest faithfully whatsoever thou doest to the brethren and to strangers," or that further one respecting Demetrius, he "hath-good report of all men, and of the truth itself, yea, and we also bear record."

This branch of the Castlemaine Circuit had become almost self-supporting, and, as it had a membership of nearly one hundred persons, and was distant so far from Castlemaine as to make oversight by the Superintendent resident there a great difficulty, it was by the Conference of 1856 made into the Avoca Circuit, with eight or nine congregations. Although Mr. Dyson had been invited to remain here, the Conference thought fit to send him to Belfast, and the Rev. Barnabas S. Walker was appointed to the new Circuit in his stead. Mr. Dyson closed his term in February, 1856. Has he joy that others reap where he sowed? Does it comfort him in this after time, that in planting this vineyard long years ago, he provided clusters of which many since have partaken, and perpetuated recurring harvests of fruit, whereby many have been made glad? In

Mr. Walker's time, the Circuit acquired consolidation and strength. Sunday schools were organized. Day schools here and there were begun. The Local Preachers' staff presented a large array of names, whilst some of these were above the ordinary ability of the Lay Preachers. The cousins, Henry and H. C. Clarkson, were excellent Methodists, and were unsparing of their time, energy, and means to advance the work of the Lord. After spending many years at Carisbrook, Mr. Henry Clarkson has rendered valuable service as a Home Missionary in the Northern stations of Durham Ox, Boort, Elmore, etc., and the southerly one of Seymour. Worthy of mention are Mr. Stubbs, father of Rev. A. Stubbs, of South Australia, Mr. Grewar, father of the Rev. Archibald Grewar, Mr. Bird, father of the Revs. Bolton Bird, and Thomas Bird, who for a time were in the Methodist ministry, and were men of marked ability. Mr. Bird, senior, Mr. Ferber, and Mr. George Middleton, will be admitted by those who know them, to be men of considerable mental force, and of sterling Christian character. They were powerful and useful as Local Preachers and Class Leaders in the places where they resided. The strength of the Circuit is manifest by the facts that in the year 1856 it raised by its liberal donations to the Foreign Mission Fund, the sum of £49 13s. 10d., whilst the adjoining Circuits, (reputed stronger), of Sandhurst raised £55 18s. 6d., and Castlemaine £127 11s.; that at the District Meeting of 1857 the number of members was returned at 167; and that application was made for a second Minister, who was accordingly appointed to the Circuit by the Conference of 1858.

The Rev. B. S. Walker did not stay long in the Wesleyan Ministry. The Rev. Joseph Albiston was his successor in the superintendency, and came to the Circuit in 1857. His colleague as junior Minister was the Rev. William Woodall, who gave the first year of his colonial ministry to this part. Mr. Albiston is a Minister of gentlemanly, courteous bearing, strict in his attention to all points, great and small, of the Methodist economy, and of excellent gifts as a preacher and pastor. He, in the second year of his term, thought fit to take about his wife, who was a faithful companion in Christian work and frequent travel. Rumour has it, that they shared in sundry misadventures in their travel among the difficult roads, tracks, and byways of the extensive Circuit, but that was a trifle when the work of God was prospering in their hands. Mr. Woodall was known as an earnest, fervid preacher, who had the solid blessing and reward during years of active toil of winning many souls to Christ. But he, too, had the searchings of heart and temporary depression of mind which came to many young Ministers in the difficult posts of duty in which they were placed on the goldfields, for the rough accommodation, the new conditions of society, the prevailing and abounding wickedness tried men's souls and bodies too. In a following year in the Ararat Circuit he was ready to faint in mind and fail in physical strength under the acclimatizing process, but a little rest was given to him and he rallied again with renewed strength and energy. In 1868 he again was stationed in the Maryborough Circuit.

The work of building Churches went on rapidly. During 1857-8 six new Churches were put up, two of brick, the rest of weather-board; amongst these were one at Carisbrook, and one at M'Callum's Creek; also, a new one at Amherst, displacing a building that had been lent by Mr. Vickery. The canvas tent at Alma was superseded by a more substantial structure. Back Creek rush followed in 1858-9, and a structure must needs be put up to accommodate the Wesleyans. The opening of the Church at Amherst in September, 1857, had been followed by great spiritual prosperity, and the members in that place had increased from 15 in 1857 to 68 in January 1859; the congregation had become too large for the building, so that the latter was extended. This strengthening of the cause at Amherst made it, for the time being, the principal place in the Circuit; here accordingly the parsonage was built, and the Superintendent Minister was located.

Messrs. Fisher, Halse, and Robinson were active in the cause, and long remained to serve its interests. The Circuit, which at first was named Avoca Circuit, became in 1858, the Carisbrook; in 1861, the Maryborough and Amherst; and later on was divided into the Maryborough, and the Talbot and Amherst. The Rev. John C. Symons was appointed to the Circuit in 1860, with the Rev. J. J. Edgoose as his colleague. He describes the Circuit as then consisting "of small digging communities, with comparatively sparse population, and for the most part the people were in humble circumstances." Under Mr. Symons' charge, a new brick Church was put up at Maryborough, that at Talbot was enlarged, a Circuit debt was swept away, and other tokens of prosperity set in. He was assisted in the later years of his stay by the energetic labour and popular gifts of the junior Minister, the Rev. E. I. Watkin. These went the round of the itinerancy in a wide Circuit, working vigorously amongst the agricultural and mining settlements, and making full proof of their Ministry. Whilst they were revolving swiftly in their small Circuit, the slowly-moving chariot wheels of the sun had traced two yearly courses round, and the point was reached anew for change to come. The period of man's work is measured by the sun. It is so in the itinerancy of Methodism. Three revolving years, at the most, completed, the old Ministerial staff must depart, and the new one come. The Revs. Samuel Waterhouse and Alfred R. Fitchett came to take up the work. Mr Waterhouse worked the Circuit with his usual ardour for two years when failing health compelled him to desist from the active life and charge of a Circuit. He has been for years in retirement in Tasmania. Mr. Fitchett was a man of brilliant gifts, who was the next year transferred to New Zealand. In 1865, the Revs. F. E. Stephenson and E. Davies were the stationed Ministers. Both were acceptable and useful, both were sons of Wesleyan Ministers in England, but after a considerable period of faithful service in the Church below, they have at length rejoined one another in the Church in heaven. Mr. Stephenson's was a calm, judicial mind, he had courteous manners, he was the soul of honour, and his ministry was "eminently evangelical, discriminating, faithful, and earnest." He reached high official position as Chairman of a District, and promised to reach the highest in our Conference, had his life been spared, but he was taken to his rest and reward in 1885. Mr. Davies died in 1880.

The limit of space forbids our detailing the further progress of Methodism in these parts. The Avoca portion had been separated from that which was afterwards called the Carisbrook Circuit, and was made a distinct Circuit in 1860. It has had for its Ministers—Messrs. Worth, Inglis, Currey, Vickers, Francis Fitchett, H. Greenwood, Ralph Brown, J. A. Marsland, D. S. Lindsay, and others. It extended to St. Arnaud, but after that was excised, it still formed a compact Circuit, which reports a strength at this day of 8 Churches, 159 members, and about 1000 adherents. Some portions of the Circuit are pleasant and picturesque. It is a snug vineyard of the Lord. The remaining section of this once wide Circuit grew apace, until in 1872 it was formed into two Circuits, the Maryborough, and the Talbot and Amherst. The former has continued a flourishing Circuit, under the care of Messrs. Dyson, Catterall, Annear, Bennett, Lancaster, and others, but the latter has been a weak and struggling Circuit, although it has had the fostering care of able Ministers, such as—Rev. Messrs. Ironside, Turner, James W. Tuckfield, and H. K. Hutchison. To-day, Maryborough Circuit has about 200 members, but Talbot only 88. Yet in both Circuits are a people who are earnest and willing, and present fair samples of country Methodism. The Rev. Richard Fitcher had notable success and popularity in the Maryborough Circuit. Messrs. Burdess, Medley, Mason, and others have been faithful Laymen in the Talbot Circuit.

SANDHURST CIRCUIT.

CHAPTER XIV.

ON Bendigo, as in many other places, the first to occupy the ground for Methodism, were the Local Preachers. South Australia gave to this part the Local Preacher who held the first public religious service here, and the Minister who first had ministerial charge of the district.

That Local Preacher was James Jeffrey, who had been resident in South Australia, and had come over with others to Bendigo in search of gold. Jeffrey was a good sample of an earnest Methodist; one that would not wait for ecclesiastical orders and regular ordinances before he sought, by private counsel and public exhortation, to bless the souls of men around him, in making known to them the precious Gospel of our Lord and Saviour Jesus Christ. Methodists are trained to seek each other's good; to be at it, and always at it; to enter every open door of opportunity, or to make one where they can exercise their gifts.

Mr. Jeffrey, cast by the providence of God amongst a crowd of men, rough, sturdy, free in their manners, and to a large extent ungodly and profane in their character, regarded it as a fine field of usefulness. Jeffrey raised his Master's standard as a rallying point for the few pious men that were about, and to gain recruits for Immanuel's army from the thoughtless and money-grubbing multitude that spread over the place. He stood on a stump near Golden Square, which was then part of the green, open forest, or bush, sang lustily a Methodist hymn, offered an earnest prayer, and preached a gospel sermon, no doubt in his quaint and homely style, which was one well calculated to enchain the attention of the class of men likely to have gathered round him. The people were quiet and orderly, the service impressive and lively, and the effect such as to encourage the pioneer to proceed in his gospel enterprise. This was in March, 1852.

Services were conducted from Sabbath to Sabbath, mostly in the open-air, by Local Preachers and others : of whom may be mentioned as coming to Jeffrey's help, or shortly after taking an active part in those early efforts—Messrs. Swann, Reynolds, Kitchen, Hibbert, Mowbray, Brookes, W. Rowe, W. Moyle, Wright, Brown, Gillett, and Bell. Reynolds and Gillett died at Sandhurst. Gillett was a wonderfully-gifted old man, and had considerable abilities as a preacher. He was eccentric, full of life and zeal, and rich in experience as a Christian. In England he had been Squire Brooke's Class Leader. Besides these, came then or later, Messrs. Fizelle, Nevinson, Catterall, and Burns, the former remaining as a local pillar in the Church, and the two latter having since done good service as Ministers of the Gospel in different Circuits in these colonies. The services, conducted on the whole with increasing interest and attendance—though subject to some fluctuations incidental to that early time—led to the purchase of a building (of wood) that had been used as a store, but, which, when removed, renovated, and cleansed, made a rather pretentious place, for those days, in which to conduct divine worship. It cost £130, of which £50 were collected by Mr. Joshua Chapman during one morning. This first building used as a church was erected at the end of the year 1852, on the ground of the present school-house at Golden Square. I know not who was the first Leader of the Class here started, but I am credibly informed that Mr. Swann met the Class in the middle of the year 1852. It was afterwards entrusted to Mr. Catterall's care, and then Mr. Nevinson took charge of it, and remained for a long while its leader.

Meanwhile, Mr. Jeffrey had removed farther down the Bendigo Creek, to White Hills, and had pursued the same pioneer work. Services were held by him and others, at first in the open-air, but afterwards in a log hut, covered with a tent or canvas covering. This had not been long commenced before opposition began. The keepers of "shanties" and the tipplers did not like the preaching in their neighbourhood. So one Friday night, when the wind was high and the weather boisterous, they cut the ropes of the tent covering of the ironbark hut, where preaching had been held. The covering was blown away, torn into ribbons and rendered useless. One of the ringleaders in this mischief was brought before the Commissioner and fined £5. And the fine inflicted was a check upon such proceedings, so that the worshippers suffered no further open molestation from them. Mr. Jeffrey was the leader of the first Class formed at the White Hills.

Where were the Methodist ministers at this time? The van of the Methodist itinerancy was led into these parts by Messrs. Symons and Chapman, who had been sent to the Mount Alexander Circuit. They arrived at Forest Creek in March, 1852, and shortly afterwards Mr. Symons came to Bendigo on a visit of inspection The requirements of Forest Creek, however, and the very assiduous and self-denying labour given to it, as well as the personal illness of Mr. Symons, delayed another purposed visit till the month of May. Then he spent a Sabbath well filled up with ministerial labour. Starting at early morn from the hut of Messrs. Howard and Anthony Forster, with whom he had been a guest, he rode from the Camp Reserve to Kangaroo Flat, thence to Eaglehawk, where his first open-air service for the day was held ; the second was at Long Gully, and the third at Golden Gully ; after which he officiated at the burial of a man just deceased, who had been known to him formerly in South Australia. At this visit Mr. Symons met with many old acquaintances, and was received with open arms and earnest co-operation by members of the Methodist Church, and also by some of other religious bodies. Mr. Chapman had also by this time preached on the Sabbath at Bendigo, his first appointments on May 20th being at Ironbark in the early part of the day, and at Golden Square in the evening ; and thenceforth ministerial labours were given on the Sabbath and week day to the Wesleyan congregations in this district, and the church's operations were organized and more vigorously carried on. The stay of Messrs. Symons and Chapman was brief, but they did good service as pioneers; and on their departure Mr. Currey laboured for a considerable period, and he in turn was succeeded by Mr. Raston, who was the first resident Minister and Superintendent of Sandhurst as a distinct Circuit.

Under the leadership of these Ministers, Methodism had come to battle with sin, to make converts of sinners, and to nurture in godliness and practical piety all who had received the new life in Christ Jesus. Preaching in the open-air, in canvas tents, or more substantial buildings, her evangelists spoke plainly the gospel message, plied well the gospel motives, and spiritual power was furnished to them from above. They addressed either small companies of people, or masses of from 400 to 800, which frequently gathered round them. At times a few persons might be irreverent and listless; but for the most part the general heed given to *the Word* would compare favourably with that of the established congregations of settled towns and cities, whilst the more fervid of the members, restrained by no cold and stately decorum of the place, were often loud in their ejaculations of prayer and ascriptions of praise. Occasional instances of conversion followed; some even "who came to scoff, remained to pray," and a cumulative power of religious earnestness was gathering which at length found notable manifestations in a genuine and extensive revival which took place at White Hills in the winter of 1853. Mr. Fizelle, a veteran in the service, who has resided at White Hills since May 1853, writes:—"It was at White Hills that I saw the first 'Cornish conversion,' in the person of Aaron Cole. A tall, strongly-built, man, smitten by the Word of God, he came forward in the meeting and fell flat on the gravel floor, as if he had been shot. He groaned through the disquietude of his soul, but soon found the Divine peace, and then jumped up and leaped over seats, and kissed and shouted, so as to frighten some of us who had never seen it after this fashion. It reminded me of the Psalmist's word,

'O clap your hands all ye people, shout unto God with the voice of triumph.'" This is not quoted as a sample of every conversion, but some type of what frequently occurred amongst the excitable and demonstrative Cornishmen.

Mr. Raston, writing in the December following, says of this revival—"Some hundreds were converted to God. Many have I heard to thank God that on these goldfields they obtained the pearl of great price, more to be valued than all the gold in the universe." Here, again, the value of lay agency appeared, for it was mainly by official laymen and private members that the services were carried on, and, under God, this revival was chiefly due to their zeal and piety.

The usual concomitants of a revival were there; more fervent and believing prayer, greater spiritual power in the services, a more active piety in the members, their religious life and sensibilities greatly quickened and intensified, and exultant joy over the sanctification of believers and the conversion of sinners. The Rev. T. Raston arrived opportunely in August to foster the work thus auspiciously begun, and he was able to record that during the four months following there were "many additions to the Society, and many signal conversions to God, and many had become members who had previously belonged to no branch of the Church of Christ; not a week passed without conversions to God."

Of the labourers in this Revival, John James, Esq. M.L.A., gives this interesting account :—"The writer certainly has no notes, therefore has to fall back upon what memory furnishes. But as I was more a participator in the benefits than a sharer of the toil, I can speak more freely. 'There were giants in those days,' but I was not one of them.

This chronicle will simply deal with the work, and some of the workers, of the Church at the Seventh White Hill, during the winter of the above-named year—*i.e.*, 1853.

About four months was all the time I spent there; but these months gave a tone and direction to many lives which has endeared to them the men who were God's agents in bringing about the change; and the ties of affection then formed will never be broken.

I will not undertake to say who among these noble men is entitled to rank first in the order of merit; but William Moyle must not be left until the last. He has long since gone to his reward, which, for the work he did on the goldfields alone, is not inconsiderable. He could launch out in denunciation of sin, he could not only advise, but lead the way in the path of virtue and honour, or he could with the stone in the sling penetrate the joints of the harness which encased sinners and bring them down literally in the dust, where, after the word had taken effect, they would tell the Lord their trouble, and He would come and heal them. (Mr. Fizelle said of him :—' A simple-minded man, a beautiful character, eloquent and gifted as a preacher.') Good Father Moyle was always richer in grace than in gold; but having done his best to succeed he did not murmur. He left Bendigo for Ballarat in 1853, where he again trumpeted forth the alarm to the godless and offered Christ to the penitent; but soon left for South Australia, where he was called home. ' The chamber where' this 'good man met his fate' was a place of glory, for the angels of God came down where he lay and showed themselves to him. It was so real (to him) that he called his daughter who was his nurse, and said, ' Mary, they are here; look at them"; and she said, ' What? father.' He replied, ' Oh, the angels have come; don't you see them ?" Then they took him from the vestibule to the inner court, where, doubtless, he has welcomed many a fellow-labourer in the old Bendigo campaign.

I think no one will be found to disagree with the order of names when I mention in such close conjunction with Father Moyle, James, or ' Jimmy' Jeffrey.

Though a comic character, he was a sort of Barnabas, full of the Holy Ghost and of faith.' ' The sword of the Spirit, which is the Word of God,' was as real to him as his own life. He accepted that weapon, and sought no other; but he had a way in wielding it all his own. He never forgot what he was before the grace of God, which bringeth salvation, came to him; and having experienced both bondage and liberty, he boldly avowed, 'No book is like the Bible,' with a freedom and heartiness, and often with such quaintness that smiles and tears would commingle. The first time I heard 'Jimmy' was in April or May, 1853, in the old dark tent that stood on the left of the road going from the camp down the flat. I don't remember the text, but I remember how 'Jimmy' had hold of my attention. Then he broke forth in praise to God for deliverance from sin—' Bless the Lord, how happy I am'; and with the next breath most quaintly said—' How do you feel, brother, just behind the third button of the waistcoat ?' But though humorous, he never trifled. During the revival of that winter he threw his whole soul into the work, and is entitled to great credit. He did not 'settle' there; but having made a little money at digging, went to New Zealand and tried farming. He failed, came back to Victoria, and about 1855 or 1856 took up his quarters at Ballarat, broken down in pocket, or, as he called it at a meeting at Mount Pleasant, 'shigged.' But, like Paul, 'none of these things moved' him. He died in harness a short time since in South Australia.

William Rowe was an earnest, intelligent preacher, of whom I have heard nothing since I left Bendigo. He came over from New Zealand, where he had been 'holding forth the Word of Life' for several years, and I think he returned there. Many remember him with pleasure as a chaste expositor of the truth of God.

Of the living much might be said. The standard being raised, a goodly number of the standard-bearers went forth to other fields to gain further conquests. Among the more prominent of those who are still with us are—Matthew Morgan, of Ballarat; J. D. Mowbray, of Melbourne; and George Fizelle, of Sandhurst. The latter brother remains at the same old spot, like a faithful sentinel guarding the old camp, and in every possible way devoting himself to the Church's interest.

Brother Mowbray has continued to this day, and both in the Church and in State continues to do work of the greatest importance. I know much less of him than of the other; but to me, in the days of my youthful manhood, he was a teacher in the pulpit; and though young himself then, his public utterances, and the force of his example, influenced and helped to give direction to my subsequent course.

Brother Morgan is a very modest man, and would blame me for inserting a panegyric in his praise. But a word, please, in the interest of this subject, and for the encouragement of young men struggling upwards in the same cause. He was an enthusiast. Night after night, during these winter months, in his digger's blue blouse, he was in that tent labouring to bring souls to Christ as though the fate of the world depended on his efforts. That his and the efforts of others were successful, everybody who has studied Methodism on the goldfields knows; but to what extent is only known to God.

Of the men who were brought to Christ I cannot now speak; but will conclude by stating that the gathering together of these men at the Seventh White Hill in 1853 was one of God's plans for establishing His Church on a firm basis. Men had come from all parts of the world to seek gold, with the intention of speedily returning laden with it. Hundreds of Christians in their wild haste had grown cold at heart; while thousands, in the flush of prosperity, rushed headlong into vices that, unless checked, must have ruined body and soul. Christian men in their individual capacity found it hard work to maintain their integrity in the teeth of the force of dissipation that raged and swayed the masses. But 'the Lord' who 'hath His way in the whirlwind and in the storm,' had also a way in the diggings, and He brought these veteran fathers, and the more numerous young men of the princes of His Israel together, where He blessed them, and strengthened them, and where they entered into a compact to prosecute the commission they had received.

In due course God scattered them, sending many away, but keeping a few there. But the wisdom of God is justified by the results which we already see and enjoy. The standard of the cross waves in every goldfield of our land, numbers have steadily increased, ' and God, even our own God shall bless us ; God shall bless us, and all the ends of the earth shall fear Him.' "

The revived Church was greatly cheered by (shall we call it ?) the episcopal visit of the Rev. Robert Young at Christmas, 1853. He was at this time on a tour of inspection amongst the Australian and adjacent Missionary Churches preparatory to their formation by the Home Connexion into a distinct but affiliated Conference for this Southern world. He paid a visit to Bendigo, and then hurried on in his world-wide tour. But that visit was a memorable occasion of lively interest and spiritual profit to the Wesleyan Church, and we gather, also, of considerable satisfaction to himself.

Mr. Young attended the Quarterly Meeting, in which he remarked the piety, zeal, intelligence, and liberality of its members; was at a tea meeting at White Hills, plentifully supplied with saffron cake, and got up in the best Cornish style; visited the diggers, and saw the several operations for procuring the gold; made acquaintance with ferocious flies, whose torments through one night surpassed all his former experiences in warmer climes; made his observations on men and things; baptized five children ; preached a sermon ; delivered an address which lasted an hour and a half, recounting the chief incidents in his then recent visit to Polynesia ; and bade adieu to Bendigo and his many friends there upon December 28th, 1853. The Rev. W. Butters, then Chairman of the Victoria District, accompanied Mr. Young on this visit.

What was Methodism doing at this period for Sandhurst proper and Eaglehawk ? We find that services were first held at Sandhurst, nigh to View Point or Pall Mall, on what was then called Commissioner's Flat, in the open-air in 1852 ; that occasional services were held in Mr. Fraser's store when in course of erection, which stood near the junction of Bridge and M'Crae-streets ; that in the beginning of 1853 a very large canvas tent formed the Church, which stood near the site occupied at present by the Freemasons' Hotel, and afterwards near or on the ground occupied by the Wesleyan Parsonage ; and that by the time of Mr. Young's visit the proposition of a good-sized Chapel, either of wood or stone, had been mooted and discussed, and was likely to be taken in hand as soon as land could be obtained from the Government. Also, that worship was held first in the open bush, then in a tent or slab place at the head of Eaglehawk, not far from the present St. Mungo claim; and secondly, at Sailors' Gully, in the open-air. Afterwards it was deemed desirable to amalgamate the two causes, and have a central building, which was accordingly put up on the site of the present Church. Before this took place, however, a temporary Church had been built at Sailors' Gully, the projection of which was on this wise:—After preaching, one Sabbath afternoon, by Mr. Raston at Sailors' Gully, a brief consultation was held by a few friends, which led to the conclusion that they would have a smaller Church than the one which they had been using, for they had been worshipping 'neath the blue vault of heaven, with many noble trees around, which seemed as stately pillars of their Church, and reminding them that "the groves were God's first temples." Accordingly, pledges of assistance were given, which subsequently were largely added to: and time, energy, labour, good-will, and these contributions making a goodly amount, speedily brought about a tangible result in the erection of the Sailors' Gully Wesleyan Church.

Thus, by the end of 1853, as outward evidences of the enterprise and usefulness of the Wesleyans, 5 Churches had been erected—1 of wood and 4 of canvas—of these one had cost £250. 4 Sabbath schools were in full operation, conducted by 24 earnest and painstaking teachers, and having 170 scholars. 2 Day schools had been established— 1 at White Hills and the other at Golden Square— together numbering 120 scholars, whose efficiency was such that when Governor Hotham visited Bendigo in September, 1854, he gave utterance to his conviction that throughout the goldfields which he had visited the Wesleyans were prominent in the great work of education, and were effecting more than any other Church.

At the first Local Preachers' meeting, held after the arrival of the Rev. Mr. Raston, in the Wesleyan Church, Sandhurst, Friday, September 2nd, 1853, the names of preachers reported on the Circuit Plan were :—Hutchens, Burall, Thomas, Rowe, Morgan, Hibberd, Jeffrey, Mowbray, Kitchen, Lucas, Moyle, Bawden, Merry, Davis, Brown, Fizelle, Pascoe, Bell, ; and the preaching places—Golden Gully, White Hills, Commissioner's Camp, Eaglehawk Gully, Fourth White Hills, and Long Gully. This latter was an experiment which was, for the time, a comparative failure. At the Quarterly Meeting held on September 9th, the names of Nevinson and Gubbins, with several of those on the Local Preachers' List appear amongst the officials in attendance. Messrs. Burall and Nevinson were appointed Circuit Stewards. Another Quarterly Meeting was held on September 27th, at which the Minister's salary was fixed at £400 per annum, and £70 were paid to Mr. Burall for his expenses in attending, at the request of the White Hills' society, the annual District Meeting in Geelong. The members were then—Golden Gully, Class of Mr. Nevinson, 28 ; White Hills, Classes of Messrs. Jeffrey, 26 ; Burall, 19 ; Rowe, 20 ; Kitchen, 25. Sandhurst, Mr. Gubbins' Class, 14. Back Creek, Mr. Moyle's, 41. The first Minister's residence was put up in October to December, 1853.

We find the first mention of Brother Whyman's name as a Class Leader in December, 1854. He has remained staunch, true, beloved to this day, one of the faithful three who have stood by the White Hills cause from the early days. The others being Brothers Fizelle and Trahair.

In October, 1853, 200 members were meeting in Class, but these had been reduced to 60 at the Christmas following, owing to the rush to other fields. This indicates one great difficulty of many amidst which the work of God was carried on and sustained. The fluctuations incident to the gold-fields were great. The work was amongst a strange, promiscuous, and migratory population. The pastoral oversight was of a number of members and adherents who for the most part passed to and fro in individual wanderings, or in great waves of movement. The best laid schemes might thus be completely overturned. Leaders, Local Preachers, members, congregations, might for the most part be gone ere very promising plans could be executed. It needed a prudent steersman to keep the vessel from the shallows or rocks of disaster, for the most sagacious and far-seeing could scarcely tell what was ahead; and we adore the goodness of God, that to so great a degree wisdom was given to those at the helm. They were "men of understanding to know the times." They were wise builders, and by them, slowly and warily, yet with good heart and hope, the foundations of the Methodist cause were laid amongst this young community.

There were difficulties for the members also in the right conduct of their temporal affairs and the maintenance of their piety. Influences, unfriendly to piety, were found in the contagion of the gold fever—its excitement tending to neutralize religious feeling in its intensity and eagerness; in the vicissitudes of gold-digging—its sudden rises to fortune, or depression into poverty, the elation of mind upon a lucky find, or rack under disappointing labour; and in the uncertain home and vagrant life marking that time. Some, unhappily, gave way under the strain put upon their good principles, others were made hardy veterans thereby. One great hindrance to personal piety was often the lack of a place for private devotion. Under difficulties the Word

o

of God was read, or prayer offered in private. But "where there is a will there is a way," and where there is a worshipping heart it will find some Bethel which shall be to the wayfarer "the house of God and the gate of heaven."

We have known soldiers who knelt at their bedside or in their bivouac for prayer when noisy companions surrounded, some of whom would pull them along the ground by the legs, or the hair of the head, to interrupt their devotion. We have known a ship's cook go behind the oakum heap for a place of prayer. The closet for devotion of another seaman was on the mainyard, or in the shrouds. We have known diggers, who had no privacy in the tent which two or three uncongenial spirits occupied, to sit on a log, or kneel behind a bush for the soul's quiet meditation and worship of God. Drivers of horse-teams on the roads have assembled at the camp fire with their passengers, and joined in family prayer. A man who became an earnest Local Preacher in the Western District, was recovered from a backsliding state by overhearing a bullock-driver at his evening devotion when he had camped for the night. And could we tell the private history of scores of Methodist diggers in the early days, we should have to relate many such incidents and methods of maintaining the religious life and communion with God.

Mr. Raston was aided by the kindly advice and timely visits of the Rev. Mr. Draper, who, in 1855, became the Chairman of the Victoria District. We gather from his life, written by Mr. Symons, an extended reference to a visit made by him to Sandhurst in August, 1855, and an incidental notice of one in October, 1856. In that of 1855 Mr. Draper records his acquaintance formed with Messrs. Allingham, Hollis, and Pease, local pillars of the Church in that day, and the former two remaining to the present, his great enjoyment in the religious service on the Sabbath and the two following days, and his aiding in other movements, such as a bazaar and tea meeting, which greatly augmented the funds of the Church.

Mr. Raston had the spirit of a pioneer strong within him. During his stay in the Circuit, which ended in March, 1857, services were commenced—in addition to places already named—at Kangaroo Flat (September, 1854), Lockwood (same date), Spring Creek, Epsom (July, 1856), and California Hill (January, 1857). Usually these began with open-air services, then were continued by tent or cottage preaching, and subsequently a church of wood, plain but serviceable, was secured. This was the order of things at California Hill, where services were established mainly through the efforts of Mr. Falder. He mentions in his diary that he commenced preaching in his own house, November 23rd, 1856, a week afterwards he began the first Class, four persons entering their names. About this time Mr. John Dawborn joined our Church. He became a Minister of the Anglican Church. Messrs. Andrew Inglis and Uriah Coombs had, during this period, been called on to exercise their gifts in preaching, and were the first raised up by the Churches of Sandhurst Methodism, who, afterwards, were called into the regular Ministry. Mr. Inglis has been for years an earnest, diligent, and successful Wesleyan Minister, and Mr. Coombs was the esteemed and evangelical pastor of the Congregationalist Church at Warrnambool, but is now in Tasmania. Mr. Raston was the forerunner of Mr. Dare, and the *régime* and labour of the one served to introduce those of the other.

Mr. Dare was one of the most popular preachers of the connexion. He was a kind of Hercules in the cradle, of giant strength from the beginning of his ministerial career; but if at any time he could be said to be in the prime of his powers, and the first vigor of his mission, it was while at Bendigo

His ministry attracted many adherents of other Churches, and gained the ear largely of the public outside the Methodist pale; but there was no proselytism in his proceeding—no petty arts to steal away the sheep of other flocks. That was utterly beneath him. We are not aware of any communicant of another Church, possessed of living piety, that was then drafted into our Church; and the many who professed to belong to other religious bodies, but were occasional or stated hearers, for the most part returned to their own Churches afterwards. Mr. Robert Lisle, and some others who had aforetime been Presbyterians, or of the Church of England, in sentiment and form of worship, became firm and staunch Methodists, because they had been converted to God through Mr. Dare's instrumentality. But his powerful preaching told with great and good and lasting effect upon his Methodist audiences. The Church members entered on higher Christian experience, and put forth a greater missionary zeal and activity. His sermons often produced a result among hard-hearted sinners as does a blast in a quarry. They separated by one bold stroke or mighty effort a number from the mass of the inert and ungodly, and prepared them for the hand of the heavenly workman, who trimmed them into shape and beauty, and gave them to occupy a fitting and useful place in the temple of the Lord. The drunkard became sober, the vicious virtuous, while rough and formerly blaspheming men began to sing from renewed hearts and cleansed lips the high praises of God.

Soon the revived religious interest spread, so that in September, 1857, Mr. Dare was able thankfully to record that eighty conversions had taken place, of whom not more than four or five were under twenty years of age.

One immediate outcome of the revival which we mentioned was that at California Hill, a spacious Church, said to have been in the Gothic style, and costing £430, had been erected and opened by September, 1857, and in that month of the following year there was a flourishing society, a crowded congregation, a Sabbath school numbering ninety, and a Day school of sixty children.

Before 1857, the first stone building used for worship had been erected in Sandhurst. The membership there was small, and so it continued for several years; but the congregation rapidly increased in that year, so that it became necessary to add a gallery at the end of the building, which, when done, made one half of the present one known as the Forest-street School house, and which, to give some idea of the costliness of building at that time, represented an outlay of over £2600. We would rather have the money than the building. Messrs. Harkness, Featonby, and Willan arrived about this time. They have been very active members of the Church as Local Preachers and Stewards. Mr. Harkness has been Mayor of the City of Sandhurst; Mr. Willan Mayor of the Borough of Eaglehawk. Mr. Featonby, devoted, liberal, and highly esteemed, passed to his heavenly reward on July 4th, 1886.

The work extended, so that the services of a second Minister were needed, and the Rev. Mr Dubourg was appointed in 1858, and a third Minister, in the person of the Rev. Mr. Atkin, came in 1859. Mr. Dubourg gave two years of very useful labour to the Circuit. New places were occupied, and fresh labourers were raised up. Long Gully was again a preaching station, and, though feeble at first, yet through the care of Messrs Stevens, Matthews, and others, it gradually rose into importance and strength. Big Hill was supplied with services, in order to benefit the labourers and others engaged in excavating the tunnel, and in the formation of the railway line. A small Chapel was opened in February, 1859, and, though subsequently the Chapel was sold, and the services were given up, they had produced valuable results. One or two members, now at Kangaroo Flat, were there converted, and so was Mr. Bogle, who became a Wesleyan Minister in South Australia. Mr. Henry Baker, the respected and pious Wesleyan Minister, passed through his probationary period as a Local Preacher at this time. Mr. West was given his first appointment, and, since, he has graduated in the Local Preachers' ranks the Congregational College and to a respected Minister of this latter body. On Mr. Dare's leaving in March, 1860, the members numbered 394, with 22 on trial. The great event in Church building during Mr. Dare's stay was the new Church at Golden Square. This was of larger size, and had more architectural pretensions and embellishments than any Wesleyan Church then in the Circuit; and consequently, as it was built in what were still "dear times," and some trouble and expense were occasioned by failure of contractors, it cost a large sum of money. Great pecuniary help was received from the liberality of Mr. Allingham and a group of claimholders, who held the Union claim—Messrs. Lisle, Nevinson, Porter, Tongue, and Kenny; and the financial burdens of the undertaking were nobly borne by the trustees and congregation.

The foundation-stone was laid on April 19th, 1859, by Mr. Draper, and the Church was opened by dedicatory services, conducted by the same excellent Minister in the December of the same year. He was greatly delighted with the devout and liberal spirit of the people; with the large congregations attending the opening services; with the amount of the collections, which came to the munificent sum of £262; and with the fine prospects appearing in this centre of the mining population for the spread of religion. So far as I can learn, Mr. Draper paid only two visits to Sandhurst, subsequently to this, for religious purposes. He continued at the head of Methodist affairs in this colony, labouring most assiduously and prudently for their advancement, till March, 1865, when he departed for England, never more to return to these shores. The public know the tragic scene which closed his long and useful life. The foundering of the ill-fated *London* is an event yet fresh in the memory, still piercing the heart.

The period up to the time of Mr. Dare's departure we regard as the pioneer one in Sandhurst Methodism. The foundations had been laid and some of the superstructure built by skilful and diligent hands and earnest minds; afterwards the building was to be carried on by other good men and true.

The Rev. James Bickford was the successor of Mr. Dare in the superintendency. He visited Echuca with the purpose of planting the Methodist Church in that place; and his valuable coadjutor, Mr. Hart, paid several visits with the same object, and extended his pastoral care and journeys to Inglewood also. Both places are now at the head of growing Circuits. Mr. Bickford marshalled his forces well, and kept the varied movements and agents of the Church in excellent work.

In the first attempts to reach the outside and non-churchgoing multitude of Sandhurst by theatre-preaching, he took a prominent part, holding the first of a series of services on July 29th, 1860; and in promoting philanthropic and Christian objects he was ready for every good word and work. Towards the close of his labours in the Circuit he could record that "his trials had been comparatively few, and the mercies had been many; souls had been saved, and God had been glorified."

April, 1861, found the Rev. George Daniel transferred to Sandhurst from Creswick, as the superintendent in Mr. Bickford's room, and his *régime* was signalized by enterprising and prosperous efforts in the building of Churches. The Church at Eaglehawk forming the front part of the present one was then erected, and has been the place of worship for some years of a lively and prosperous society. Our Cornish friends muster strongly in the congregation; and as might be expected from such large element in its composition, the singing is hearty and the style of worship demonstrative. Revivals have been frequent, but declensions of the young converts rather numerous, and this notwithstanding that the Church members have been under the care of some very diligent, pious, and devoted Leaders. Still the net gain will compare favourably with any society in the Circuit, and the holy lives of many, as well as the happy or peaceful deaths of not a few, show that religion is an elevating and sanctifying power in the hearts of the greater number in this society.

The present Forest-street Church was at this time built under the auspices and with the aid of great men and good men. The foundation-stone was laid by His Excellency Governor Barkly, several of the civic dignatories being present: and at the subsequent public meeting the Hon. J. P. Fawkner, the grey father of Victorian society, and pioneer of this colony, presided. Speeches on the occasion were also given by the Rev. W. Butters, one of the fathers of Victorian Methodism; the Rev. W. Hill, since so well known amongst, and so deeply lamented by the Sandhurst people; the Rev. G. Daniel, the superintendent of the Circuit, and by others. This meeting was largely attended, and it was announced that £650 had been gathered to meet the outlay on the building. The Church was opened by sermons from Ministers of note in this and other lands—the Rev. W. Taylor, of California, who continued religious services during a whole week; and the Rev. J. Dare, who officiated on the second Sunday. This dedication was eminently signalized by what Methodists love best and crave most,—the crowning blessing on their work and worship—the conversion of sinners and the sanctification of believers. It was computed that nearly one hundred persons, broken-hearted on account of their past transgressions, found the healing and saving mercy of God during the eight or ten days of special services. From this time the Sandhurst congregation increased, until it became the largest in the Wesleyan Circuit, and is believed to be at the present the most numerous Protestant congregation in the Bendigo district.

Able men have filled its pulpit, as the Rev. Thomas James and the Rev. William Hill, who (have had the pastoral charge of Forest-street in succession to Mr. Daniel,) were remarkable for the intellectual force of their sermons, and for the nervous or attractive style of their pulpit oratory.

Juniors assisting these superintendents were stationed at Golden Square—Mr. Worth, a man of genial spirit and quiet labour; Mr. Lane, whose earnest, incisive, lively public discourses were made a great blessing unto many, and the means of conversions; and Mr. Edwin I. Watkin, who will always live in the affectionate remembrance of the people amongst whom he was stationed. He has a fertile mind and retentive memory, and is an adept at composition, which makes him very ready in pulpit and platform exercises. His addresses are full of vigorous thought, and his delivery has much of effectiveness, especially when speaking from the platform, where he reigns supreme in striking, humorous anecdotes. He is social, diligent, a good companion, a faithful colleague, and an earnest Minister of Christ.

The extension of the borders of the Circuit to farming districts such as Emu Creek, Marong, and Shelbourne, took place under the pastorate of Messrs. Daniel and James, as also to the mining district of Lower Huntly, where, after one or two attempts, Methodism was established through the efficient support of Messrs. W. Clay, Thompson, and others. New Churches at Long Gully, California Hill, and at White Hills (the fourth in succession erected there—the present one is the fifth), were built during the superintendency of Mr. James. Messrs. Swift and Fitcher were at this period preparing themselves for the Christian ministry. Mr. Fizelle assisted for a while in working the Circuit during the latter part of Mr. W. Hill's stay. Mr. Somerville has been a faithful and active servant of the Church at Strathfieldsaye, where are a healthy society and a neat Church.

The Rev. W. Taylor paid a second visit to the Circuit in May, 1864, officiating on the occasion of the re-opening of Golden Square Church, after many internal improvements had been made. The house of prayer was again the spiritual birth-place of precious souls. This society has been second to none for its noble staff of Leaders, for its men of intelligence, influence, and piety, and the loving concord and unity with which Pastors, Leaders, and members have co-operated in Christian work.

From the first there has been a steady increase of members and attendants at worship, save only when the exodus to New Zealand drafted off a large number of miners from the neighbourhood.

Mr. Henry Hooper was a good example of the class of men, noble, pious, devoted, faithful, with which this society has been blessed. His heart was wrapped up in this revival work, and greatly rejoiced over the extension of Christ's kingdom amongst his neighbours. Strong men wept, the Church made great lamentation, the whole neighbourhood mourned, when it was known that he had been suddenly killed in a mine. This sad event took place in January, 1865.

Messrs. Hill and Watkin commenced the Chinese Mission at Sandhurst by the employment in evangelizing agency of James Moy Ling, a Christian, who was for years an inmate of Mr. Hill's household. These Ministers laboured diligently to make the first visit of Mr. Matthew Burnett the evangelist, and his singular but devoted efforts, a success in the salvation of precious souls, and they rejoiced with the joy of harvest at the ingathering to the Church at that time and during the period of their stay in the Circuit, the numbers increasing during their pastorate from 503 to 639 members, and 209 on trial. But their joy (Mr. Hill's especially) at the prosperity of God's cause was tempered by that mysterious bereavement which befel him in the sudden removal of Mrs. Hill. This excellent lady had gone into the work of revivals with great fervour of spirit; but the exciting toil was too much for the weak bodily frame. The hand of death struck her down when her soul was most given up to the Lord and His work, and, no doubt, ripest for heaven. But a bereaved husband and family and a mourning Church felt her loss keenly; and, alas! that Church was soon again to groan in trouble and bereavement, when, a few short months after, Mr. Hill fell by the assassin's hand at Pentridge Stockade.

Tracing to later dates the history of Sandhurst Methodism, we record a great increase in all the departments of Methodistic influence and enterprise in the years 1870 and 1871. Rev. W. P. Wells was the superintendent, Rev. W. L. Blamires the second Minister, and the Revs. C. Lancaster, D. O'Donnell, C. P. Thomas and A. Brown, the junior Ministers during Mr. Wells' management. Several Churches were enlarged, or new ones built in lieu of the old ; the societies in town and country greatly advanced, so that the Church membership was reported at 1080 ; between 5000 and 6000 people were adherents of Methodism, and a still larger number influenced thereby, and at no period have the several departments of the Lord's work been in greater vigour and prosperity. The Churches at Golden Square, California Hill, and Long Gully, spacious and elegant, were erected between 1870 and 1876.

Eminent Ministers filled the superintendency in these and after years. Rev. J. G. Millard, possessed of a pleasing, mellifluous style of oratory ; Rev. H. Bath, with a vigorous mind, giving masterly discourses ; Rev. W. H. Fitchett, B.A., clever, brilliant, sanguine, enterprising ; Rev. E. S. Bickford, an active and indefatigable worker ; Rev Joseph Waterhouse, who had given but one Sabbath's service to the Circuit, when his valuable life and labours were brought to an untimely end in the wreck of the *Tararua* ; the Rev. R. C. Flockart, cheery, genial, a staunch Methodist, an earnest Scotchman ; and the Rev. W. L. Blamires, who has spent a second term of three years labour in this Circuit. The number of members advanced from 1013 in September, 1883, to 1206 in September, 1885, but since that date has somewhat declined. The Revs. John Harcourt, Thomas James, and Spencer Williams have been efficient Superintendents at Golden Square. Other valued Ministers in the Circuit have been—Revs. E. W. Nye, P. R. C. Ussher, J. H. Ingham, Arthur Powell, John S. Greer, John Cowperthwaite, and J. P. M'Cann. Prominent Laymen are—Mr. M. Thomas, Mr. J. Ellis, Mr. J. Bamford, Mr.

C. Perry, and others. The Church has had no more faithful servant, noble, liberal, pious, the same in the sunshine and storm, in wealthy and in adverse circumstances, than Mr. Richard Allingham, now very near to his heavenly home. In this Jubilee year, this Circuit, in point of numbers, and some other facts and items indicating a prosperous Circuit, is the premier one of the Southern world. (See also "Former Days of Methodism in the Sandhurst Circuit" by the Rev. W. L. Blamires.)

KYNETON AND DAYLESFORD CIRCUITS.

CHAPTER XV.

THE travels of the Minister, Rev. S. Waterhouse, who acted as Bush Missionary prior to the era of the goldfields had extended to the flourishing district of Kyneton. A Church was opened in 1855, but it was not finished at the time of the Rev. D. J. Draper's first visit to the town in August of that year. The Rev. John Mewton accompanied him. Mr. Draper found Mr. Furphy as Church Steward and Treasurer, and Mr. G. W. Johnston as an active member or adherent. He left Mr. Mewton as the resident Minister, when he journeyed onward to Castlemaine. 35 Church members were reported to the Conference of 1856. Rev. Henry Chester came in March, 1856, in succession to Mr. Mewton, and the Rev. John Catterall was appointed in the following year. Under their ministrations the work of the Lord extended in town and country, services being established in Taradale and Tylden by the year 1857, and in the direction of Blackwood about the same time. In Kyneton, a good parsonage, costing £700, was erected in 1856, the Church was lengthened by 20 feet in 1857, and numerical and financial prosperity had set in. After much inconvenience had been endured for want of a suitable building at Taradale, the friends determined in 1859 to erect a Church, which was accordingly done at a cost of £420. The opening services were on October 9th and 10th of that year. The society increased, as the neighbourhood had considerable mining prosperity for some years, until in January, 1865, a new Church superseded the older structure. It is the present neat Church so pleasantly situate on a low spur of the range which forms the back ground to this picturesque town of Taradale. Other places were, in these years, occupied as preaching appointments, and eventually Churches were erected—At Tylden, of wood, at Malmsbury, of stone, at Blue Mountain, of wood (September, 1863.) At Newham, some active, intelligent, and earnest Laymen had reinforced the staff of Local Preachers. Mr. John Thrum, who had been for a short time in the Wesleyan Ministry in South Australia, was most acceptable in his pulpit exercises; and Mr. Whitfield Raw, a racy, effective, and fluent speaker. In Kyneton were—Mr. W. Ward, pious and earnest, Mr. Southern, and others. These were resident before 1860, and after that date came Mr. John Bond, who, having been a Wesleyan Minister, has since followed the profession of a School Teacher, and gave services to this Circuit, which were highly valued, for a while as a paid agent, but gratuitously during many years. His sermons are well studied, remarkable for their chaste diction, and are delivered with much expression and power. Other Laymen have served their God, their Church, and their generation very faithfully within the bounds of the Circuit—Messrs. Joseph Rogers, Johnson, Chambers, and Blencowe in Kyneton; Hoopell, and Fleming, in Malmsbury; Ham, Kistle, and others in Taradale. A devoted lady, Mrs. Elizabeth Watson, made an imperishable name for herself in connection with her labours as a teacher in both Day and Sabbath schools in Kyneton, and her intelligent and untiring activity for the welfare of her rising family, the young people of the district, and the community generally. She was a good mother, a highly esteemed Class

Leader for young females, and a most amiable Christian. Many, besides her own family, call her blessed. Her spirit passed away from earth in triumph on June 21st, 1858.

While, so to speak, the vessel had such an excellent crew on board, she was steered by skilful pilots and officers. Three bells rung out, and the watch was changed. So, in succession after Mr. Catterall, came the Revs. Samuel Waterhouse (1860-2), returned from Fiji; Charles Dubourg (1863-5); John Pemell (1866-8); Peter R. C. Ussher (1869-70); James D. Dodgson (1871-2); Martin Dyson (1873-5); Thomas Kane, (1876-7); John Catterall (1878-80); Charles Lancaster (1881-3) and James W. Tuckfield (1884-6). All will acknowledge the wakeful fidelity and wise management of these trusted men who have had the charge of the Kyneton Circuit. This, to-day, is one of the most stable and flourishing of the country Circuits.

DAYLESFORD.—The first places taken up by Methodism within the present Daylesford Circuit, had been missioned from Castlemaine. The earliest was Mount Franklin (township Franklinford) the residence of Mr. E. S. Parker. This hospitable gentleman and his family kept open house and a well-spread board for Ministers of any denomination, and many stayed there during the first years of colonial and goldfields history. The preaching was at first in the house of Mr. Parker, then a Church was opened in Franklinford in 1858. As the station for the natives was within a mile or so, many of these attended the service. A number could understand English, and speak it well. They had received the rudiments of education in the Day school. They were frequently found in the congregation at the small Church. The Castlemaine Ministers from 1857 to 1860 made a monthly visit to Franklinford, Yandoit, and at the latter portion of the time to Spring Creek (then the Jim Crow diggings, now Hepburn). The country was very interesting, for miles spreading out in a high table land, that was ended on one side by the abrupt gorges of the

Jim Crow Creek. Mount Franklin stood a prominent object towards one point of the compass, Wombat Hill in another, and at farther distances were the Mounts Alexander, Macedon, Tarrengower, and the Smeaton Hills. In 1860 a flourishing society had been formed at the Spring Creek diggings—Messrs. S. and J. Barkla (Local Preachers), J. Andrew, and Browning were leading members, Messrs. Bumstead, Warren, Gannon, Morrison, and Taylor were active in the other places, Franklinford and Yandoit.

At this time, Daylesford, distant some four miles from Spring Creek, was not touched by Methodist agency, although a few Methodists were living there. The place had an unenviable notoriety for lawless proceedings, some of the 'tar and feathering' order. Drinking, gambling, profanity, reckless living, largely held sway. The Rev. John Harcourt paid a preliminary visit to the place in 1860, holding service in the Court House, and gathering together the few Wesleyans that were in hearty sympathy with the Lord's cause. This led to the appointment of the Rev. Samuel Knight in the same year, although his Conferential appointment was in 1861. There could not have been a more suitable man sent. In the fire and ardour of his youthful zeal he laboured with all his might, soon a congregation was gathered, the revival power which was abroad in the colony, came in signal force upon this place, and very shortly moral revolution and spiritual regeneration took places in multitudes. When the first Methodist Church was opened in October, 1861, Mr. Parker, chairman at the public meeting, referred in gratitude to God to the swift expansion of the work. "A few months before, 14 persons comprised the society, but at that present time 76 were in Church communion; then, the congregation of a score met in a hired room; now, hundreds were assembled within the walls of a commodious and beautiful building." This was 40 x 30 feet, and cost £1100. The converting power of God was also amongst a small congregation at

Stony Creek, so that the Circuit made its first return to the District Meeting and Conference of 94 Church members. Soon the Circuit spread, and the mining districts of Blackwood, Smith's Creek, with those of Yandoit and Hepburn mentioned before, and the more important agricultural districts within a radius of some miles around, were occupied as preaching stations. The mining prosperity and the increase of Church members and adherents influenced the sanguine mind of the Rev J Mewton (who was the successor of Mr. Knight) to a great undertaking. This was the erection of the present large Church, one of the finest that the Wesleyans have in the colony outside of Melbourne, and vying with the ecclesiastical buildings in that city. The dimensions are 80 x 48, with a tower 42 feet in height, to complete the structure. The enterprise began well, the foundation stone was laid in June, 1865, a large amount was promised by local subscribers, but before the edifice was finished, a large collapse of mining affairs took place, and many of the people left for other fields; some of the promises were not redeemed, and when the Church was opened, it was heavily encumbered with debt. Over £3000 had been expended on the Church itself but on all the Church property—Parsonage, Church, and School—nearly that amount remained as a liability. Nobly have the people grappled with their difficulties, so that through a strain of constant effort locally, with some assistance from Connexional funds, that liability has been reduced one half; but it has been a tremendous struggle. Messrs. Rashleigh, Waddington, Betheras, and others have been devoted labourers and efficient officers in this Church, and have willingly put their hands and shoulders to the burden, yet, happily, they have had a series of enterprising and judicious Ministers, who have contributed largely to lessen the financial burden, and to extend the spiritual life and interests of the Church. Such were Messrs. Flockart, Royce, Dodgson, Bickford, T. Adamson, Crisp, and J. H. Tuckfield. The junior Ministers too, have been of exceptional ability in the pulpit, as Messrs. T. E. Ick, M.A., Richard Fitcher, and D. O'Donnell. Blackwood was detached from the Circuit, and has of late years maintained but a feeble existence, although able Ministers such as the Rev. J. de Q. Robin, M.A., H. Saloway, and W. Burridge, have been in the field, and Laymen like Messrs. J. Barkla, Robinson, Garland, and others, have wrought with self-denying devotedness for its establishment. The decline has been largely accounted for by the failure of mining interests at Barry's Reef, Simmons' Reef, and elsewhere. Daylesford itself has a strong, healthy, lively society, and the Circuit tree has vigorous and widespread arms and branches.

THE DUNOLLY AND TARNAGULLA, AND INGLEWOOD CIRCUITS.

CHAPTER XVI.

THE father of the cause at Tarnagulla was Mr. Jonathan Falder, who emigrated from Cumberland, stayed for a time at California Hill, Sandhurst, and thence removed to Sandy Creek, as Tarnagulla at first was called. He was an acceptable and earnest Local Preacher, and at the time that he began the services at Tarnagulla, had a proper status on the Sandhurst Circuit plan. On September 12th, 1858, he took his stand near Poverty Reef, and unfurled the banner of the Cross, to rally and enlist soldiers for the Lord. He preached from I Timothy, chapter 1, verse 15, to an attentive audience, and again conducted service in the evening, but this time in a private house. He was one of the staunch, true, tried men, who are not long in a place before they make their influence powerful for good, and want no outside authority to tell them to use their gifts and opportunities for the welfare of souls. A Class was formed, and the first meeting held on September 16th. Then a small building in the main street was fitted up, and opened for Divine

P

service by Mr. Falder, on October 24th. Thither came the Revs. Joseph Dare, C. Dubourg, and others from Sandhurst to minister to the little flock, and Sandy Creek appeared as one of the preaching appointments on the Sandhurst plan. Mr. T. Pybus, a popular and eloquent expounder of Scripture, who resided in the neighbourhood, rendered valuable aid. The work prospered, so that a new Church was opened on March 13th, 1859, by sermons from Mr. Falder in the morning, and Mr. Pybus at night. The first building used as a Church was of slab sides and of bark roof, and had a capacious chimney, affording a cool seat for a select few, always provided no roasting fire was placed there. The second building was more comfortable and capacious, but still of very primitive design and materials. If any ask, "Why do you tell us about a slab hut, a weather-board Church, a canvas tent?" we reply, "Because from such humble beginnings grew many a cause and Church that became subsequently flourishing," and further, "Because we have to deal with the wares ready to our hand. We do not manufacture them as we go on. We take what facts and incidents occurred, be they plain or ornamental, prosy or romantic."

This story of Victorian Methodism can present no Stonehenge, monument, still existing, of a religion passed into oblivion, no round towers, cromlechs, nor grey ruins which tell of dead persons and dead things. We have to write of a living religion in its infancy of life, with poor and flimsy buildings at the first, which suited that early state, but which have been for the most part superseded by more durable structures. We write not of minsters venerable with age, of ivy crowned and covered ecclesiastical piles, for our life is young; we are but of yesterday; nevertheless these plain buildings were more frequently the birthplace of precious souls born into a religious life, than are many more pretentious and stately buildings. The word "Circumspice" is said to be graven on the monumental tablet of Sir C. Wren, at St. Paul's, London. We, too, can write

"Circumspice" as to Methodist temples and institutions on the goldfields, with no shame-facedness, but with glowing thankfulness of heart. Yet the chief test of an ecclesiastical building with the Methodist people is found in the inquiry: Is it the birthplace of precious souls? "Methodism rears no monument where she saves no souls!" So of these humble structures at Tarnagulla and similar places, we record with grateful satisfaction, as did the Psalmist of old time of the Zion he loved. "This and that man was born in her. . . . The Lord shall count when he writeth up the people, that this man was born there."

But to return to our narrative, Tarnagulla Circuit was formed in 1860, and the Rev. Robt. S. Bunn was appointed as the first Minister. He laboured assiduously for one year, and was then transferred to another Circuit. He was a native of the Emerald Isle, and had the warmth of manner and wit of speech which mark so many sons from that soil. The places on the plan on the formation of the Circuit were—Tarnagulla, New Inglewood, Old Inglewood, Korong, Dunolly, Kingower, and Newbridge. The next Minister was the Rev. John Mewton, during whose time these additional places were put on the Circuit plan, viz. :— Jones Creek, New Chum (Llanelly), Kangaroo, Bridgewater, Serpentine, Old Dunolly, Burnt Creek, Wattle Flat (Inkerman), Cochrane's (Bealiba), Moliagul, and Woodstock. The Circuit thus extended from Mount Korong on the north, to Burnt Creek on the south; from Bealiba on the west, to Woodstock on the east. It was not likely to contract or diminish under Mr. Mewton's care. He was in labours more abundant during his three years' stay, and left with the esteem of the whole Circuit.

By June, 1864, the project of a new Church, to cost about £1400, was entered upon with spirit, and before the work was begun, £700 was promised towards this outlay. On October 19th, the foundation stone was laid by the Rev. W. Hill. The main structure was 55 x 32 feet in extent, and the whole was finished in the next year. The Church remains to this day a memento of the liberality and pious enterprise of the Tarnagulla people. It was a great leap of progress in seven years, from the slab hut to the stately and ornate sanctuary. Mr. Edward Davies, a son of a Wesleyan Minister in England, had been converted under the ministry of the Rev. Joseph Dare; he soon afterwards exercised his gifts as a Local Preacher, and was eventually received into the Wesleyan Ministry in 1865. None rejoiced more than Mr. Falder, to see the new Church erected, to find that God was raising up of Zion's sons those who went forth to preach the everlasting gospel, and that the Word of God was not bound, but mightily prevailing in the overthrow of sin, the conversion of sinners,. and the edification of believers. Born in Cumberland in the year 1815, of a yeoman stock, he carried into his religious life, much of the sterling honesty, and unswerving fidelity which mark the sturdy, hardy race of the extreme north of England. Goodly in appearance, well knit in strength, deeply rooted in godliness, useful in most departments and branches of our work, he was as a cedar in our Lebanon. Said his pastor, the Rev. Thomas Grove, " He was one of the hardest working and most successful of our Lay Preachers in Victoria, a veteran in the work. He was noted for his faithfulness in reproving sin of every kind, and his diligence in improving every opportunity of doing good to those with whom he came in contact. His mind was active and inquiring, leading him to familiarize himself with the standard works of our Church, both theological and historical, so that it was a pleasure to converse with him. During forty-five years he seldom preached less than twice on the Sabbath, and not a few were brought, under his preaching, to the experience of the new birth. His twenty-two years of devoted labour in this Circuit caused him to be greatly beloved by the people, and to be regarded as a patriarch in our Israel. ' He was a faithful man, and feared God above many.' He represented the Circuit, though then in great feebleness of body, at the

Melbourne Conference of 1879, and his health soon after became worse. He gradually declined in bodily strength, but his faith and peace continued strong as ever, until he sweetly fell asleep in Jesus on Sabbath evening, August 15th, 1880. 'The memory of the just is blessed.'"

Mr. Mewton's zeal was largely instrumental in the erection of a new Church in Dunolly, in which he was liberally sustained by the officials of the society. The building cost about £700, and was opened in March, 1863. From that time this society gradually increased in strength and importance, until it became the chief in the Circuit. Mr. Mewton was assisted one year by the Rev. W. Weston, and under their united labours conversions multiplied throughout the Circuit, especially in Kingower, as also in Dunolly, Korong, and Tarnagulla. When Mr. Mewton left, he could report about 200 members in the Circuit, and large numbers in the congregations. In 1864, the Rev. Edward King took charge, and a work of grace spread through many portions of the Circuit. 270 members were returned at the Conference of 1865. The Rev. D. Annear was his colleague residing at Inglewood. This portion became so strong that it set up as an independent Circuit (1866), having the Rev. James Graham for its Minister.

Dunolly has had a flourishing Sabbath school for years past, having been favoured with Mr. Job Hansford as its first superintendent, who was a Christian having a great love for children and the work of scriptural instruction. This godly man had been converted in Guernsey, through the zealous effort of the pious captain of a vessel. Migrating to this land, and settling at Dunolly, he soon identified himself with every good work. He was a man of cheerfulness, bright intelligence and devout spirituality. Beloved by his class, and his school, and by all good men, his name in this town is still as ointment poured forth. He was removed by death in May, 1874, but has left behind worthy descendants to carry on his work. A mine, the Queen's

Birthday, which gave for years, large returns, had a large number of shareholders who were Methodists, and the dividends placed many of them in comfortable circumstances, and a few in affluence. The yields of the mine contributed also, through the liberality of those shareholders, to put many of the enterprises of the Church in Dunolly and neighbouring places in an easy financial position. A feature of the work of God in Dunolly of late years has been the great attention given to the religious care of the young people in Catechumen or Juvenile society classes, which will surely yield fruit in after years. The Dunolly Circuit has been favoured in such appointments as the Revs. W. Woodall, J. S. H. Royce, H. Baker, T. Kane, C. Dubourg, Thomas Grove, and W. Williams, and the people have greatly valued their ministry. Laymen, such as Messrs. Bristol, Peters, and others have added greatly to the strength of this Circuit. It now includes 10 congregations, and has 334 members, with 1700 adherents.

INGLEWOOD.—So far as we glean information, Mount Korong, with its township of Wedderburn, was the first place in which Methodism had a foothold within the bounds of what is now the Inglewood Circuit. Scattered Methodists were to be found upon the several goldfields, comprised within this area, prior to regular services being established. Some one has likened Methodists in such circumstances to spilt quicksilver, where the particles, separated for a time, retain even in these minute portions, their brightness and attractive power, and show their innate faculty for cohesion, and as two portions get near enough will almost spontaneously join together again. That may be so with the more earnest members, but usually the bulk of Methodists want some active agent to gather and band them together. The story of early Methodist life in these parts is illustrative of that statement. An active Local Preacher, gifted with more than average ability, went from Dunolly to Wedderburn, and during a three weeks' stay, preached on three successive Sundays in a large storeroom, kindly lent by the landlord of a chief hotel in the place. These are supposed to have been the first regular Methodist services held there, although they were preceded by some open-air services. The preacher, Mr. George Middleton, before he left, formed a Church Building Committee, which undertook the erection of a Church in 1856 or 1857. This they proceeded to do with spirit, energy, and liberality, so that a Church was built, a small society formed, and Methodism permanently established. Before this, according to a resident observer, in the absence of religious ordinances, profligacy and vice abounded. The Sabbath was desecrated, licentiousness increased, and moral desolation reigned. After the services began a most salutary change was effected. The progress of iniquity was arrested, and Sabbath desecration diminished. Some who were deeply sunk in depravity and wretchedness were raised to a condition of divine purity and holy enjoyment; and where spiritual sterility and death had reigned, life, fruitfulness, and beauty appeared. The Mount Korong society in its early years was more indebted to Mr. George Bunting than to any other person. He wrought hard as a digger during the week, and on the Sabbath he laboured even more strenuously to bring sinners to repentance. He had good natural gifts as a speaker, being clear, emphatic, and homely in his style. Soon after he came, the people found that he was a devout, consistent Christian, and could edify the congregation by his forceful instructive sermons, so they wished him to act as their pastor. They did not offer him a thousand pounds stipend, but they did that with which he was quite content. They bargained that he should have a certain time in the week for pulpit preparation, and they would pay for that time at current rates, so that he should be no monetary loser, or not to any great extent, when he gave one or two days to earnest study of his subjects for the Sabbath discourses. For months and years he preached twice on the Sabbath, as well as conducted meetings on other days of the week. Many were by his agency turned to the Lord, and a prosperous society was gathered, and kept together. with an occasional or passing visit by an ordained minister. One such took place on July 18th, 1858, when sermons, on the occasion of the Church Anniversary, were preached by the Rev. Joseph Albiston, and Mr. T. Pybus. According to the report read at the succeeding public meeting, in the Korong Society were five Local Preachers, two Class Leaders, and twenty-four members. The Sabbath school had thirteen teachers and sixty-nine scholars. The congregation had increased, so that a more commodious place of worship was projected. When Mr. Bunting left in 1862 all classes joined together in presenting him with handsome volumes, in token, as an inscription in them testifies, "of their esteem for the consistent and self-denying manner in which he laboured as a Local Preacher in connection with the Wesleyan Methodist society, for a period of more than five years." Mr. Bunting removed to Williamstown, and handed over the care of the Society to the Minister at Tarnagulla. Mr. Bunting had the emotional fervour of his race. He is a West Indian. At social prayer meetings we have heard him pray like an apostle, and have known him to be so overcome with spiritual transport or ecstacy, that after prayer, he could not for a while rise from his knees. He seemed "lost in wonder, love, and praise." When he was examined before his reception as a Local Preacher, his replies were after this style, "Do you believe there will be a general judgment at the last day, making awards to the evil and the good ? " Yes, I do ; this I know, that Bunting will be there." Personal application of important religious truth was frequent with him.

Inglewood had been, with its outlying appointments, a part of the Tarnagulla and Dunolly Circuit, but in 1866 it was made a distinct Circuit, having the Rev. James Graham as Minister. It then comprised Inglewood, Jersey Reef, Kingower, Korong, Yarrayne, and Jericho. Since its formation the mining interest has declined, but the agricultural interests have increased, so that relatively strong societies are to be found in Bridgewater, Wedderburn, Korong Vale, Boort, for the most part agricultural settlements. The Circuit has had very excellent appointments in the Revs. Robert W. Campbell, A. R. Edgar, and William Burridge; as also earnest and capable men in Revs. H. Saloway, James Lowe, D. Gilsenan, and D. S. Lowe; but, owing largely to the fluctuations of mining interests, has been for years a struggling Circuit. Of the old pioneers, Messrs. Galloway and Pearce still remain, and Messrs. Clark, Wingfield, and other prominent Laymen have stood nobly by the cause. They have given largely of their means, time and energies, to support and extend it. Dr. Cox, of Wedderburn, was very kind and helpful. The flourishing agricultural communities around Boort have in 1886 become a new Circuit, and it is confidently believed that a bright future is before the two sections that formerly made up the Inglewood Circuit.

NORTHERN AREAS.

THE ST. ARNAUD, CHARLTON, ECHUCA, AND OTHER CIRCUITS.

CHAPTER XVII.

THE St. Arnaud Circuit is an offshoot of the Avoca Circuit. Our Circuits spread like the Banyan tree grows. The propagation is often like to that of some creatures, low in the scale of organized life, multiplication by fissure or excision. When the Rev. A. Inglis was Minister of the Avoca Circuit in 1861, he was invited to visit St. Arnaud by Mr. Pemberthy, an adherent of the Wesleyan Church, who was then the mining manager of a claim employing 150 men, and is now a respected storekeeper of the town. Mr. Inglis went accordingly, and held services, at first, once a month. The

Church of England prayers were read sometimes, as many in the congregation belonged to that religious body. After a short trial of such services, a meeting was held to project a Church; seven persons were present; £150 were promised, but owing to the fluctuation of mining interests, and othe causes, we understand that only £57 were actually paid. However, the Church was built, and the opening services, with a tea meeting, produced a large amount, which put the finance of the Trust in a somewhat easy position. Gold and silver mines were the large stay of the place in those years, the silver mines being the principal. The congregation was maintained, and presently a Society class was formed. One of the first converted was a Mr. Hobbs, who had been a Freethinker, but afterwards became an acceptable Local Preacher. Whilst it was an adjunct of the Avoca Circuit, St. Arnaud had the ministrations of the Revs. A. Inglis, C. Dubourg, W. C. Currey, and Robert L. Vickers. It was made into a distinct Circuit in 1866, and the Rev. Albert Stubbs was appointed as the first resident Minister. It was then a weak, infantile Circuit, with big head and little body, for it consisted of one Church, which had most of the membership, and of two preaching places beside. The return at the Conference of 1867 was of 47 members, 1 school of 94 scholars, and 330 adherents in the whole of the Circuit. In July, 1866, only two Local Preachers, C. H. Brown and W. Richards were resident, but the Circuit had received help by the visits of Local Preachers from places of the Avoca Circuit. An important addition to the staff of Local Preachers was made by the arrival of Richard Rowe, in 1868, who is a gifted preacher, and by J. Jennison, who is a devoted labourer, a man of good judgment and effective speech, and has proved a pillar of the Church in these parts since the time of his coming in 1872. For a season, although the central Church had good appointments in Richard Fitcher, George Schofield, Alexander Brown and W. Williams, it made little extension; still Carr's plains was made a preaching place in 1869, then Waterloo plains and Gregre. Stuart Mill was put on the plan in 1870-1, Mogg's plains (afterwards Swanwater), and Wallaloo in June 1871. Then the land selection movement spread over the district. The plains were of a rich soil, suitable to the agriculturist, and this becoming apparent, numbers of Wesleyans from the south—Talbot, Clunes, Ballarat, etc.—swarmed into this region for its occupation.

Rev. David S. Lindsay was the principal agent as Circuit Minister (1873) in the erection of the present commodious Church in St. Arnaud; but with the appointment of the Rev. Ralph Brown in 1874, came the time of rapid growth and wide extension. This Minister is a Circuit Rider, admirably suited for a growing district, and a widespread field of labour, for nothing delights him more than swift movement, whether on horseback, or in driving a pair of horses. Fifty or sixty miles of journey, with three preaching services, he accounted as an easy or ordinary Sabbath's work. As settlement was rapidly taking place, he put the preaching appointments abreast, almost in the van, of settlement. So in 1874 were placed on the Preachers' Plan, Nicholl's plains (Conooer), Mount Jeffcott, Sutherland's plains, East Charlton, and Donald; in 1875, Stratford, Wycheproof, Dooboobetic; in 1876, Wooroonooke (Watson's lakes), Avon plains, Tyrrel Creek, Bungaluke, Quambatook; and in 1877, Armenian and Barrackee. In most of these places are strong societies, and at Donald and East Charlton are now resident Ministers, with active Laymen, Messrs. Carne, Williams, and Stamp at the former, and Messrs. Procter, Martyn, Curnow, and others at the latter place. The Revs. J. S. H. Royce, R. O. Cook, T. Angwin, followed as energetic Superintendents, and the Rev. E. Clement De Garis as an active junior. Mr. De Garis was the first Superintendent of a new Circuit divided from St. Arnaud, of which Charlton is the head. Rev. Ebenezer Taylor has successfully carried on the work of extension in the Charlton Circuit, and the Rev. J. H. A. Ingham has exercised a soul-saving ministry in St.

Arnaud, and now these Circuits are two of the strongest and healthiest in the northern or north-western portions of the colony. The labours of the new form of agency, the General Missionaries, have also been greatly blessed in this district, so that in recent years Methodism has grown with the swift expansion noticeable in the vegetation here, when the warm spring sunshine alternates with genial showers. Our Church has gone up to possess the land, and is far the strongest of any Evangelical Church in this region. The St. Arnaud Circuit returned in 1885 (September) 351 members, 890 Sabbath scholars, and 2180 adherents, whilst the Charlton Circuit was of about equal strength in 403 Church members, 891 Sabbath scholars, and 1960 adherents of the Church.

ECHUCA.—The first Methodist Minister who visited Echuca and held services on the Sabbath was the Rev. James Bickford. The Rev. Thomas Raston had previously paid a visit to Messrs. Booth and Argyle's station in the direction of Swan Hill, and administered the ordinances of religion. The beginning, however, of Methodism in Echuca itself, dates from this visit of Mr. Bickford in May, 1860. He was welcomed by Mr. and Mrs. Oliver Veale, Mr. Kipling Powell, Mr. Lambert, Mr. and Mrs. Webb, who had been in other places attendants on the Wesleyan Ministry, and by persons who belonged to other Christian Churches. Mr. Bickford preached on May 27th, in Echuca, from I Timothy, chapter i, verse 15, in the morning, and from Revelation chapter vii, verses 13, 14, at night, and held a service at Moama. No Clergyman at that time was resident between Sandhurst and Deniliquin, a distance of 100 miles. No regular public worship was held; only an occasional visit was made by a Minister to Echuca, or to adjacent districts. Mr. Bickford's missionary heart was stirred within him, as he found the people "hungering for the bread of life, and anxious for the settlement of a Minister." His representations led to subsequent visits by Wesleyan Ministers, and bore fruit in the appointment of the Rev. Francis W. Jenkin to Echuca in 1864. This brother afterwards entered the Presbyterian Church. Mr. James Burchett succeeded him. He went subsequently to the Congregationalist Church. The cause was numerically weak. 29 members and 180 adherents constituted the return after three years of labour. Thomas F. Bird was the next Minister. He was of commanding intellectual gifts, but he also transferred himself to the ministry of the Congregationalist Church. Then in 1868, William H. Fitchett was appointed, when our Church gained a good position by the eminent gifts and enterprising spirit of this Minister, blessed by God to the conversion of a few persons, and to the gathering of many hearers into the congregation. Mr. Fitchett stayed three years, and was followed by Ministers of good standing in the Church. Echuca was favoured by having in succession, Revs. C. Lancaster, J. F. Horsley, H. Baker, J. D. Dodgson, J. Waterhouse, J. Cowperthwaite, who are, or have been, strong men in the Church, and have filled some of its most important stations. At this time, under the pastorate of the Rev. W. M. Bennett, Echuca has a roll of 102 Church members, 291 Sabbath scholars, and 660 adherents. The Church was erected in the pastorate of the Rev. W. H. Fitchett, but its additions have been considerable in subsequent times, and the congregation has done nobly in meeting the required expenditure. Messrs. Moorhouse, Heyward, Dr. Allin, Kyle, Kelly, Adams, Matthews, and Payne may be mentiened as having actively promoted the interests of the Church.

Two Circuits flank Echuca on either side. That of KYABRAM has been mostly under the care of junior Ministers, who have been active, energetic young men. Messrs. Adams, H. K. Hutchison, F. Watsford, W. R. Cunningham may be named amongst them. The Circuit was formed about the time of the migration to the northern areas by selectors in the years 1872-3, and owes much to the unstinted and self-denying labours of the Messrs. Lancaster. At one time the father and two sons were Local Preachers within its bounds, and another son, the Rev. C. Lancaster, was the Circuit Minister. Like sire, like son, in simplicity of character and aim, and in fervid labours, could be said of these male members of this choice Methodist family. Mr. William Baldwin, formerly of Heathcote Circuit, has been an acceptable Local Preacher in this Circuit also. The places embraced in its bounds are—Kyabram, Pinegrove (near Sheridan township), Timmering, Cooma, Mooroopna North, Spring Vale, Tongala, and Carag. The people are a willing, liberal, loyal set of Methodists. Kyabram Circuit is to the west of the Goulburn, YIELIMA Home Mission is to the north of that river, where it makes a bend to the westward and runs for a short distance almost parallel with the Murray river. This mission is taking good root amongst the settlers of the Yielima, Yalca, and Nathalia regions.

Durham Ox and Kerang Circuit is to the west and south-west of Echuca. That, too, has been favoured with representatives of a choice Methodist family within its bounds. The Holloways were there prior to the appearance of the selectors, when these latter came, the utmost good feeling existed between the squatter family, and the selectors. Every facility was rendered for the commencement of services and the settlement of a Minister by the liberality and zeal of the Holloways. The first location of a Home Missionary, Mr. H. Clarkson, and afterwards of a married Minister, was at Durham Ox, near the station of Mr. George Holloway. As a Home Mission station it was one of the first formed under the auspices of the Wesleyan Home Missionary Society of Victoria, and under the oversight of the Rev. John Watsford. It grew and prospered during the lengthened administration of Mr. Henry Clarkson. Other good Methodists had selected land within its bounds, the Woods and Midgleys of Terricks and Yarrawalla, Neale of Kerang and Loddon Vale, and many others. Mr. Edwd. Holloway has a station at Tragowel, and is a Local

Preacher, most unsparing of his personal efforts and means, for the spread of true religion. He has conducted winter campaigns of special services in conjunction with the Circuit Ministers, and Mr. Baker, a devoted Home Missionary, which have resulted in very marked success in the ingathering of precious souls to Christ and to his fold. The Revs. E. Taylor, E C. De Garis, and H. J. Cock have been indefatigable in their labours in this field, and during their administration the Circuit has strengthened greatly in membership and piety. It returns now 253 Church members and 1000 adherents, and has 13 Churches within its bounds. Mr. De Garis has gained well-deserved repute for the advocacy of irrigation, a vital question on these northern plains. Raywood Circuit and Elmore Home Mission are situate in an agricultural district between Sandhurst and Echuca. The former, after some vicissitudes, is now a thriving Circuit. Swan Hill has been missioned by Mr Baker within the last two years, and with the sympathy and help of Mr. Murdoch, Mr. George Holloway, and Messrs. Dennis, of Millool (N.S.W.), promises to become a flourishing station.

GIPPSLAND DISTRICT.

CHAPTER XVIII.

WE are indebted to the Rev. J. S. H. Royce, the esteemed Chairman of this District, for most of the following sketch of its history :—

In the minutes of Conference for 1863, Gippsland makes its first appearance by one of the stereotyped forms used in the columns of the stations, viz., " One earnestly requested. At that period no returns of members, or adherents, or Church property, were given, simply because Methodism had no organization in that remote part of Victoria

Twenty-three years have passed away since the above record was made and our Church was in the position indicated; but that state has been reversed by a deposit of Methodist leaven, which has permeated the country from Omeo in the far north to Wilson's Promontory in the south; "the little one has become a thousand"; now, Gippsland is a separate District with six Circuits and three Mission stations, where there are also six Ministers and five Missionaries. In these several Circuits and stations there are now 21 Churches, 54 other preaching places, 585 members, 1225 Sunday scholars, and 4289 adherents. It was "the day of small things" when the first Methodist service was held in Sale, which being the principal town of the province, became the centre of operation; the original Circuit embraced the whole of Gippsland. Twenty years before this, the squatter found his way into the country, but it was from the coast line he had to push his way through almost impenetrable forests, and surmount other barriers in the mountain ranges, which only men of enterprise would have undertaken. These early pioneers had the pick of the country, which possessed magnificent pasture land, watered by numerous streams, while a productive soil and bracing climate made Gippsland the Goshen of Victoria. No wonder that under these favourable circumstances the settlers found themselves in affluent positions, and that a tide of population flowed towards this land. Some of the Wesleyans who first came joined other Protestant Churches, whose Ministers preceded the Wesleyan. The advent of some of our loyal and influential Laymen led to a movement for the establishment of a Methodist Church in Gippsland. Among these was the late Mr. Nehemiah Guthridge, and Mr. William Little (both of whom had been influential Laymen in Melbourne), with Messrs. G. Ross, J. Waters, Derrick, J. J. Drew and other gentlemen. Rev. James Bickford, in Oct. 1863, made a prospecting tour around the settled parts of the province, and urged the Conference to send two Ministers. Several of the above Laymen entered heartily into the project of erecting a

Church in Sale, and by their untiring efforts and liberality the movement was crowned with success. In 1864, Sale appears in the list of stations with the Rev. Henry Baker, as the Minister. The services were conducted at first in the Mechanics' Hall, but on the completion of the Church, the congregation removed to its own premises, occupying the most central position in the town, and on a site which has become exceedingly valuable. In the same year, Port Albert also appears in the stations with "one to be sent." In the following year of 1865, the Rev. James W. Tuckfield was sent to the Port which was then the principal place of intercourse with Melbourne. The shipping at that period supported a thriving community, as all the stores, for Sale and other parts of Gippsland, were conveyed from this spot. For several years the Methodist cause flourished. Churches were built, both at the Port and Taraville; but when the iron-horse found its way from the city through the forests, the trade at Port Albert was all but closed; the Minister for a time had to be withdrawn; but now a tide of agricultural and pastoral prosperity has set in, and, under the name of Yarram Yarram, this promises to be one of the best Circuits in Gippsland. The Revs. Messrs. Ingham, James Lowe, and H. J. Cock have given devoted labours to this part; also, Mr. F. Wood, who was employed as a Home Missionary.

In the minutes of 1868, Walhalla appears after Sale, not as a Circuit, but simply as indicating a future station; while the following year it is a Circuit "to be supplied from Sale and Port Albert." Very few can form a conception of the journeys which had to be taken then to reach Walhalla, which is in a gorge of the mountains composing the Baw Baw range, and where the roads were not merely of the most primitive type, but positively dangerous. In the year 1870 there were three Circuits with a Minister at each, viz., Sale, Rev. C. Dubourg; Walhalla, Rev. D. S. Lindsay; Port Albert, Rev. Henry Moore. Subsequent appointments at Walhalla were—Revs. John Leslie, Arthur

Q

Powell, Samuel Adamson, John A. Osborne, and A. Inglis. The incidents that occurred in those days were unique in connection with the Circuits in the mountains, as Walhalla and Omeo, and those on the plains or lake country; and perhaps no backwoods' preacher of America could surpass them in interest. The difficulties attending the establishment of Methodism were of a romantic character, and the pioneer Ministers and Laymen of Gippsland, have had that in their heroic work which could "point a moral and adorn a tale." In addition to the places mentioned we have Ministers stationed in the thriving towns of Bairnsdale, Warragul, and Traralgon; while the positions occupied by Home Missionaries will, no doubt, soon be filled by Conference appointments, and other outposts occupied by enterprizing pioneers. The Revs. W. Brown, John Harcourt, Robert C. Flockart, William Williams, S. T. Withington, and Thomas Kane have been foremost Ministers in the Lowland Circuits. In Gippsland there are the elements of permanency, rich pasture and agricultural lands; forests of valuable timber; while in the mountains there is incalculable mineral wealth—gold, silver, copper, lead, tin; and it is not improbable that extensive coalfields may yet be developed.

The recent extension of our work in the new parts of the District, chiefly through the agency of the Home Missionaries, should be noticed. Mr. J. S. Holmes, of the Belfast Circuit, was the first Home Missionary in the District. He was the pioneer of the Warragul Circuit in 1871, when the country was a dense and almost unbroken forest. The roads were of the rudest, roughest character, and the travelling was unusually laborious and exhausting. The Messrs. James and Hugh Copeland had settled at Warragul (then Brandy Creek and Buln Buln), and were as hearty and liberal friends of our Church as they had been in Melbourne and Ireland before. Messrs. Garside, Witton, Walters, in this neighbourhood, and many other members of our Church from various parts of the colony, dispersed themselves through Gippsland and began to cry out for the means of grace. That veteran pioneer, the Rev. J. C. Symons, who had done such faithful service in other parts, and left his name and mark on many of our Church projects and institutions, was also early in this field, and frequently preached at the home of Mr. James Copeland, and again at what is now the "Poowong and Jetho Home Mission." Mr. William Hill, son of the late Rev. W. Hill, describes how he persuaded Mr. Symons to don a "pair of moles" that he might look more homely and harmonious with his rustic congregation, and not appal them by the terrors of a black suit. The services took well, and one especially was profuse in his compliments on the preacher, as being a right good sort of a fellow in fustian, instead of a mere formal parson. A good central site was forthwith secured, Mr. Hill purchasing an allotment on one side, and Mr. Burchett on the other, that our Church might be well flanked and protected, and the Church which had such a good start, has taken a good position and made good progress. The Anglicans and Presbyterians are equally active and aggressive, and all seem to use, indifferently, each others Churches when necessary. One Missionary will preach in three or four places on the Sabbath—our own Circuit system, without the name.

The Rev. H. Howard's ministry at Warragul gave a good impetus to our work there. Mr. Witton, pioneer of our Church in Victoria, resides in that part, and still labours in the cause of Christ. Many who saw him at the Jubilee celebration in the Exhibition Building were glad to note how hale and hearty he looked after fifty years of service given to Methodism. The progress of Methodism in this province has been rapid in these later years, and the work gives bright promise of a prosperous future.

WESTERN DISTRICT.

CHAPTER XIX.

PORTLAND.—This place holds a venerable and honourable rank in Colonial annals, as the first spot in the colony visited and settled by Europeans. Some two or three years before Melbourne was founded, Portland Bay was a familiar name and resort to sundry hardy and adventurous spirits from "the other side" and the stream of Methodist life and work may be traced almost up to those dim and early days. A respected and intelligent member of our Church still living, who came from Launceston to Portland in 1841, and has a vein of historic curiosity in him, has been kind enough to record and compile sundry facts and incidents, illustrative of the subject, and which are, in substance, as follows :— The coast and bay had been visited for whaling purposes, some years before his arrival, by a small fleet owned by persons in Van Dieman's Land, as it was then called. In 1832, one Dutton, in the employ of Mr. John Sinclair, overseer of convicts in Launceston, settled at Portland, probably in charge of the old Whaling Boiling-down establishment, the site of which may be seen on the shores of the Bay. Then in 1834 came the Hentys, with a staff of men, boats, and material to found a complete whaling establishment, and in 1836, Major Mitchell, on his exploration tour from Sydney, turned up at Portland, and found this establishment in active operation. The narrator observes, that the natives were very numerous, and were much dismayed and diverted to see Mitchell on horseback, and imagined that the horse and rider were one body, after the pattern of the ancient centaur. They were also amused at the grey head and beard of the Major, and described them as the result of a flour bag shaken over him, flour being a luxury with which they had just become acquainted. Major Mitchell's track may be still traced, and the writer has seen the spot known as Mitchell's tree, between Dunkeld and

Yuppekiar, where the party camped and inscribed their names, an historic landmark like unto the tree which is sacredly preserved at Wodonga, marked by Hume and Howell, on their first crossing the Murray in 1824. It was on this occasion that Mitchell was so charmed with the country through which he passed, that he called it "Australia Felix" in the spirit of grateful prediction and glad exultation. The little colony established by the Hentys, and thus visited by Major Mitchell, contained, it is said, some who had heard the Gospel from Wesleyan Missionaries and other faithful men at Launceston. One of these, tradition states, was ploughman to Messrs. Henty, the first to turn a sod and plough a paddock in the colony. He died in 1882, and the site of his work is still shown on the bluff, near the railway terminus, while the plough itself has long been cherished as an heirloom in the Henty family, and was exhibited with pride at the Melbourne Exhibition of 1880. Another more definite character was known as "Jimmey Chapman," the brickmaker, and when Messrs. Hedditch and Wilkinson arrived from Tasmania they found prayer meetings going on in his little hut. Beside the Missionaries, there were, at that time, two earnest lay workers in the Launceston society, Messrs. Oakden and Leach; they were very diverse in style and manner, but both very useful. Mr. Leach was the instrument in the conversion of Mr. William Witton, and, it is believed, that this Jimmey Chapman was another seal of his labours. Then in 1839 came over in the service of Messrs. Henty, Mr. Henry Deacon, the first man married in Portland, and for many years a faithful member of our Church. From 1836 to 1840 a small but growing stream of emigrants arrived from Tasmania, Sydney, and Geelong, the true pioneers of settlement in the Western District to be followed fifteen years later by a large and direct influx of population from Great Britain. Shortly after Major Mitchell's visit in 1836, a stranger was cast for a while on the shores of Portland Bay. Mr. J. J. Peers, wife, and children, had left Tasmania for Adelaide in the brig *Isabella*, intending to settle there. The brig was wrecked at Cape Nelson on the night of April 1st, 1837, but the passengers and crew, twenty-one in number, escaped safe to land. Mr. Peers lost all his goods, but his wife and children were saved in their night dresses. The whalers, like the barbarous people of Melita, "showed us no little kindness, for they kindled a fire and received us every one, because of the present rain, and because of the cold." If "Jimmey Chapman's prayer meeting" was going on at that time we may be sure that there was a fine thanksgiving service on their behalf. From the whalers' huts they were taken to Mr. Henty's house and hospitably treated. In a short time they returned to Launceston. (See the Rev. J. C. Symons' Jubilee speech.) One would not duly inflate this incident or import into it any far-fetched element of heroism, it was no exploit of classic song or story, such as the landing of the pilgrim fathers, or of the hero of Juan Fernandez, but it was a coincidence, or rather a providence, that Mr. Peers, instead of reaching Adelaide, was stopped at Portland, and turned back, that he might take a leading part in the introduction of Methodism into Melbourne, while the Rev. W. Longbottom, who about the same time had left Tasmania for Western Australia, was shipwrecked and detained at Adelaide in the same way, and instead of proceeding to his intended place of abode, was an honoured instrument in the introduction of Methodism into South Australia. In 1840, Messrs. Saunders and M'Dowell arrived from Launceston, the former removing to Narrawong, twelve miles from Portland, on the shores of the Bay, gathered, in after years, a primitive Sunday school together in a barn, and taught them the way of life, while the latter began religious service at once in his own shop, a cooperage at the corner of Gawler and Percy-streets, by reading one of Wesley's sermons to the few people who would gather there. At this time, 1841-2, Mr. Hedditch arrived from Tasmania, and Mr. Kitson and family from Geelong, in quest of land. Mr. Kitson was a staunch and hardy Methodist from the North of Ireland, and settled at "the Lakes" near Bridgewater. He opened his house for Methodist preaching, himself reading and exhorting in turn. His family were active members of our Church, and the week-day afternoon service at "the Lakes" was very precious for many years. The solemn ocean, with its long wash and swell, is for ever swathing the noble Cape Bridgewater, and its serried waves, like crested and mounted battalions, pour into its lovely Bay, while, in vivid contrast, "the Lakes," round whose margin the wombat and platypus revel with impunity, lie with unruffled repose just within the coast line, and make the scenery very varied and romantic. In 1842 Mr. Thomas Wilkinson arrived from Melbourne and Tasmania. Finding two worthy men (Messrs. Saunders and Deacon?) he united with them in establishing regular service, first in Jimmey Chapman's hut (before mentioned), then in a slab kitchen, and at last in Messrs. Henty's wool store, which was occupied in the morning by the Rev. J. Y. Wilson, Anglican Chaplain, and "where a Wesleyan Sabbath evening service was commenced with glorious results." In 1843, Mr. William Witton came to Portland to overlook the building of the new Court-house and gaol, and was, says a witness, "a genuine Local Preacher." Messrs. Akers, Raddenberry, Stack, and Lilley occasionally visited the place from Melbourne, and fed "the little flock." A Sunday school was started by Mr. Cole, classes were formed, and prayer meetings held. A Sunday school was also started at Double Corner, near the little Wesleyan Cemetery. The first Church was erected in 1842, mainly through the exertions of Mr. M'Dowell, on the site of the present Bank of Victoria. It was 30 x 20, "lath and plastered on both sides." In 1854, it was sold and removed, and was existing as recently as 1867, a combination of lodging-house and flour store. In 1844, Portland appears on the Melbourne Circuit plan with No. 6 (Mr. Thomas Wilkinson) appointed as almost perpetual curate, for Mr. Witton had removed to Belfast. Mr. Wilkinson's Church principles were of the solid and conservative type, (for he had been a London Methodist of the old school, and was wont at times to conduct the Anglican service in the morning, and the Methodist service at night), while Mr. Witton's were more free and elastic, and the two did not always harmonize. Mr. Wilkinson founded the Portland *Guardian*, the first newspaper in the Western District, and in 1851 was elected to represent that town in the Legislative Council. In 1848-9, the Rev. F. Tuckfield visited the place, followed, in 1850, by the Rev. J. Harcourt, whose visit is gratefully remembered by one still living, who found Christ under his preaching, but had not the courage to confess it. As early as 1845, application had been made to the General Superintendent for the appointment of a Minister, and £50 forwarded to him for that purpose. Mr. Harcourt took up the case, and, in answer to his urgent presentation of the matter, the Rev. W. Lightbody was sent down from Sydney in 1851, to take charge of the cause. He was young and strong, and entered with great heart into the work. A strong tide of emigration from the old country to Portland Bay had set in, and Mr. Lightbody is gratefully remembered by many, for the kindly interest he took in them on their arrival, and for advice and help in the outset of their career. Messrs. Salmon, Bye, Cook, Satchell, Jarrett, and other valuable brethren arrived at this time. Mr. Lightbody's Circuit extended to Belfast and Warrnambool (then budding into existence). He encountered no little fatigue and peril in crossing the rivers, and in going from one side to the other of the Circuit, a stretch of nearly 100 miles. His heart, however, turned fondly towards the far west, as the needle trembles to the pole, for there at Bridgewater was the fair "lady of the lake" (of the family above mentioned), who became his faithful wife, and is now his bereaved widow. Mr. Lightbody did good and faithful service in his generation, and ended his days in peace as a Supernumerary n the same Circuit. At Bridgewater and Drik Drik his

ITS ORIGIN AND HISTORY. 257

family have entered into his labours. In 1851, the first stone Church, 25 x 25, was built, and in 1852 a bazaar was held to raise funds for the addition of a transept. Mr. Lightbody, who had married and removed to Warrnambool, was succeeded by the Rev. W. Tregellas, who had been recommended to this Conference by the Rev. R. Young. The times were hard, Belfast and Warrnambool were formed into another Circuit, the Quarterly Board was appalled at the prospect of supporting a married Minister, and some soreness and trouble ensued. Then followed in 1856, Mr. Samuel Knight, a "supply" from the Prahran Circuit. He began, the next year, his successful Ministerial career, and in 1877 was President of the South Australian Conference. His labours were greatly blessed and are still fondly remembered. In the years which followed, various Ministers were in charge, and the Bridgewater, Heywood, and Wattle Hill Churches were built. In 1865, the Rev. F. Tuckfield was the Minister, and was esteemed very highly in love for his own and his work's sake. The present Church was then projected and commenced under very promising auspices. Mr. Tuckfield took a severe cold at a funeral, and in a few days, died in great peace. (For a fuller sketch of this faithful servant of God, see the story of the Buntingdale Mission before referred to.) The following sketch from the Rev. W. L. Blamires, of Hamilton, who preached Mr. Tuckfield's funeral sermon, may be added :—"'When those snows melt there will be a great flood,' remarked one, referring to Robert Bolton's grey locks, and remembering the great affection with which he was regarded by his flock. This prediction had a fulfilment in the circumstances attending the death of Francis Tuckfield. There was great weeping when it was known that this good, laborious, and faithful pastor was dead. The Church made devout lamentation over him, the town was filled with mourning, and in distant places many a sorrowful pang was felt in the breasts of those who had known and loved him. To say that he was well known was to say that he was greatly beloved, for the one followed the other. He was not of the great men who excite wonder, but of the good men 'who inherit love.' 'A man to be beloved' was the uppermost thought, as one remembered him. Not the man of brilliant talent or of florid eloquence, but the man of goodness, the peacemaker, the warm-hearted friend, the Christian of loving spirit and courteous bearing, the affectionate and unwearied pastor of Christ's Church." The death of the pastor proved the new life of many, and at the close of the funeral sermon just noted some eight or nine decided for Christ; among them the young son of the deceased, who then and there sought and found mercy, and consecrated his best powers and remaining life to the service of his father's God and people. He is labouring with enthusiasm and success as the Rev. John Hannah Tuckfield. Mr. Tuckfield's sudden death, together with a serious reverse in the prosperity and prospects of the place, brought the new Church undertaking to a standstill for twelve months. During the Ministry of the Rev. J. B. Smith the project was resumed and completed. The old Church was turned to good account, the materials of the first part were used in the new Sabbath schools, the two wings form the front of the present parsonage, while the porch is turned into a pantry or passage. The Rev. Messrs. Binks, Knight, and Blamires conducted the opening services of the new Church, and in the subsequent ministry of the Rev. R. M. Hunter, a valiant and successful effort was made to bring down the debt. Mr. Hunter's ministry took a wonderful hold of the people, and greatly advanced Methodism. An interesting work was undertaken in the writer's time at Drik Drik, near Dartmoor, more than forty miles from Portland. It was a veritable "Church in the wilderness," raised by a small but hardy band of settlers on the lonely and romantic banks of the river Glenelg. The writer has a vivid recollection of the opening service. The Church was built of slabs and bark, with very rude seats and earthen floor. The afternoon service was attended by twelve swarthy bushmen, each one accompanied with a shaggy hound. The evening service was held around a blazing bush bonfire, for want of better light and room. The tea meeting was held next day at three o'clock, two young friends of the softer sex were imported for the occasion, and after a ride on horseback of some forty miles, proceeded to arrange the feast which was spread out on imaginary table-cloths in nature's own lap, and under the shady limbs of the trees of the wood. The Rev. W. Lightbody sitting in his buggy, presided over the after meeting, and from the same forum, glowing and telling addresses were delivered. It was a real, primitive, backwood's scene, but it proved the start and nucleus of what has since developed into the Portland Bush Mission with some dozen preaching stations, and has done a large amount of good. A fine stone Sabbath school and a living Church of thirty members are flourishing there, while the Kitsons and Lightbodys of a younger generation are heartily carrying on the work which their fathers began. A similar bush Church has been erected at Mount Clay, at a cost of £20 for forty sittings, or at the rate of 10s. a sitting. The Revs. George Schofield and Samuel Adamson entered the Wesleyan Ministry from this Circuit, and are worthy representatives of families long resident in Portland, that are strongly attached to our cause. Heywood is the centre of the Bush Mission, and has had, from an early date, a good society, of which Messrs, Remfry, Satchell, and others were leading members. Mr. Thomas Alday graduated here as a Local Preacher, and has since become a Home Missionary, and a probationer in the Wesleyan ministry. The Circuit keeps a premier position in the Western District, in strength of numbers, although the commercial prosperity of Portland has been recently at a low ebb. The town is beautiful for situation, has a fine and sheltered harbour, and should become a summer and seaside watering place. Brighter days are yet in store.

BELFAST.—The beginning of Methodism at Port Fairy, as this place was first called, is somewhat obscure. The tiniest of grains of mustard seed, otherwise the kingdom of God, began to grow in the heart and home of a Mrs. Harris, of Duckholes, now Rosebrook, near Belfast. Her house was on the River Moyne, "a place where prayer was wont to be made." Every Sabbath "a tract was read to a few assembled in the house, and then a Class or Prayer meeting was held for serious persons. She was a devoted Christian woman, whose look, lip, and life were employed for Christ, and who was very zealous in inviting the neighbours to this religious meeting." Her persuasions brought Daniel Love to the place. He was much impressed by the reading of a tract on "Eternity," though afraid to stay to the after meeting. Conviction, however, deepened into distress, and then into alarm, and on Easter Sunday the crisis came, suppressed groans and broken cries proclaimed, "Behold he prayeth," and friends gathered round him and pointed him to Christ. He was soon blessed with the joy of God's salvation. His old companions said he had lost his senses, but he had only lost his sins, and became henceforth a truly wise, sober, and holy man. He has long "adorned the Gospel of God his Saviour," and been permitted to turn many to righteousness,—his name is still revered in the Western District. His case is a contrast to that of another brother who, at that time, like Diotrephes, loved to have the pre-eminence, and when, after a sermon by the Rev. F. Tuckfield on "the little foxes," he was rebuked for a fault, he resented it, and left the Church, seeking to scatter and divide the little flock in doing so. He has pursued an erratic course ever since. In 1848-9, visits were paid to the place by the Rev. F. Tuckfield and J. Harcourt. Mr. Witton resided on his farm at Bootapool, seven miles from Belfast, and at length took charge of the Class and work. In 1844, Mr. Jealous and Mr. William Watson and family arrived from Tasmania, and two years after, through the winning influence of Mrs. Harris and the mercy of God, Mr. and Mrs. Watson both realized the great change. Mr. Watson became a great help and stay to the cause for many years. A fortnight after his conversion he was appointed tract distributor for the whole town, then Prayer Leader, then he took part with Mr. M'Mahon in reading alternately from Jay's and Wesley's sermons in the little Church which had been built at Rosebrook. That building is now used as an hotel, and a larger Church has been erected near the site of the first. Of those days, Mr. Watson writes :—" Belfast consisted then of about fifty dwellings, mostly thatched huts, the streets were covered with grass and she-oaks, there was no money in the place, but business was done by ' mullock' as exchange was called. For leather, I had to take wheat, bran, butter, cheese, pigs, and anything I could get. As pioneers we were satisfied and brought our mind to our circumstances. Colonists of the present day cannot form any conception of the trials and difficulties the early settlers had to endure." And then he tells of his finding out the people of God, with its happy results. Belfast became, in a few years a sort of Immigration depot, for receiving and distributing new arrivals from the United Kingdom and Tasmania, and from 1850 to 1854 many good Methodists in this way passed into the Western District. In 1854, the Rev. J. Albiston was appointed to this Circuit, and in 1855 the Rev. R. Hart (residing at Warrnambool). The Church at Belfast was at that time a long, queer building 45 x 11, built skillion fashion, and familiarly called, " The Sailors' Chest." It was sold in 1869 for £9; on August 24th, 1855 the foundation of the present Church was laid by Mr. Witton. It was considered an imposing and elaborate structure, built in troublous or rather expensive times, at a cost of £1935 1s. 8d, or £7 11s. per sitting. The ornamental frontispiece or figure-head of "our venerable founder," as he appears in the old hymn books, was wrought in stone by an amateur sculptor, and valued at £60. It looks down benignly on the worshippers as they pass in at the Church door, or else at his first love, the Church of England on the other side of the street. Among the receipts towards the erection of this Church are £66 13s. 4d. from the Buntingdale Mission Estate. In 1856, the

Rev. M. Dyson was appointed as a young Minister to reside at Belfast. No Circuit horse was kept, and the young preacher's walks were long and sore. At Yambuk, Mr. Hindhaugh, from Geelong, had settled, amid a little cluster of Methodists, and preaching was held for a time in his house. The stone Church which is now a ruin, was erected during the Ministry of the Rev. Charles Lane, who was moved thereto by the failure of a scheme of a Union Church, and by the attempt of an impetuous little cleric to brand us with the sin of schism. In 1863-4, the Churches at Koroit and Kirkstall were built, and in 1865-7, under the ministry of the Rev. R. Hart. the old Church at Koroit was superseded by the present handsome structure, while the Kirkstall Church, through some mishap, was sold by the Government with the land on which it stood and turned by the lucky purchaser into a potato store. After long and harassing negotiations, the Government admitted the wrong it had done, and made compensation. During the Ministry of the Rev. R. Hart, three houses were purchased for the Parsonage. These were converted into the present Parsonage in the time of the Rev. J. G. Turner, and the present Sunday school was erected. Some of our leading Ministers have taken their turn in this Circuit, and of devoted Laymen who have stood by it from the first, grateful mention should be made of Mr. J. Bedford, W. Watson, and J. Scott, and of Messrs. R. Skilbeck and William Midgley, of Koroit, two out of several worthy branches of a large family of Yorkshire Methodists who settled at Yangery Grange in the early days, whose generous hearts beat warm and true to all the interests of our Church. Elect ladies in this Circuit as Mrs. Youngman, of Belfast, and Mesdames W. Midgley, Skilbeck, and Gray of Koroit, have been distinguished by their Christian devotedness and large-hearted hospitality. Of late years the Circuit has been blessed with the ministries of the Rev. H. Baker, W. Brown, J. W. Tuckfield, R. Osborne Cook, and Charles Sanders.

WARRNAMBOOL.—This thriving township was laid out in 1847, and settled mainly by arrivals from Tasmania, Melbourne, and Portland, among whom were a few Methodists. Mr. Witton is said to have preached the first sermon in this place in an hotel. Mr. John Smith, of Byaduk, a name dear to Methodists in the Western District, resided here in 1850-6, and his little child was the first corpse interred in the Wesleyan Cemetery. In the year he worked for Cassidy (Cassidy's punt on the Merri River), he astonished the neighbours by his prodigious feats in the threshing line, threshing in one season with the flail (threshing machines were not yet in fashion), 1700 bushels of wheat. He was one of a little flock of faithful men, who "feared the Lord and spake often one to another." The others were Messrs. Goodall, Goldstraw, John Hughes, &c., remarkable men, brought to God in Tasmania in the old times. We have heard the one tell in graphic style of his conversion to God in a saw-pit, and another give touching stories of early Methodism at Deloraine and Wesley Dale "on the other side." They were rejoicing in the simplicity and glow of their first love, and kept alive the kindled flame. Another member of the little band was equally earnest and forward; but proved weak and unstable, and often fell away. Speaking of himself at the Class meeting as "a brand plucked from the burning," the Rev. Wm. Butters, who was leading the Class, replied, "A burnt log will soon catch fire again, take care lest you catch fire again and your last end be worse than the first," a warning which seemed prophetic of his sad end, for he died a few years after, friendless and miserable in the Hamilton Hospital. Mr. Denny, an earnest and useful member of our Church in Launceston, arrived at this time. He had been the friend and companion of the Rev. C. H. Goldsmith, of the S.A. Conference, associated with him in Messrs. Henty's office, and converted to God about the same time. In 1850 he was a prominent tradesman in Warrnambool, (Messrs. Craig and Denny, and then Messrs. Denny and Stevens), and states that at that time a small Sabbath school was in existence, under the care of himself and his young wife. When the Rev. J. Harcourt, on his visit to the Western District in 1850, preached in Mr. Denny's auction room, the little children were perched upon and stowed away among the sacks of wheat, which were heaped up in the store. Mr. and Mrs. Denny and John Smith possessed capital singing powers, and made the service interesting and attractive. At this time the first stone Church was put up,—rough and rude in its construction, it soon began to crack and fail, and had to be supported by props and crutches. Mr. Watson, of Belfast, says that it was built over a wombat hole, or at least surrounded by wombat holes and sheoak trees. When in 1855 the present Church was erected, it was built over or around the old one, so as to have the latter for service while the new building was going on. The first resident Ministers were severally, Messrs. Lightbody, Albiston, and Hart. During the ministry of the latter the Dennington Church was built, in faith, at a cost of £100, and then a tea-meeting held to pay for it. John Hughes, who resided in this place, offered £5, and waxing warmer, added, "Nay I would give £10." until pacing the Church in his emotion, he exclaimed, "Nay, I believe I would give £20 if the Church could be paid for," and thus provoked and challenged, the sum was soon raised. "John Hughes" is a name on which one loves to linger, for the grace of God had set him in point of moral worth among the princes of the people. In 1863 the writer found him his Circuit Steward, although he could neither read nor write, such was the deep interest he took in the work of God, and the honor and reverence with which he was regarded. The Rev. W. Lightbody and others, who knew him in his prime, loved him to the uttermost, and cherish his name and memory, and the photo of his homely, happy face with pious and enthusiastic affection. The Dennington Church did good service for some years, although in the midst of an alien Roman Catholic population. One simple soul, emulating the generous style of the "alabaster box of ointment very precious," provided us with some choice currant cake for the sacramental bread, while another humorous or penurious brother, in a year when all the crops, except "spuds" (the staple of the disrict), had failed, proposed that instead of the ordinary teameeting, we should have one of fried potatoes! Churches also were erected at Wangoom and Woodford, and the usual incidents of Circuit history, bazaars, revivals, changes, deaths, &c. have taken place. The reserve in which the Church stands is very central and valuable, and portions of it have been disposed of to advantage. The ministry of the Rev. Thomas James attracted influential families to the Church during his stay. In 1872, the Western District was constituted under the chairmanship of the Rev. G. Daniel, and ever since the chairman has resided at Warrnambool. Space precludes the mention of the worthy Ministers and faithful Laymen, past and present, who have helped to "build the temple of our God," in this Circuit. Though no longer within our borders, mention may be made of Mr. F. P. Stevens, a leading townsman, who, grateful for a noble Methodist parentage, was, in early years, a liberal supporter of our Church, and an active worker in our Sabbath school. The Rev. Charles Jones, of New South Wales, made his first effort in preaching the Gospel, within the bounds of this Circuit.

HAMILTON.—In 1855 a grant of £20 was made by the Missionary Committee in Sydney, to enable the Rev. W. Tregellis, of Portland, to visit and report upon Hamilton, or "The Grange," as it was then called. He found a small mixed lot of Methodists, lately come from Belfast, and settled at Muddy Creek, near Hamilton, consisting of Wesleyans, Primitives, Reformers. A few Independents, and Baptists also resided there. With such conflicting views, they were unwilling to combine for common worship, even though enjoying the common salvation. In the township proper

R

were found an English Methodist lady, Mrs. Wiggins (Blastock) and a few others, who heartily sympathized with the object of the Minister's visit. These, in the town were further strengthened by the welcome arrival and addition of Mr. Peter Learmonth to their number. He has, from the first, been a devoted and generous supporter and member of the Church. In 1859, the Rev. E. B. Burns, from Belfast, visited the place, and in 1861, the Rev. H. Baker was appointed the first Minister of the Hamilton Circuit. Mr. Baker was well received, and his services were highly appreciated by the general and christian public. They were held first in the old National school, and then in the old Mechanics' Institute. Hamilton is the centre and capital of a famous pastoral district, in which Presbyterianism predominates, while Methodism, as in Scotland, takes a somewhat restricted and qualified form. The district is also somewhat unique in its physical, as well as its social and religious features. Bishop Moorhouse has described, in beautiful word painting, the rolling, billowy aspect of the far-famed Muntham Downs, and the magnificent country around Tahara and Merino; while the Wannon and Nigretta Falls, and the curious volcanic phenomena of the region, were described in the Methodist *Spectator* of 1881. Under the attractive ministry of the Rev. H. Baker, our Church made a good start, and took a high place in public esteem. Mr. J. H. Scott, a worthy Wesleyan conducted for some time a Sabbath school for the Church of England. Some of the people were scandalized at his use of extempore prayer, and, to compromise the matter, the good Bishop Perry composed a short form of prayer for the occasion, and on inspecting the school, highly commended Mr. Scott's good work. Mr. Baker also visited Muddy and Murphy's Creeks, but with small results. The nondescript character of the religious elements found there, induced an experiment in Union Churches, which may "point a moral," if not "adorn a tale." At Murphy's Creek two such Churches were erected within a few yards of each other, the one, used by the Independents and Baptists (about one family of each), has long been closed, the walls pretty well enfolded in emblematic sweet briar, and the furniture and library waiting to be claimed and appropriated some day. The other is used alternately by the Wesleyans and Primitives; but the joint stock affair is very unprofitable, for with a mere handful of hearers, the building is dilapidated, and neither Church cares to incur responsibility or expense At Muddy Creek a Union Church was built with the understanding that any of the subscribers removing to another part should still retain their interest in the building, or else be bought out for £7. Many removed to the Horsham district, but the financial stipulation was not kept. The building fell into ruin and decay, for it was hard to tell to whom it belonged. It is now renovated and occupied exclusively by the Primitive Methodists. In 1862, the Rev. E. B. Burns was appointed to Hamilton, and the present Church built. Other Ministers of varied gifts and excellencies followed. We may specify the ministry of the Rev. W. L. Blamires and R. M. Hunter, 1865, as being representative of these, and as possessing important and intrinsic attributes, which told for the lasting advantage of the Circuit. These Ministers were together on the ground, Mr. Hunter residing at Dunkeld, and they have both since attained the Presidential office. It is but bare justice, and surely not at variance with becoming modesty, for a colleague in this narrative to state how much Methodism in the Western District owes to the wisdom and strength of the Rev. W. L. Blamires, both as Minister at Hamilton, and afterwards as Chairman of the Western District. Of the sterling qualities of his mind and heart, and of pen and tongue, there is no need to dilate. Long known to his closest friends and held in due reserve until wanted, they have, since his elevation to the chair of the Conference, become public property, and are patent to all. The Hamilton Circuit at that time reached from Yuppekiar on the east to Green Hills on the west, and from Rosebrook, near Horsham, on the north to Macarthur on the south, an area of 90 x 56 miles. The places composing the Circuit were regularly visted once a month, entailing a great amount of travelling and fatigue. In small Churches or School houses, in the shepherd's hut, the shearer's woolshed, or the station parlour, the word of life was spoken, while the little ones were catechised, taught to say or sing their hymns, or heard their Scripture lessons appointed at a previous visit, and sometimes baptized in little clusters. After a cheerful cup of tea, kindly talk about "good things," and earnest prayer, the Minister would go on his way, leaving the leaven of the kingdom (Mark iv., 26-29) to work until the next visit, and the fruit was often found after many days. In May, 1865, was the famous Hamilton "Land Racket," being the great rush to take up land under "Grant's Act." Thousands of intending selectors swarmed into the town, or else scoured the adjacent country to spy out the land. The weather was very wet and stormy, and the roads, owing to so much traffic, became frightful with Hamiltonian mud of the worst description. Day after day multitudes pressed into the Land office to take their chance at the Land Ballot box, the name coming out first from the wheel of fortune, having a right of selection in first class agricultural areas around. The huge iron building, erected as a temporary Land office, and in which, it is said, land to the value of some millions sterling was disposed of, was standing only a short time since. The Ministers endeavoured to improve the occasion by preaching near the spot at eight o'clock in the morning, on the week day, and at three p.m. on the Sunday, in the open-air, to the crowds waiting the opening of the office or visiting the town. They were urged to "buy the truth, and seek an inheritance in heaven"; and the word was not in vain. The Cavendish Church was also built at this time, and afterwards used as a Sunday school at Hamilton. In Mr. Albiston's time, the new parsonage was erected, and in Mr. J. B. Smith's day a successful bazaar relieved the Circuit of the debt on the same. The visits of Messrs. W.

Taylor, M. Burnett, and W. Osborn have left tide marks of religious blessing and influence. The cause at Byaduk is of a hearty and pleasing character. The service was held for a time at John Smith's, and then, during the ministry of the Rev. E. B. Burns, the present Church was built, and has been consecrated by many blessings. The members were united and numerous; a strong leaven of vital godliness pervaded the village, and from this place "sounded out" the word of God, and in the Horsham District and Gippsland, their "faith to God-ward is spread abroad, so that we need not speak anything." John Smith has been for many years the Leader here, and deserves more than passing mention. As a farm lad in Devonshire he had rueful experience of hard and almost cruel toil, and his prodigious feats of strength and work in after years have surprised many. This energy characterized him in the cause of God, and he spared neither time nor toil, nor means, nor life, nor limb, when there was a chance of getting or doing good. He could travel to Ballarat to get a blessing, or to Portland to find a kindred spirit who "had the power." Power was the ruling element of his new nature, and ran through his prayers and experience like golden threads through a royal robe. He loved a revival, as the songster loves his song, but it must be, as Ivan Preston called it, "a *menseful* (solemn) revival" and was judged, not by the noise, but the power there was in it, the power of the Spirit and the force of truth. He had a clear grasp of the plan of salvation, and a touching and pathetic way of speaking of the "wrath to come." In company somewhat silent and suppressed, but on his knees a prevailing prince with God. The well-worn family Bible, used morning, noon, and night for family worship, told of his love for the Psalms and the words of the Lord Jesus, and few could use them (even the deep vast words of the fourth gospel), or the plaintive phrases of the Psalms, or the less familiar lines of shaded beauty found in our Hymn Book, with greater feeling and effect. With all this solid worth there was a vein of play in him, and he had the old

English love of sport. He can use a gun, put up a hare, or draw out a trout with enthusiasm and delight. The writer remembers the keen zest with which he joined him in stocking the Byaduk Creek with English trout. His jubilee offering was in memory of Richard Heales, "who gave the poor man a chance of getting a home!" for it was under his administration that the Occupation licenses took effect. That home with its prophet's chamber, and generous hospitalities, stands on the banks of the beautiful and perennial Byaduk Creek, whose waters Mr. Smith has turned to good account. In that home faithful sermons have been preached, and souls have found the Saviour; young beginners and dying saints have been cheered and comforted, and the daily incense of praise and prayer have made it a Bethel of blessing, and power; and, to those who have known it for twenty years, it seems thus seasoned and "consecrated for evermore." " He shall be like a tree planted by the rivers of water, that bringeth forth his fruit in his season, his leaf also shall not wither, and whatsoever he doeth shall prosper." The influence of this holy man of God and of other kindred spirits make Byaduk a bright spot in the Hamilton Circuit, while the personal worth and social standing of Mr. Peter Learmonth as a Christian and a citizen, and the active sympathy and generous help of the Wiggins' and Learmonths' on the one hand, and the ungrudging labours of devoted Local Preachers on the other, have served to sustain the cause and comfort the Minister's heart. The Rev. J. Y. Simpson was converted to God, and began his course as a Local Preacher in Hamilton. He has long been a popular and successful Minister in South Australia.

MORTLAKE was visited by the Rev. J. B. Smith from Warrnambool in 1864, and by the Rev. W. L. Blamires, when passing through to Geelong on October 31st, 1865. Mr. Lowe, storekeeper, was the chief representative of Methodism in the place, he kindly welcomed our Ministers who visited it, and urged its claims as a field of labour.

Mr. Blamires presented the case at the following District meeting, and the Rev. W. H. Fitchett, who, while assisting the Rev. T. Raston at Warrnambool, had visited Mortlake, was appointed its first Minister (1866). Mr. John Pearson, a liberal friend of our Church, resided for some time at Shadwell Park, and Mr. Mark James was for many years a faithful stay and help to our Church. Mr. Thomas Shaw, of Wooriwyrite, brother of Mr. Jonathan Shaw, of the Richmond Circuit, was a liberal friend to our Church in early times, as Mr. Montgomery has been in later times. The Circuit has been supplied with energetic young Ministers, but much migration of the people has taken place. It is not strong in numbers, and Terang and Camperdown, which had existed for nine years as a separate Circuit, were in 1876 added to it. Messrs. Hillard, Wykes, Hughes, Heard, Hindhaugh, Edge, (of Jancourt), and others, have stood by the cause from the first. In 1880, the Rev. W. L. Blamires, the Chairman of the District, with the Rev. E. O. Knee, visited the area now known as the Heytesbury Forest, on an exploring mission, and under his management, Cobden, Carpendeit and other places, reaching as far as Port Campbell, were detached from the Mortlake Circuit, and put under the care of a Home Missionary, Mr. A. J. Wade, while Mr. Cole, of Carpendeit (an indefatigable Local Preacher), and others, were his faithful co-workers.

PENSHURST.—The PENSHURST Church was built during the Ministry of the Rev. H. Baker. The place had been previously visited by the Rev. E. B. Burns, from Belfast. He found there the Wesleyan families of Walters, Shaddock, Porter, and others to welcome him. Mr. Walters, who had been a Local Preacher in England, had suffered some relapse through the rough hardships and changes of Colonial life. On one occasion he came upon a bullock dray encamped in the bush, and was attracted and arrested by the voice of prayer. The camp fire and the silence of the bush, broken only by the weird clang of the bullock bell, invested the figure of this wrestling Jacob with strange interest. It was "John Smith" of Byaduk, at his evening devotions. He was on his way with the team to the diggings, and the fervour of his spirit then and often caused him to pray aloud. The scene and prayer recalled other days, revived former impressions, and re-touched a chord which had long lain silent and unstrung. He was brought again to rejoice in God his Saviour, and became an active labourer and acceptable Local Preacher in Penshurst, Hamilton, Horsham, Warragul, etc. The Rev. J. W. Tuckfield was the first resident Minister at Penshurst. In his time a gracious revival took place, and amongst those converted were Earl, Deutscher, Schonfeldt, and others who have kept the faith and abide unto this day. In 1871, Penshurst began its career as a separate Circuit, with the Rev. T. Adamson its first Superintendent. Churches were now built at Dunkeld, Yuppeckiar, Hawksdale, etc. The Circuit has long been in an easy position, thanks to the steady and generous help of Silas Harding and Co. The Circuit is fortunate in having such living and active friends as Messrs. R. Howell, Woodburn, M'Intyre, Thurgood, Cameron, and others. Mr. R. Howell, of Devon Park, has fostered the rising interests of this Circuit by his unwearied labours as a Local Preacher, and by his munificent gifts and hospitality. This healthy neighbourhood has proved a choice nursery and training school for Ministers' wives, for Mesdames Hunter and Reed, of South Australia, and Leslie, of the Blackwood Circuit, were of families resident in this Circuit. In that respect it has been a garden of the Lord.

MERINO.—In the "minutes" of 1864 the words "one wanted" stand against the Portland Circuit, evidently referring to Merino, which had just before been visited by the Rev. F. Tuckfield, and afterwards by the Rev. J. B Smith from Portland, and then in 1866 by the Rev. W. L Blamires and R. M. Hunter, from Hamilton. Mr. Blamires preached in the Presbyterian Church, Merino, and then in the Anglican Churches, at Digby and Casterton, by the kind permission of the late Rev. Dr. Russell, a true "father in God" for the large district of the Wannon, a man of Christian spirit and liberal views, and greatly respected by all classes. Further visits followed and services were held at Casterton, Merino, Rifle Downs, etc. In 1867, Merino was made a Circuit with the Rev. R. M. Hunter, its first Minister. In 1868, the Merino Church, a "dummy" and blank for beauty, was built and opened. The tea meeting was held in the billiard room of Mackwood's Hotel, and addressed by Mr. P. Learmonth, chairman, and Messrs. J. J. Watsford, Hunter, and J. B. Smith. During the years which followed up to 1882, Churches were built at Digby, Coleraine, Casterton, etc. Mr. Hunter was indefatigable in his labours, and very popular. The Rev. James J. Watsford was very earnest, and established what Mr. Hunter founded. Enterprising Ministers followed in the Rev. J. H. A. Ingham, who tried to extend the borders of the Circuit to the northward and met with some adventures on the Chetwynd in doing so, being on one occasion nearly drowned in the Glenelg; in the Rev. E. Orlando Knee, active, genial, sound as a Preacher, and diligent as a Pastor; in the Rev. Robert Brown, vigorous, portly, hearty; and in other young Ministers who found this an excellent field for physical and spiritual exercises. The families of Mr. Mark James and Mr. Maxwell of Coleraine, Illingworth of Casterton, Ford, and Jelbart of Merino, and the Methodist families of Karapook, have been staunch supporters of our work in this Circuit.

OVENS AND MURRAY DISTRICT.

CHAPTER XX.

The site of Beechworth is on the centre of radiating ranges or on a crowning height of surrounding eminences. A high table-land itself, the region immediately adjacent for the most part falls into more or less steep declivities and deep contracted gullies, whilst towards Reed's Creek the landscape is scarped by an immense precipice. Go into it from almost what quarter you may, you can only reach it by climbing miles of steep gradients and winding about gullies and hills. The railway train which has so great a liking for the smooth even track must here go out of its ordinary course of dead level or easy ascent, and the iron horse puffs at a tremendous rate as it is propelled up the steep incline leading out of Tarrawingee plain to the Beechworth table-land. Once reaching it, one is well repaid for the toil. From the township or near to it can be seen the ranges bordering Black Dog Creek and Indigo on the N.W., and those enclosing the upper waters of the Yackandandah and Clear Creeks on the east, whilst further away to the other points of the compass are the Warby Ranges and the magnificent peaks and bluffs of the Buffalo Range. The region of which Beechworth is the metropolis is well watered, in that respect the best in the Colony, next to Gippsland, and the scenery is exceedingly diversified. Hill and dale, plain and vale, high ranges and river flats, towering mountains where the rain-clouds make their home and drop their fatness, and long reaches of levels where rivers such as the Murray, Mitta, Kiewa, Ovens, are in winter time hasting on their racing floods, or in summer wandering lazily along, 'melancholy, slow,' please the eye and inspire the soul of the cultured traveller with their placid grandeur, or impress him with the fertility of the virgin soil and the rich pastures that are spread around. In this district are many tracts of country that well repay the toil of the agriculturist, while others delight the eye of the artist and those spirits which haunt the woods and waterfalls. The changing leafage and verdure, as the seasons keep their march, the beauteous and variegated flowers, when spring has gemmed the carpet of the earth, the clustering grapes, the ripened fruits, the beauteous crops of corn, which show that Pomona and Ceres have been "greeting 'neath autumn's spiriting smile," are a varied, yet complete, rural picture. But the harvest has been gathered only of late years. In the early years of occupation, wool and gold rather than grapes and grain were the prime factors in bringing population and in promoting settlement. The first settlers came across the Murray border, somewhat in the track of Messrs. Hovell and Hume, and Sir Thos. Mitchell. Mr. Faithful, one of the pioneers, met with a tragic fate early in the period of settlement, being killed by the black natives. Other settlers, such as Mackay, Reid, Osborne, Mitchell, (of Little River), had more peaceful and prosperous times, but the region was sparsely occupied until the era of the gold discoveries. Adventurers, as hardy and busy as the first settlers, although more migratory, came at the beck of gold. The *"auri fames"* brought first a few prospectors then a horde of gold diggers, who searched the gullies and climbed the hills and spread over table-lands and "flats," wheresoever it was likely that gold could be found. An early encampment of them took place at Reed's Creek, and its upper part, entitled Spring Creek. Very rich yields were found by the lucky delvers who came first, turning over the earth and making it into mounds and anthills in search of the precious metal. At a later period, on the same creek but below the 'woolshed falls,' some almost fabulous amounts were secured by those who paddocked, that is took out rectangular blocks of the surface soil, till, perhaps, at a depth of from 50 to 100 feet, they reached the payable washdirt in which had mingled the golden sands. Later on in years, and lower down the creek in position, the Eldorado, as it was called, became a payable goldfield, costly and difficult in its working, but yielding for a season handsome returns. The alluvial diggings in this region for the most part followed the course of existing streams, and had not that feature, so marked in other regions, of the workings being in old river beds, where the former current, blocked up, had been turned into another and somewhat distant channel by lava or basaltic overflow, or by freak, convulsion, or other action of nature, so that the old stream having laid its deposit of gold had been thrust aside and left a dry channel or gutter, where exploring diggers or miners could find the stored-up treasure on which their hearts were set. From a claim on the Woolshed Creek (that is, Reed's Creek in its lower part) a few yards in length, were taken out by Johnson & Co. some £70,000 in a few months' of working. Other claims near to this worked by Messrs. Cameron, Lonie, Strickland, Chandler and others were almost equally rich.

Beechworth was the name given to the Government township surveyed near the Spring Creek diggings. It is a splendid spot for a town, and has been much beautified and adorned with the nice cottage residences, wide streets, having substantial stores and shops, and the trees, mostly from stocks that are indigenous to other lands, that have luxuriantly grown up within its precincts.

Methodists were among the swarm of diggers that came to Spring Creek in 1852-3. Amongst the first arrivals belonging to our Church, and who stayed sufficiently long to take part in founding and establishing the local church. were Messsrs. Chas. Williams, E. Abbot, Coade, Gillard, Hunt, Stevens, Reynolds, Taylor, Symons, Tinckler. Mr. C. Williams had been a prominent member of the Church in Tasmania, on his removal to Spring Creek (or May Day Hills as the locality of Beechworth was then called), in 1852, he commenced services by taking his stand under a gum tree in Madman's Gully, and with Bible and Hymn Book in hand he sang, prayed, and expounded the Word of God. He describes the prevailing indifference to religion and wickedness. "At this time I had no one to help me, most about me were engaged, some in cutting wood, others in cleaning gold, others were drunk and fighting, but no one interrupted me, and a few gathered round me." The services were continued and the gathering increased in number on the subsequent Sabbaths, so that he felt emboldened to purchase a large tent for £20 and fit it up for use as a place of worship. Some friendly miners cut slabs and made seats without charge. Shortly after a Local Preacher from Cornwall came to his help, and then a second from another part who rendered important aid, so that the Sunday Services were regularly kept up. It was the old story repeated. The private member and the Local Preacher extemporized services, gathered the band of praying people together, founded the Church, and then sought the aid of the Minister and the full development of Christian ordinances. No stationed Minister was nearer than Mt. Alexander or Melbourne in a southward direction, although Ministers of other Denominations were, we believe, by this time living in Albury. The lay brethren sustained the services for nearly two years before any Ministerial visit was paid to them. Application, however, to the Chairman of the District was made for the appointment of a Minister, and one was promised on the arrival of six Ministers expected from England. As a proof of the eagerness of Mr. C. Williams herein, he gave liberally to the expense of these gentlemen in their cost of transit from the old country, and then, on the arrival of the Rev. Mr Akrill, provided for him, for six months, free of charge. Meanwhile Mr. Williams had procured first the use of an auction room lent for the holding of the meetings, and then with others set about the erection of a substantial schoolhouse of wood which cost from £1,100 to £1,200. Contributions of £50 each from Mr. Williams, Mr. A. Palmer, Mr. E. Vickery headed the list, and many others gave handsome donations. This school was erected on the valuable and central block of land on which our Church premises now stand. It was the only place of worship in the town for several years. Early in 1854 Mr. Butters came on a visit to induct the promised Minister, Mr. Akrill. The journey was a difficult and formidable one, and accompanied with a few adventures of rough shaking and peril incident to the travel of those days, but they arrived duly and safely in Beechworth, to the great joy of the little flock which had been long awaiting them. The stay of Mr. Butters was short, but he visited Snake Valley (now Stanley) and Yackandandah, and good meetings were held there, but nothing remarkable or immediate came as the fruit of them. Unfortunately, for this small society, the mental and physical health of Mr. Akrill proved unequal to the strain of this pioneer work to which he was called. After a stay of a few months, temporary mental aberration compelled his absence from Beechworth, and finally from the Colony. This was a sad sequel to so promising a beginning, and much disheartened the few members. It was found impossible to procure another Minister for some time, yet again thrown on their own resources, the active members manfully grappled with the difficulty, and Messrs. Abbot and Gillard, with the help of Mr. Symons, preached regularly for some months, so that the services were maintained. Mr. and Mrs. Brooke had been appointed Master and Mistress of a day school opened in the Wesleyan building and did much for the education of the rising youth of the neighbourhood during several years. Mr. John Wilton with his amiable wife succeeded them. In October, 1855, the Rev. Mr. Symons paid a visit as the substitute for the Rev. Mr. Draper, who was prevented from fulfilling personally his engagement because of sudden illness. This Minister found the travel rough and uncomfortable even for his experience. Jolting over bad roads and bush tracks, wading through creeks, threading the forest by the light of lamps which made the dimness a little way off denser and darker, rattling along at the rate of ten miles an hour, just clearing the stumps, avoiding the trees, falling into the ruts, the coach kept marvellously on the right track, during a ride which lasted night and day for about forty hours. This was a feat of endurance for the traveller not to be welcomed every day, but nevertheless having its enjoyment as a variety in travel. As the Jehu had a parson under his care, probably for the first time on this line of road, he managed to get his coach bogged in a creek about three in the morning. It was a good experiment to see whether the parson would sink or swim, or what he would do under the circumstances. He turned to with the others to get the coach out, wading up to his knees in water, until after an hour's immense effort the coach was hoisted on to solid land, and the travellers continued on their way. Mr. Anthony Trollope many years afterwards wrote of travel in Victoria :—"A Victorian Coach with six or perhaps seven or eight horses, in the darkness of the night, making its way through a thickly-timbered forest at the rate of nine miles an hour, with the horses frequently up to their bellies in mud, with the wheels running in and out of holes four or five feet deep, is a phenomenon which I should like to have shown to some of those very neat mail coach drivers whom I used to know at home in the old days. I am sure that no description would make any one of them believe that such feats of driving were possible. I feel that nothing short of seeing it would have made me believe it."

This long and fatiguing journey mentioned brought Mr. J. C. Symons to kind friends and a hospitable home and people at the end. He preached in Beechworth on one Sabbath and opened a small Church in Albury on the next, and visited the Woolshed (on Reed's Creek), Yackandandah and Snake Valley diggings, and spent about ten days altogether in this part. This visit led to his appointment here in 1856, and to his residence for three years.

Mr. Symons was appointed to this Circuit (if so it could then be called, which had but one outlying preaching appointment beyond Beechworth) in the year 1856. He brought his power of administration and business habits to work the usual machinery of our Societies and to build a new Church. This was opened on Easter Day, 1857, by services conducted by the Rev. D. J. Draper. This enterprise of building was accomplished by the aid of liberal contributions from the members and adherents, but as the outlay was large and the building costly, a considerable debt was left to after-times. When this new Church of stone was erected, business was brisk, Beechworth was very flourishing, the storekeepers were doing a fine trade with the country round, the Woolshed diggings were at their best, besides fair prosperity at the Nine-Mile, Yackandandah, and Buckland goldfields, so that the debt, which appeared to be relatively light in those prosperous times, became burdensome in the depressed times that came in after years. Beechworth had several strong business firms then connected with the Wesleyan Church, so that money was plentiful to sustain the Minister and carry on building operations. Indeed, in his first year of residence, Mr. Symons' stipend was fully met by the income derived from marriage fees, which, with the Wesleyans in this Colony, have been diverted from the private fee of the Minister to the ordinary income of the Quarter Board which supports the Minister. This has been done by the concurrence of the Ministers concerned, who simply ask from their congregations a regular and sufficient income for their family wants and the needs of a respectable appearance in society. The lucky diggers in those early days not infrequently gave £10 as a marriage fee, so that the amount derived from fees was a considerable source of Circuit income. Mr. Symons is always an instructive Preacher, and frequently deals in the pulpit with topics of the day, so that the congregation was well fed and sustained during his stay. He sought the mental improvement of the people and gave, now and again, his interesting lectures on "Nineveh," "Plurality of Worlds," etc., etc. These were chiefly given in connection with a Young Men's Association, which had, as the writer remembers, young and middle-aged men enrolled in its list, some of whom have attained to positions of eminence in the Legislature and Government of the Colony, as the Hons. G. B. Kerferd and J. McKean. As Mr. Symons helped to start the Young Men's Christian Association in London, he might be expected to have a fatherly interest in them on this side of the world. The chief workers and supporters amongst the laymen at this period were Messrs. J. Wilton, C. Williams, Hunt, McLean, Nixon, J. Higgins, W. Higgins, Taylor, Gregory, Coade, Abbott. The Local Preachers were Abbot, Symons, Tinckler, Gillard, Bailey, and one or two others. There was but little opportunity for these brethren to exercise their gifts, as few places were on the Circuit plan. Beechworth was a Circuit with big head and puny body. Mr. Blamires came in May, 1857, to assist Mr. Symons in the working of the Circuit. Then, in addition to Stanley and the Woolshed, Yackandandah was taken amongst the preaching appointments. At the Woolshed was a canvas tent as preaching place and a feeble cause, which latter in a year or two dwindled away as the population went farther down the creek. The Stanley cause remained stationary for many years, but afterwards developed into a strong society. At Yackandandah Mr. Blamires opened the ground by preaching at the township, first in the open air, then in the billiard room of Jarvis' Hotel, and also in a Restaurant at Allen's Flat, five miles down the creek from the town. A few scattered Wesleyans were drawn together as a congregation, of which one or two, as Meldrum and some of his relatives, had been members in other places, but as yet no stable class could be formed. However, from this time a hold was kept upon the people, the fervour and power of the Methodist preaching began to tell, and under following Ministers and Agents the Methodist tree struck root, branched out, blossomed, and bore fruit, so was formed the Yackandandah Circuit. But the ploughing throughout the early period was on hard soil. Mammon largely and strongly held the ground. Yet the servants of God ploughed in hope. A few conversions took place, some souls were saved by pastoral visitation and in the sick room, but no revival came. Indeed, we are not aware that any great revival powerfully moving many classes and great numbers of the people has marked the annals of

s

Beechworth Methodism until a very recent day, during the visit of the young Evangelist, Mr. Nall. A gracious work has taken place from time to time in several places, and Eldorado was the scene of a great awakening of sinful men and in-gathering of converts during the time of the Rev. J. D. Dodgson's Ministry, but the Ovens and Murray Methodist District had not been swept over by a tide of revival until the visit of the young Minister abovenamed, in the years of grace, 1883-4.

Prior to Mr. Symons' leaving, as his health required rest and change, the Rev. E. B. Burns was sent as a supply, and exercised an acceptable Ministry for some months. Then the Rev. J. W. Crisp was welcomed as the next Minister, and his stirring activity caused the branching out of the Circuit to Chiltern, Growler's Creek, and other outlying parts. The Rev. Robert S. Bunn was stationed at Yackandandah in 1861, and the little Church grew in numbers and piety under his fostering care. Mr. W. Welshman then joined the Church. When Mr. Crisp left the Beechworth Circuit the returns had increased to 7 Churches, 6 other preaching places, 111 members and 40 on trial. The Rev. Geo. B. Richards was his successor, and the Rev. Thos. Kane, was also appointed as the third Minister, but this added to the financial burdens by the swift increase in the Ministerial staff, so that the Circuit was presently under the incubus of a heavy debt. Nobly Mr. Richards met the difficulty and travelled hundreds of miles in his efforts and excursions to extend the work and secure aid in removing the debt. His success was worthy of his effort. Ere he left Beechworth the debt was gone. The slowly-moving chariot wheels of the sun had gone their three courses all too quickly, in the estimation of the people, when the time for Mr. Richards' removal came, for he was held in great regard for his courteous spirit, faithful preaching, and indefatigable exertions. The Revs. D. Annear, James Taylor, and Thomas Edmeades had been his colleagues in the work of a very widespread Circuit.

In these years, Mr. Morrison, Local Preacher, would occasionally ride sixty miles on the Saturday from Yackandandah to the district of Growler's Creek and the Buckland, ride several miles and hold services on the Sunday, and return over the sixty miles on the Monday. Others showed a similarly laborious and self-denying example to further the cause of Christ in outlying regions. It was time that the extensive Circuit was divided. In 1865 the appointments of Conference were—Beechworth, Andrew Inglis; Growler's Creek, Thomas Edmeades; Albury, Francis Neale. This latter location, especially, gave a new impetus to the work in Albury. Influential laymen rallied round Mr. Neale, in the persons of Dr. Hutchinson, Mr. Blackmore (Mayor for one year), Mr. H. Moffit, Mr. Samuel Burke, Mr. H. Lumley, and others. By the end of the year a new Church had been built, and was consecrated to Divine Worship by services held on December 3rd. Dr. Waugh, then President of the Wesleyan Conference, was the Officiating Minister. This was a centre from which Methodism spread to Wodonga, Indigo Creek, Corowa, Bethanga, and other places on the Murray River, or on tributary streams.

GROWLER'S CREEK Circuit had several changes of name, becoming Morse's Creek in 1866, and afterwards being designated Wandiligong and Bright Circuit. It embraces a considerable territory nigh to the Ovens River in the upper reaches of it. It has extended from Harrietville, bordering the high and snowy ranges to Myrtleford in the Ovens Valley. Messrs. Gillard, Nuttall, Cook, Schofield, have been devoted laymen who have wrought with others to make this the flourishing Circuit, with its fine central Church and outlying stations, which it has become. The Revs. T. Grove, D. Annear, J. Seccombe, Henry Moore, W. Williams, A. Inglis, H. Merriman, C. Sanders, W. S. Worth, and R. Osborne Cook have been successively the Pastors.

ELDORADO AND WANGARATTA were integral parts of the Beechworth Circuit for a time, afterwards they were formed with Everton into a Circuit. Whilst Eldorado was flourishing as a mining community it was the head of the Circuit, but since its decline, and the steady growth of the neighbouring agricultural township, Wangaratta has become the chief place. It has a neat and beautiful edifice as a Wesleyan Church, opened in 1885. Messrs. Sennett and Foxcroft have been useful supporters of the Church and active labourers in this township and Circuit. The Revs. C. H. Ingamells, W. Burridge, J. Adams, J. A. Osborne, may be named as active Ministers in this region.

BENALLA was long left untouched by the Wesleyans, although as a township it dates prior to Beechworth. But when agricultural settlement took place so extensively upon the Broken River and in the Goulburn Valley, and in the places adjacent, Methodism sent its forces to occupy those fields contained now in the Benalla and Shepparton Circuits and the Yarrawonga Home Mission. Benalla was the first station occupied by the Wesleyan Home Missionary Society of Victoria, and the Agent selected, Mr. Donnes, was peculiarly fitted for pioneer work. Full of grace, ardent by disposition, with indomitable zeal, he soon planted the Methodist stock in Benalla, Euroa, and other places, and after some years of successful labour he handed over the Station in so flourishing a state to his successor that it was at once equal to the support of a married Minister. He was assisted by many good laymen, and the Benalla Circuit continues one of the most prosperous in the Ovens and Murray District. The region between the Goulburn River and the Murray River has been strongly occupied by Methodism, owing largely to energetic young Ministers as the Revs. John J. Brown, D. S. Lowe, J. Nall, S. Cuthbert, A. M'Callum, and D. J. Flockart, and the influx of many earnest Laymen. The Shepparton and Numurkah Circuits are prospering, and have well repaid the zealous labour spent upon them.

The whole District received a great impetus by a recent visit of the Evangelist, the Rev. Mr. Nall. When that form of Agency was decided upon by the Conference, this was the first District to which Mr. Nall was sent, and he fully proved the wisdom of his appointment, and the fire and fitness with which he could carry on such work by conducting a most successful Mission in the several Circuits of the District. The results of that Mission and the transfer of the Shepparton Circuit, formerly pertaining to another District, have made this Ovens District, formerly weak in numbers, to become of the respectable numerical strength of over 1,000 members and 6,600 adherents. Methodism was attracted to this region at first because of the mining adventures and settlements, but it now finds its chief strength in the agricultural areas. The District is well watered, or capable of advantageous irrigation at relatively small cost, so it is likely to support a prosperous farming population, for centuries to come. The Methodist Tree has been firmly planted, has taken deep root, and will flourish with the District. Its fruit in an orderly, strong community, will be " unto holiness, and the end everlasting life." Many that have sat, and will sit, under its branches with delight will eat of the tree of life in the paradise of God.

NORTH WESTERN CIRCUITS.

CHAPTER XXI.

ARARAT was the first part occupied by the Methodists in that wide region adjacent to the Grampians which lies to the east, north, and west of that Mountain range. The rush of miners had brought thousands of people to the Ararat goldfield in 1855-6. Amongst these some earnest Methodists instituted the public worship of God, and their social means of grace. The first place of worship erected was the Wesleyan Chapel, towards the end of the year, 1856, a Sunday School was established, and 18

Members met in Class. When the people dispersed and migrated in quest of gold, the Chapel was taken down, and the services on the Lord's Day were conducted for a while in the open air. In June 1857, the Chapel was again erected on the Canton Lead. The population increased, and the accommodation was too scanty in the canvas tent, so it was superseded by a larger structure, one of weatherboard which could seat 200 persons, and cost £160. This sum was raised by the time the opening services had been completed. Mrs. Wardman of Cathcart near to Ararat, was one of the first to open her place or tent for preaching, and gather together the few young people for a Sunday School. She is a fine spirited woman, shrewd, hearty, with good business capacity and earnest piety. Her Yorkshire Methodism shewed itself of a hardy stock when transplanted to this new soil. For over twenty years, she has been an earnest Teacher and Class Leader at Cathcart and Stawell. Other Methodists had banded together at Ararat, so that when the Rev. W. C. Currey visited the place in March, 1858, journeying overland from Belfast, he found a neat building as a Chapel, and a cluster of members joined in church fellowship. He preached on Sunday, 11th, and in the Evening administered the Sacrament of the Lord's Supper to 35 persons. The Rev. W. Calvert from the Avoca Circuit was expected on the following Sabbath. Mr. Currey states that at the time of his visit Ararat had 52 hotels, 40 doctors, and an indefinite number of lawyers but only one Minister of the Gospel. At the time of his visit Ararat was losing its population through the scarcity of water; and about 20,000 persons had congregated at Pleasant Creek, 18 miles to the northward. The Wesleyans amongst this mass of people had repeated their tactics and efforts; they stood up as witnesses for truth and righteousness, gathered a congregation; put up a tent as preaching place, and then sent off a message to the nearest Circuit for Ministerial help. This cry "Come over and help us" was heard at Avoca. The " Cooee" from the Grampians was echoed by the

Pyrenees. The Rev. William Woodall, an earnest Minister recently from England, then living at Avoca, took counsel with his Superintendent, the Rev. J. Albiston, and it was agreed that the former should respond to the call from the westward. Accordingly, one Sunday morning Mr. Woodall started *en route* for Pleasant Creek ignorant alike of the way and the distance to be traversed. He however arrived at his proper destination about 7 o'clock in the evening after a wearying ride of over 50 miles, and found himself the welcome although unexpected guest of Mr. Brown, storekeeper. The same evening he went to the Canvas Church and found a number of people met for prayer, and he was glad to join in their petitions that the tent they had erected might become a Bethel to many a weary Jacob, and the birthplace of many souls. The Minister's coming was a surprise to the people, but the occasion of great joy. The next day the opening Services were held, and the gladness of both pastor and flock was greatly augmented, as several persons were converted. Amongst the number was one who became a Minister of the Methodist Free Church, the Rev. D. Porteous. The place cost £110, and was estimated to hold between 200 and 300 persons. Another place of worship was opened by Mr. Geo. Middleton (now of Carlton) on June 31st, 1858, at Cathcart, and a Sunday School was gathered. Preaching was also begun at Great Western, midway between Ararat and Pleasant Creek, and by March 1859, a tent had been set up for worship, and from its first site had been removed to a spot more convenient for the population. Mr. Middleton, as Local Preacher, and Class Leader, was held in the highest esteem, and was unwearied in his labour. He was a wise counsellor, and most acceptable Preacher. After Mr. Woodall's first visit he came once a month, until, on the petition of the people, he was appointed as the Circuit Minister in December, 1859. He took cheerfully the oversight of the work and the care of the Churches. Around the preaching of Christian truth and doctrine as a centre, he set in motion branching and radiating Christian ordinances and activities, which, as wheels to a conveyance, made the Chariot of the Gospel move onward. He had willing helpers in the Local Preachers who not only conducted Sabbath Services, but gave freely of their money to build the Churches. A devoted Class Leader, Mr. Batten, did the work of erecting a Church at Canton Lead, free of expense to the Society. Preaching was begun at Moyston and Armstrongs, and at many places now embraced in the Ararat and Stawell Circuits. At Moyston the Methodist Church owes much to the liberality of Mr. M. Bowe and Mr. and Mrs. Clarke, of Lexington Station, who have also been most bountiful in their entertainment of the several Ministers and visitors who came to conduct services at the house or Church. Mrs. Wardman gave Mr. Woodall a home under her hospitable roof for several weeks. The grace of liberality has been conspicuous in the history of these Circuits. Yet they have had their financial difficulties. In after years the new Church at Ararat had a heavy burden of debt. In Stawell also, the strain for the reduction of Church liabilities and the support of the Minister by one congregation has been severely felt, especially in times of mining depression. Those were the struggles of after years. Of the early Churches, Mr. Woodall writes—"The Canvas and Wooden Churches of those days, with their benches having no backs, with their gravel floors, were indeed unpretentious Sanctuaries, but God made them glorious with His presence and by manifestations of Christ's power to save. Young and old, the miner in his jumper, and the Bank Manager in his broadcloth alike knelt at the penitent form and found mercy."

The second Church at Pleasant Creek was of corrugated iron but having the front of weatherboard. The Rev. C. Lane opened it on February 5th, 1860, it was displaced by a better structure of brick at a subsequent date. Another Church, this time of wood, was opened at Great Western on Sept. 28th, 1862, by Rev. A. Inglis. That has been superseded by one of brick, built quite recently. The substantial Church at Moyston, of brick, was opened on 30th March, 1863, and cost £363.

The Rev. Charles Dubourg succeeded Mr. Woodall, and as the strength of the Circuit was at Pleasant Creek, he resided there. He was indefatigable in his labours, and could report, when he left, some 6 Churches, 50 members, and 700 adherents. The Rev. Andrew Inglis kept well in the lines of his predecessor, but also extended the Circuit. Progress was made on the whole, and a second Minister was obtained in 1863, in the person of the Rev. Jas. A. Taylor, who lived at Ararat. For a season the cause here had been feeble and knew many of the fluctuations which marked goldfields' history in the early time. In 1863, the congregation had no settled home, but worshipped now in one building and then in another. Soon after Mr. Taylor's arrival another Church was erected which did service until the present commodious one of brick was erected in Mr. Fitcher's time. The Superintendent for the most part resided at Pleasant Creek, but in the early part of Mr. Catterall's term his residence was at Ararat. Under that energetic Minister a new Parsonage was built at Stawell (formerly Quartz Reefs, Pleasant Creek) which then became the permanent residence of the Superintendent. In succession to Mr. Inglis were the Revs. E. B. Burns, J. Catterall, W. Brown and W. L. Blamires as Superintendents. During the latter Minister's stay, the Circuit was divided, and Ararat with adjacent places, was made an independent Circuit with Rev. Thos. Adamson as Minister. The membership for the whole Circuit was 125, at the Conferenee of 1863, which had increased to 279, just prior to the division of the Circuit in 1876. Messrs. W. Brumby and C. C. Forster were active Stewards at Ararat before the division, and more recently at Stawell, whilst other gentlemen, Messrs. Dash, Hillard, Murton, Dungey, in Ararat, M. Lennox, Metcalf and Wilkinson in outlying places, have been zealous labourers. Stawell too has been favoured with earnest workers in Messrs. Rickard, Lodwick, Stephens, Jory, R. Taylor, G. Bond, T. Sussex, T. Hutchings, Dartnell,

Dalkin, Akins, and has for years past had a flourishing congregation and Sabbath School. The residence of Rev. Richard Hart and his family for some years has given an important addition to the strength and activity of this Society. These Circuits have sent three estimable and zealous brethren into the ranks of the Wesleyan Ministry, Messrs. J. A. Marsland, A. R. Edgar, and R. W. Campbell.

HORSHAM.—About 1872, selectors began to occupy the pastoral lands around Horsham that had so long been in the tenancy of the squatters, and some of the first to do so were Wesleyans from the Western District. Messrs. Dyer, Chapple, and Leeson were pioneers of the settlement by farmers, and of the Methodist cause in the neighbourhood of Rupanyup. They had migrated from the Hamilton Circuit. A few Wesleyans were residents in Horsham, Mrs. Bowden, a sister of the Rev. E. E. Jenkins, M.A., Mr. Bond and one or two more, when the Rev. James Hillard was sent by the Conference of 1874, to mission the field. He did this indefatigably, and made an extensive Circuit with preaching stations at Horsham, Rupanyup, Murtoa, Kewell, Kalkee, Warracknabeal, &c. After a year and a half of labour he lost his life by drowning in the River Barwon. He was an estimable and devoted young man. Active young Ministers succeeded in Messrs. A. Powell, J. P. McCann, James Lowe, Wm. Presley, R. Thompson, J. Nall, &c., who worked the ground well, and traversed many miles of country and made many a wearisome journey to supply the Gospel and Christian ordinances to the people. Occupation spread, for the land was found very fertile, and grew splendid crops. Soon church after church was put up in places where preaching had at first been in a cottage or a hall, and at this day three circuits have been carved out of the area first covered by the Horsham Circuit, those of Horsham, Murtoa, and Warracknabeal. This latter place had a few earnest men from the first, who had come from the South Coast and Byaduk. Messrs. Devereux, S. Clarke, and Hayter resided in the town or neighbourhood, and are good men. A promising cause has also been formed at Dimboola. The Wesleyan Home Missionary Society, sent its agents to the regions between Horsham and Dimboola on the east, and the South Australian Border on the west, as such districts became gradually occupied by selectors. Through the labours of Mr. Lee and young Ministers, Messrs. Stafford, Jolly, S. C. Flockart, promising stations or circuits have been formed at Clear Lakes, Lillimur, Nhill, and Harrow and Apsley, which bring our work in touch with that of our Sister Conference in South Australia.

MISSIONS AND MISCELLANEOUS.

CHAPTER XXII.

WE interweave with our narrative some mention of our special missions, the work of Church extension recently made within our borders, and of our attitude to other Christian workers and societies. At an early date the Bethel Flag waved over our Church at Williamstown, and instances of benefit derived by seamen from our church operations are given in former pages. We have heartily supported the Seamen's Mission in the Port of Melbourne, of which the Rev. Kerr Johnston was for so many years the leading spirit, and of which, at the present time, a Wesleyan is the chief agent. Captains M'Callum, Brown, and Matthews were warm friends of the sailor, and active members of our Church. Two of them gave sons to our Ministry. Captain Brown was one of a band of earnest men who helped to "build the temple of our God," a temple of living stones at Emerald Hill (South Melbourne). The writer remembers pulling him through the surf, when his ship, the *Lady Robilliard*, on her last voyage, came ashore

on a stormy night at Portland Bay. That Church at
South Melbourne has had earnest workers connected with
it. A former generation, such as Messrs. Bee, Blair,
Woodfin, Johnson, Elder, Parry, and Morrow have found
worthy successors in the active men of more recent days,
who not only sustain their own enterprises at the parent
Church, but have branched out into new causes at Albert
Park, Boundary-street, Park-street, and in the mission at
York-street. There many trophies of grace have been won.
Mrs. Varcoe, a noble character and active Bible-woman,
in her unwearied efforts for the upraising and salvation of
the rougher and vicious classes, both at South Melbourne
and at Lonsdale-street, Melbourne, has done heroic work
that would place her name alongside those of Miss Macpherson, Miss Ellice Hopkins, Sarah Martin, and other devoted
Christian women of the old country. Captain Matthews
did faithful service at Sandridge (Port Melbourne), where
our Church was first represented by Messrs. Adam and
Newman, the latter being now a veteran of over sixty
years standing as a member, and abiding still at his post.
These, with others, such as Messrs. Poolman, Francis, etc.,
helped to sustain our cause in the midst of the difficulties
which too often beset religion in a busy and profligate seaport. Captain Matthews' son is doing good work as the
founder and manager of the Maloga Mission to the Aborigines on the banks of the River Murray. Our own
BUNTINGDALE MISSION to the Aborigines, with which the
name of the Rev. F. Tuckfield must be ever identified,
deserves to be held in remembrance as a brave and right
noble effort for eight patient years to rescue the perishing
natives, and to "save their souls alive." We can only
mention it in passing, and must refer our readers to the
sketch of the mission published in the *Spectator*. The
following are the titles of the chapters, and may indicate
the scope of the story—" Buntingdale—Previous efforts on
behalf of the Aboriginals—Origin of the Mission—Rev. J.
Orton—Outset of the Mission—Rev. F. Tuckfield—Name

and place—Progress and Encouragement—Incidents and Illustrations—Native Language and Customs—Trials and Perplexities—Other Schemes—Disappointment and Defeat."

Missions to the very poor, and to the lapsed masses are carried on by Miss Brew and Miss M'Lean in Collingwood, and by Miss M'Gahy at Sandhurst. Question may be raised whether we have done as much as we ought in utilizing the willing services of Christian ladies in our Church, yet we have furnished in Mrs. Derrick, Mrs. Williamson, and others, godly women who have laboured under the auspices of Protestant Mission societies. We have given some agents to the Melbourne City Mission, and are in touch and sympathy with all well-directed efforts to reclaim the vicious, and save the lost.

Whilst having special agents and special missions, we have branched out by ordinary Circuit extension to the 'greater' Melbourne of to-day, with its spreading suburbs radiating and growing in all directions. Carlton Church, in its first erection, was opened in January, 1861, with Messrs. A. J. Smith and Jones, as its prominent founders. The first Church has been displaced by a grander building, and the early workers have been succeeded by worthy men in Messrs. Cowperthwaite, Middleton, F. and C. Lavers, Fullerton, Lewis, and Clowes, who have helped to make Carlton a strong cause. Fitzroy has established two new and important societies at Nicholson-street, North Fitzroy, and at Clifton Hill, with which the names of Messrs. Galagher, Guille, Avery, and Abbott are closely identified. Sackville-street has, none too soon, built a new and tasteful Church, and has had steady servants of Christ and His Church in Messrs. Nettleship, Carne, Preston, Latham, Fenton, M'Neilance, Graham, and others. Collingwood has a fine Church at Gipps-street, the outcome of several small causes in the lower part of the city that have been amalgamated. The Church has a large debt, which would have been overwhelming (despite noble efforts of the congregation to grapple with it), but for large connexional assistance rendered. Messrs. Puckey, Wilson, Hendy, Nicholson, and Muntz, with their families, have been strong supporters here. The Hotham Society has become numerous and flourishing in the course of years, and has offshoots at West Melbourne and at Hotham Hill. Messrs. M'Cutcheon, Andrews, Butler, Potts, Moran, Buncle, and Edgerton have been leading members or adherents in these places. Flemington, dating from the fifties, was, for a long time, a feeble cause; but has recently grown apace, and has a younger sister Church at Moonee Ponds so flourishing, that she promises to outgrow the other. Messrs. Colclough, D. Smith, Pearce, Ekman, Edwin Harcourt, and Varey have been prominent laymen connected with these Churches. They, with Kensington, formed into a Circuit in 1883, have since made rapid advances. Brunswick and Coburg have made steady progress since their formation into a Circuit. Messrs. Overend, Bedford, Straw, G. B. Wilson, J. Holloway, and A. Booth have been good supporters. Some are removed to heaven; the survivors are earnest, godly men. The mother Church at St. Kilda has a growing daughter at Balaclava, which has come to a strength, liberality, and enterprise equal to the elder. Messrs. Crouch, M'Cutcheon, and Eggleston are strong names here, with good, venerated Father Ironside, a Minister in a vigorous old age, exercising still a beneficent interest in all departments of the work, and in all public questions of the day. City Methodism, extending her borders, has occupied not only the lowlands near the Saltwater and Yarra rivers, and the coast of the Bay, but also the rising uplands, and pleasant undulating country, which form the eastern and south-eastern suburbs of Melbourne. Prahran Circuit has stretched out to Armadale and Toorak, and the Richmond Circuit has dotted and crowned the pleasant hills of Kew, Camberwell, Box Hill, with neat and spacious Churches.

CHINESE MISSION.—This is another worthy and successful enterprise of our Zion. The mission work amongst the

Chinese began in Castlemaine under the superintendency of the Rev. Thomas Raston. The Rev. Mr. Young, who had been a Missionary in China, under the London Missionary Society, was sent by a united Committee, to open a mission in that town, but he did not stay long, and, we think, was discouraged. Mr. Raston, who had the missionary spirit and zeal strong within him, when Mr. Young withdrew, took the Chinese convert and agent, Leong-a-Toe, under his care, and encouraged him to continue the effort, so feebly begun, for the Christianizing of his countrymen. The Chairman of the District approved, and the Mission committee took the new mission under its fostering wing. The various Churches nigh to which the Chinese most congregated, were thrown open for afternoon service, when they could be gathered together. The number varied from twelve to a hundred persons. Castlemaine was the central station, where service was held regularly, and soon a few began to turn from their heathen practices to worship the true and living God. Mr. Robinson, with a few young men, Graham, Roget, and others would accompany the agent to the Chinese camps to distribute tracts and portions of Scripture printed in the Chinese characters and language. The Chinese appreciated the kindly interest of Europeans in their welfare. (See account in Wesleyan *Chronicle* 1859, pages 43-4.) Soon the converts increased in number and in enlightenment, so that a few were baptized into the Christian Church. At a meeting held in the Wesleyan Church, when some of the converts gave testimony of their former beliefs and habits and the present change in their views, faith, and mode of life, a Chinese merchant from Melbourne acted as interpreter. After the meeting, at the supper table where the merchant was present, a Christian lady asked him, "How is it that you, brought up in a mission school at Singapore, are not a Christian ? The reply was, " Oh, ma'am, 'tis very hard to make money and be a Christian." Certainly, Mammon and Christ are not reconciled to this day as supreme divinities in one and the same heart.

During the term of ministry of Messrs. Raston and Blamires a Chinese Church was built, the first, in Castlemaine, and it is believed, on the Australian Continent. The foundation stone was laid by E. S. Parker, Esq., who presided at the public meeting, when the Church was opened. The Rev. D. J. Draper and the Circuit ministers also made speeches on the occasion, encouraging the Agent and the members to proceed in this mission work. From that time onward, a Chinese Catechist or Minister has been stationed in Castlemaine, and the Wesleyan Church has had Chinese converts to Christianity in membership with her in that town and neighbourhood. In the Church at Castlemaine Leong-a-Toe had a congregation of about forty hearers. At a Missionary meeting on November 16th, he reported that amongst others, five converts baptized into the Christian Church in March previous had continued faithful, and that three or four more were nearly ready for that Christian ordinance and recognition. A considerable number of the Chinese converts returned to China, and of some, tidings were heard that they joined the Christian churches in that land, or were faithful to Christianity, returning no more to the gambling, opium smoking, idol worshipping, and other sins of days gone past. Mr. Leong-a-Toe himself returned to China about 1865. Under date of October 16th, 1866, he addressed a letter from Canton to the Rev. Edward King, then in Castlemaine :—" I have heard from Leong-on-Tong a few months ago, and he said that he was engaged by the Wesleyan ministers to carry on the Chinese mission at Castlemaine; and preach the Gospel to my countrymen there. . . . . I expected to get to China, and ask the Wesleyan ministers here to send some to go over, if I could not return; but Mr. Piercy could not get any one to go over and take charge of the Church, and lately I have heard that the Wesleyan Committee had appointed Leong-on-Tong to carry on the great work under the care of the Rev. Mr. King, so I am glad to give thanks to Almighty God. I pray that he may take care of him, and make him useful to save souls. I believe he is a faithful servant of Christ, and a good Chinese scholar. Now, I think that I shall have no time to go to Castlemaine again, for I preach at Canton in the Mission Hospital, and under the Rev. J. Chalmers and Rev. F. Turner of the London Missionary Society. I live near Mr. Piercy, about three miles off." Leong-on-Tong is well-versed in his language and is of more pleasing features and gentlemanly address than any Chinaman the writer has known. He continued in Castlemaine as the Chinese agent, carrying on the work of Leong-a-Toe, his spiritual father, until the year 1879, when he was removed to Melbourne. The Rev. Josiah Cox, who had been for years a Wesleyan missionary in China, when he visited the colony in 1871, certified to the ability of Leong-on-Tong as a good Chinese scholar; and of the love and ardour with which his spirit entered into this earnest endeavour to win to Christianity the souls of his countrymen, the following may testify. During his probation for the Wesleyan ministry, the writer heard him reply to questions put to him by the Chairman of the District, the Rev. W. P. Wells—" Do you love the Lord Jesus Christ as your Saviour ?" asked the Chairman. He responded in an unstudied and earnest manner, " With all my heart." " Do you love this work of preaching Christ to your countrymen ?" " More than life," was his fervid reply. Rarely has a probationer for the ministry, of the English-speaking race, evinced a more single-minded purpose to glorify God in preaching the Gospel of His Son. Leong-on-Tong could speak English but imperfectly, yet after his probation he married a Chinese lady, we believe, from Singapore, who could speak English fluently, was a fair musician, and was a true help-meet to her husband in his home and in his work. Leong-on-Tong was received as a probationer in 1872, and to the full ranks of the Wesleyan ministry in 1876. He returned to China in 1885.

A young minister from Great Britain, Mr. Caldwell, came to Victoria, and determined to give himself to the Chinese mission. In order to prepare himself in the lan-

T

guage, he went to Canton, and gave himself to study under the tuition of the Rev. George Piercy. But his good purposes, as well as his life, were brought to an untimely end by his death through drowning in the Canton river. A promising career was thus sadly closed, and the oversight of our Chinese work by a European speaking the Chinese language was long delayed. The Church authorities in Victoria had besought such aid from the Parent Missionary Society in London, their hopes were high when Mr. Caldwell came and during his course of study, but they were disappointed and saddened by his sudden removal. Years elapsed before the long-wished-for oversight was obtained, and then it came through the intelligent devotedness of a young Australian. The Rev. Edward Youngman went from Goulburn (N.S.W.) to study under the Wesleyan Missionaries in Canton, and, when equipped for his work, took the care of the Chinese mission in Victoria, and gave an effective oversight to the agents and their operations. Meanwhile, until he came, the Church used, for the best account, the Chinese agents that were at hand. One of the most effective of these was found in the Rev. Jas. Moy Ling. His labours amongst his countrymen have been very useful, and many, by the persuasions of his lips and the earnestness of his spirit, were turned from the worship of idols, and their pernicious habits of life to serve the living God. When the "heathen Chinee" becomes a Christian he presents as fair evidence of sincerity, docility, and honest virtues springing from love to Christ as do the average members of Christian Churches that are of European race. Mr. Moy Ling wrought at Daylesford, Castlemaine, and Sandhurst. Then for several years he conducted the Chinese mission in Melbourne, and was the chief means, in conjunction with Mr. S. G. King and Mr. John Wilton, of the erection of the Chinese Church in Little Bourke-street, Melbourne. As the number of Chinese in the colony had decreased, and it was deemed prudent for purposes of economy, that the number of Agents should be lessened, the Rev. E. Youngman was transferred to New South Wales, to which colony also the Rev. Tear Tack, a young Chinaman, converted in Victoria, was removed. The Rev. Leong-on-Tong preferred to labour in China. The Rev. Moy Ling therefore remains at the head of this mission, and is assisted by Chinese catechists, stationed at Castlemaine, Dunolly, Creswick, and Haddon. The mission increased in numbers steadily for some years, but for four or five years past has remained about the same, and now reports 8 Churches 16 Local Preachers, 112 members, and 306 stated attendants on public worship. The blessing of this mission has extended to adjacent colonies and to some provinces of China.

SOUTH SEA MISSIONS.—Although Victoria is not the seat of the executive of our Foreign Missionary Society, and is more remote from the scene of its operation, yet our people have taken a deep and generous interest in it. Before the Home mission work arose and, to some extent, divided attention, the Missionary meetings were at times enthusiastic and the subscriptions very liberal. Distinguished visitors from the old country and from the mission field as the Revs. Dr. Gervase Smith, E. E. Jenkins, Burgess, Haigh, etc., have kept alive the missionary fire. Our Church, too, in this land has furnished a noble army of able and self-denying men, who have occupied the high places of the mission field. Of these may be mentioned the Rev. Lorimer Fison, M.A., now in charge of a Melbourne Circuit. Mr. Fison is an accomplished scholar and teacher. In conjunction with Mr. Howitt, P.M., he published an able work upon the Aborigines of this Continent. It has been his high honor and life work to train a long succession of Fijian natives for the ministry. He is also an author and authority on Fijian languages and customs, and equally able and esteemed in colonial Circuit work. Other names as Messrs. Carey, Dyson, Lindsay, Langham, Rooney, Greenwood, Danks, Bromilow, and Oldmeadow are suggestive of abundant labour, honor, and success. These were sent forth as missionaries from Victoria, and our Church is proud of them ; at the same time we award a due meed of praise to those Ministers, Revs. Thos. Williams, Samuel Ironside, John Watsford, James S. H. Royce, J. and S. Waterhouse, A. Rigg, and Joseph White, sent forth from England or from neighboring colonies, who gave the flower of their days and their best energies of mind and heart to mission work among the Maoris or the South Sea Islanders.

From an extraneous point of view, our narrative may be regarded as somewhat complacent and self-absorbed, in that it has taken little account of the other religious forces and Christian Churches of the land. But the scope of our plan did not allow us this pleasure. Especially would it have been grateful to refer to our own kindred, the junior branches of the Methodist family, who also have a "story" of labour and success to tell, and have done brave and faithful service in extending the kingdom of Christ in the land. But the exigencies of space forbad it. It has often been questioned, whether the direct influence of Methodism on the world, or its indirect and collateral influence on the Churches has been the greater. It has certainly proved a prolific and propagating Church, its "seed is in itself," "its branches run over the wall," and it has done much to replenish the ranks and pulpits of other Churches, including that last development of militant Christianity—the Salvation Army. It is pretty certain that there are but few active Christians and earnest Churches that have not been indebted, at some point or other of their history, to the influence and example of the Methodist Church. Candid and generous observers will accord it merited praise for the pioneer work it did in this land. It was usually the first in the field, except in the pastoral districts, and with "undistinguishing regard" sought to bless and save all whom it could reach, of whatever class or creed. Hence the mixed and miscellaneous character of our first congregations. In course of time, many gravitated towards their own particular standard whenever it was raised, and were distributed among their several ecclesiastical species, grateful for their temporary accommodation in the Methodist Church, though a few were unmindful of it. Imitation is said to be the sincerest form of flattery, and many have been glad to adopt our methods, and to copy or borrow some features in our financial economy, to wit, the provisions of our Church Loan, and Infirm Ministers', Funds. It is worth a passing glance to note how that *Financial Economy* has been built up. Its present finished form is the result of long years of care and pains. There are those whose hands and hours have been given without stint to the moulding and adjusting of our financial machinery, and who are " worthy of double honor." Among these may be mentioned the Rev. J. Cope, who has given years of patient and exhausting study, and of Herculean labour to the Supernumerary Ministers' Fund; to the Rev. W. P. Wells is due the inception of our Loan Fund, a timely substitute for State aid, and a lasting boon to our Church; while the Rev. W. H. Fitchett deserves the credit of providing a solution of the vexed question of the Children's Fund, and his simple scheme has been favorably quoted, and, to some extent, adopted by our Church in Great Britain. The Rev. John Watsford's name must be always identified with our Home mission work, the Rev. J. C. Symons' with the subject of State education; the names of the Revs. Dr. Waugh, Dr. Watkin, and Messrs. Quick and Fitchett with our Colleges ; while a long list of writers, from the Rev. Dr. Waugh, the first editor to the present one, have given literary labour to the Church, and sought to make our organ, the *Spectator*, a power for good. *Our doctrinal position* has been unchallenged, and few cases of heterodoxy have occurred, thanks to a bright and definite creed tested by an ample and living experience. *Our polity* has been broadened and strengthened by a larger infusion of the lay element, and by wise and liberal legislation. The Rev. Messrs. Symons and Wells have been the chief compilers of a handbook of Methodist laws, issued under the authority of the General Conference. Our Conference was among the first to consider the question of Methodist Union. A Committee of the representatives of all the Methodist Churches was held, and a scheme of union was formulated. It has been sifted, weighed, and analysed with no very definite result. The question of Methodist Union must still be considered an open one. *Our worship* is little changed, except that the liturgy of the Book of Common Prayer, which was used in our leading Church and a few others, has been discontinued in deference to the wishes of a younger generation, but to the deep and lasting regret of others of the older school, who were accustomed to responsive worship. The craving for bright, brisk, brief services, according to the spirit of the age, is met in part by Gospel addresses, Evangelistic bands, and the singing of Sankey's hymns in addition to our own. The *itinerancy* of our Ministers is still a vital and settled part of our system, and, on the whole, was never more tenaciously held. A few have grown weary of it and left us, whether the change is for the better is doubtful. At the same time it must be conceded that the itinerant system is not favorable to sustained study and academic distinction among our young men. Few of them have been able to avail themselves of our University, or pursue an "Arts course." But the intended Affiliated College will, it is hoped, do much to remedy this defect. The same itinerancy may be some bar to local influence and reputation. Our Ministers cannot, except in some few instances, be specialists, or identify themselves with local objects and institutions to the same extent as fixed and permanent Ministers, for, as soon as their individualism and influence assert themselves, they have to move on to the next Circuit. Still many public and philanthropic objects engage the sympathies and services of our Ministers and people, as one may see by noting the services at gaols, refuges, hospitals, asylums, and missions which appear on many of our Circuit plans. What concerns humanity, concerns the Methodist family. In any good work carried on, they would lend a helping hand.

CONCLUSION.

CHAPTER XXIII.

WE must have some regard to our readers' patience, otherwise to what portentous length we might spin out our narrative. We have written about the young days of Methodism in Victoria, but how little about the young Methodists therein. What a fertile theme, their sprightliness, smartness, love for indoor lessons and outdoor sports and other characteristics! The work of God amongst them, and our Sabbath schools—our model ones, such as Yarra-street, Brunswick-street, Lydiard-street; our large ones in South Melbourne, Hotham, Sandhurst; the good work of the Sunday school Union of our Church; the glad fact that our losses in the gap between School and Church are far less than in former days, and that now a larger proportion of our scholars are serving Christ and doing work for Him than heretofore; what blessed topics for mind and pen! With a sigh, having regard to our limited space, we forbear.

The employment of lay agents in our Home missions, the great successes of the young evangelists who in the last two or three years have been so honoured of God in their labours :—these too must be reserved for after writers.

Must nothing be written about Methodism in relation to temperance, and literature, and music? its prayer meetings, lovefeasts, class meetings? its pulpit power and platform oratory? its devout sisters, elect ladies, earnest women? its Local Preachers, Home Missionaries, and Lay agency? its care of the poor, its relation to Benevolent institutions and to other Churches, and similar topics? Alas! only a brief mention, where chapters should be written.

Can a sketch of Victorian Methodism omit an extended notice of its distinctive doctrines, or the salient points of its Church polity? We have only space to record that a considerable change took place in the constitution of our Church, in the years 1873-5, when general Conferences for legislation, and annual Conferences for administration, were inaugurated, and a larger introduction of the lay element into the higher courts of the Church was made.

Our Church polity is based upon the New Testament recognition of the functions of the pastoral office, combined with widening regard for the increasing intelligence, scriptural rights, and spiritual welfare of the members and laity. It is conservative in its tenacious clinging to fundamental principles, but expansive and elastic in its adaptation to the varying circumstances, and liberal spirit of the times. Happily we have been spared the dissensions which have occurred in other lands upon points of Church government, and the Methodist polity approves its suitability to the people of the Southern world, by growing symmetrically, and expanding gradually, without altering its model forms, its type, its nature. It has central points, which are fixed, yet its boundary lines are not stiff, rigid, unbending but elastic, yielding, accommodating. It has wrought well for the peace and prosperity for the Church, and the spread of godliness in these lands.

The Methodist Church has been noted for its hearty belief in, and earnest clinging to, Arminian views of theology in the century and a half of its existence. It has had extremely little of heresy to deal with, and is not in its doctrine, given to change. This fixity of doctrinal teaching is owing largely to the creed fitting so closely to Scripture, and standing so well the test of experiment as applied to the spiritual needs and aspirations of men. Such facts most of our own writers upon Methodist affairs have observed, but it has not been noted as frequently what an important influence our itinerancy has had upon similarity of doctrinal teaching amongst us. Some one has remarked, "It is by fluctuation that all things become fixed, it is by restlessness that they become permanent." This is exemplified in the influence of the itinerancy upon the settlement of doctrine. A man preaching to one congregation for many years, may, if he change his own views, gradually and almost imperceptibly change theirs. He may lead them into by-ways of theology, and mould them after his own mind, vagrant or steady as that may be. But a man preaching before many congregations is kept to their common standard of doctrine, is himself shaped after their common standard of thought. He must be very original, and determined, to alter the views of many intelligent congregations, unless his views are demonstrably much nearer the truth than theirs. Any variation from accepted doctrine which may pass with one congregation will not pass without comment and criticism before many similar assemblies. He will find the many will not tolerate the vagaries which the one may. This, with the annual examination of Ministerial character and belief taking place in the District meeting and Conference, accounts largely for the fixity of doctrine and teaching in the Wesleyan Church. Strong men, and subtle minds therein, such as Dr. Clarke and Dr. Pope, have alone been suffered to differ, and that only in minor points, from the accepted standards of truth and doctrine, and these have scarcely inoculated two men besides with their peculiar views. The neat, orderly type of Wesley has stamped itself upon his followers, his conservative yet free spirit, holding fast by old landmarks, but open to conviction and slowly adapting new measures, works in them still. And his system of itinerancy, bringing new Ministers interchangeably to work with new colleagues, and to appear before many congregations, is likely to work for many generations to come in fixing the grand old Methodist doctrines in the heads, hearts, and experiences of both Ministers and people.

Good and well adapted as may be the Church polity and administration, and scriptural as may be the doctrine, they avail little without the spirit of piety. This record goes to show that the leaven of an active cheerful godliness has wrought in the Methodist Church, that the spirit of a hopeful aggressive Christianity has inspired her labours, and brought about her successes. Scriptural holiness is the test of a rising or falling Church, more even than the doctrine of justification by faith, and other cardinal truths.

The Methodist Church is a growing one, and it will grow, through God's blessing, long as the spirit of scriptural, experimental, and practical Christianity is cherished therein.

We are apt at times to speak highly of the influence for good which our beloved Methodism has been in the world, and so that we do not vainly and vaingloriously boast thereof, we have right and reason to speak of her position and power. For Methodism has inscribed her name, not only upon the surface, but upon the heart of society. Under God, she is affecting for good the institutions of the age, and helping to mould the character of the people. The pulsations of her religious life, like the lifeblood coursing through the arteries and veins, are felt to remote extremities. In the place of her birth she has made a noble stand for truth, and occupies that foremost position in every good work which makes her to be praised of good men, and she has spread out her children to many continents of the earth and islands of the sea. God can do without her, but not man. Were her agencies removed, her peculiar institutions set aside, her light extinguished, and her members lost to the Church of Christ, a great void would be made in that Church, and a great desolation in the earth. God, employing secondary means out of the exuberance, not out of any poverty of His resources, and having the choice of means, can at any time raise up a religious body, marked by an active and aggressive Christianity; but the Church itself can ill spare any zealous body of Christians, or any section thereof, that is living and working for the glory of Christ.

God has blessed and is blessing the institutions and agencies of Methodism to the salvation of men; and whilst we hold fast pure and undefiled religion, we believe that a great work and blessed destiny await us in the future.

The providence of God has raised us up as a Church, and brought us together as a people, for some high and gracious purpose in the extension of His kingdom on earth.

We mark this wonderful providence in the history of the colony. He did not design that the wide pastures and extensive tracts of land in this beauteous and diversified country should be ever the roaming haunts of the emu, or the feeding-ground of the kangaroo. " The earth hath He given to the children of men." He fitted it up for their habitation, and spread it out as goodly land for their possession; and when men were slow to colonize, or when a few would fence the land in as an immense domain for the settler and his sheep, then, by causing the discovery of the wondrous deposits of gold that had for ages been hid in the bowels of the earth, He drafted off the needy, adventurous, and enterprising myriads of other lands, so that this land should be replenished with a numerous and increasing population, and the field for industry and civilization which it presents should be well occupied by a thriving and energetic people. Providence has brought from various continents and climes a large body of men of different races, and speaking different languages (but with the Anglo-Saxon vastly predominating in speech and blood), so as to form one homogeneous mass, and be blended into one great nation which should be in the van of all true progress in the southern world. And the same wise and good Providence has brought and is welding together, in order to make the distinctive and flourishing Methodism of Victoria, representatives from many families of the human race. Our local Methodism has combined in it the vivacity and wit of the Irish, the shrewdness of the Scotch, and the manly perseverance of the English; the robust steadiness of the German and the Dane (strange to say, an American is a rarity amongst us), with a fair sample of what we may call native growth, distinguished, perhaps, like mercury among the metals, for its small attachment for any one place, and its ready amalgamation with any other people. Amongst the English, or those of English extraction, we have the fervour of the Yorkshireman, the steadiness of the Northumbrian, the liberality of the Londoner, the impulsive heartiness of the Cornish, the independence of those from the North, the docility of those from the South of England, the plodding habits of men from the East, combined with the fire and zeal of those from the West. Such are the elements making up Victorian Methodism; and we believe that to this Church a noble duty and destiny are allotted by Divine Providence.

Our Church's duty is to lay well and soundly the foundations of Methodism, and to be diligent pioneers of spiritual work in all parts of the colony; to make right materials for history; to exemplify a beautiful, beneficent, and spiritual piety which shall be a pattern to those who follow.

We cannot point back to any antiquity as a people or Church in this land. We cannot refer with reverence to any sanctuary of centuries ago, as "our holy and our beautiful house, where our fathers praised Thee." We cannot say in relation to any work of God in this land, dating from ages back, whose blessed fruits have descended to us, "Other men laboured," and we are "entered into their labours." No grey fathers of bygone generations are looking down upon us. We are but as of yesterday. Our lineage is a short one; our history, as yet, but a brief one. We have no venerable piles, no ancient temples bearing upon them the grey moss of time; no classic or sacred spots that we can visit, where noble deeds or noble names associated with them come crowding in upon the memory or mind, and make us feel that we tread as on hallowed ground. We are young. We have everything to create. We look as young hopefuls to the future, rather than as grey-beards who recall and rehearse the facts of the past time.

We accept the responsibilities of the position. We may be tremulous as we feel our weakness, and in some degree realize the issues which depend on our right conduct; nevertheless, we look to God to strengthen and aid us, to work in us and work by us for the establishment of a vigorous and aggressive Church, which shall be a blessing to thousands yet unborn, and whose right influence shall be felt in every corner of the land.

A poet has said—

" 'Tis the sunset of life gives me mystical lore,
  And coming events cast their shadows before."

We might alter and accommodate these lines to our circumstances, and say—

" 'Tis the sunrise of life makes historical lore,
  And coming events cast their shadows before."

When a people or nation is young, it supplies choicest materials for history. The transactions of its early days will be most often recounted, and will stand out very prominent landmarks in the field of the mind's vision or remembrance. The facts of its young life also are pregnant with the character of its future. They cast the mould, or give shape or form to that body of facts which will compose its subsequent history. They shadow forth the substance which is coming after.

The shadow, whilst it gives an outline of, is by no means so beautiful as the substance. The shadow of a flower, dim and black, is no where so fair as the flower itself in its variegated and harmonized colours and beautiful array. The shadow of a man is sombre, and oft distorted in figure, as compared with the "lord of creation" in his erect stature, noble form, and bright and manly countenance.

So we would like to prophecy and promise that the buildings of the past, good as are some of them, are but poor and dull shadows of the noble edifices which are to follow; and the religious prosperity with which we have been favoured in the past, we trust is but a dim shadow of the mighty things which God shall accomplish for us in the future.

We are no seers that can foretell the future in precise terms; we cannot peer down its dark and receding vistas, and tell what is coming. Still, with an ordinary amount of sagacity, we may augur somewhat of the future from the character of the present.

Were it too bright a vision to foresee, were it too great a joy to predict, that we shall have in this land Churches which, in their ample size, neat appearance, fair proportions, and adaptations to the purposes of worship, shall be second to none around; ordinances that shall be wells of salvation to a thirsty people; pastors full of faith and the Holy Ghost; leaders, local preachers, and officers baptized with the spirit of holiness; and members growing in intelligence, concord, and piety; that such days of grace will come to us as will crowd the houses of God and the means of grace with devout worshippers, so that there shall be "added to the Church daily such as should be saved?" and that in all things lovely and of good report, and in whatsoever tends to the temporal, social, and moral elevation of the people and the glory of God, Victorian Methodism shall for ages have a foremost place? "The Lord of your fathers make you a thousand times so many more as ye are, and bless you, as He hath promised you."

Whilst leaving out many records, and touching lightly upon others, nevertheless we have given the chief facts and incidents of our "story." Fifty years is but a short span in the life of nations, and yet what progress do those years cover in young and nascent communities like our own. The ordinary observer will look at our material progress and say, "what hath *man* wrought?" In a circuit now intersected by railways and telegraphs, it is hard to realize that the preacher, still living, had to find his way from one place to another by a plough furrow driven through the virgin bush; and in a city where the electric light, clear as crystal, cheats the night, it is hard to realize the vocation of the young son of the chapel-keeper of old Collins-street Wesleyan chapel, scarcely now past the prime of life, who was then candle-snuffer to the congregation, and three times in the service had to decapitate the tallow dips which did duty in those dark ages. But the Christian observer as he calls to mind the temples, institutions, and living forces of the Methodist Christianity of to-day, and contrasts them with the small beginnings of Mr. Orton's day, will exclaim with humble and adoring gratitude, " What hath God wrought !"

Looking at the mighty Methodism, typified or illustrated by the series of Jubilee meetings held in Wesley Church and in the Exhibition Building, Melbourne, in May, 1886, so crowded, enthusiastic, liberal, so full of grateful ardour, so jubilant with joyous song, so marked with the presence and power of the Spirit of God, presenting such marshalled hosts of 2000, 5000, and over 10,000 persons, young and old, convened in the several assemblies, and comparing such with the seven members under Mr. Witton's care in 1837, and with the small company that heard the first sermon from Mr. Orton, we thankfully acknowledge God's exceeding goodness, in the past and present, to this section of His Church. We give all praise to His name; we lay all the trophies at His feet. " It is the Lord's doing, and marvellous in our eyes." " Not unto us, O Lord, not unto us, but unto Thy name give glory."

We are nearing the close of our story. The reader has kept our company so far. Before we part, may the hope be indulged, that this account will prove of some permanent benefit, as well as of mere passing interest to our companions.

The writer of this paragraph was once the escort to a young maiden during a ride through the " Stony Rises," between Colac and Camperdown. We were seated at the top of the coach, and were driving along a road, firm, narrow, winding, serpentine, amongst the deep hollows and swelling hillocks which there abound; the coach swaying to and fro as we went up one rise or down another, around one sharp curve, and in view of others, until our motion reminded him of the eccentric figures on the ice, and the graceful oscillations of the body which the skater makes. The scenery was novel and picturesque, and such as the young lady had not set eyes on before. Our track was amongst a labyrinth of rough boulders, miscellaneous heaps of rock, dark masses of basalt, pitched down in great disorder, but these had intermingled with them the tall bracken and smaller species of fern. Green grass was interspersed amongst the stones, and spread over the hollows. Gems of wild flowers were scattered here and there. In places, such as small swamps, and pools of water, aquatic plants were laying out their broad leaves, and lifting up their tiny beauteous flowers. As we rode on, we had glimpses now and then of a settler's house, a farmer's clearing, and of the grand volcanic hills in the distance, covered to their tops with emerald verdure. The air was crisp and clear, and the sky was a translucent blue, flecked with fleecy clouds. It was a sunbright spring morn. The lady's face was radiant with joyous health; and animated with lovely human life. Her spirits were exhilarated by the invigorating breezes and the morning ride. Her companion's hope had been that she would be pleased with the scene and the journey, and he confesses to some quickened feeling of joy when she said in her simplicity, "Oh! I like this; it is delightful!" He was well repaid for any pains he had taken to bring the lady thither, to point out any objects of interest, and contribute to her enjoyment of the day and the drive. Now, a work of art is inferior to the grandeur and beauty of nature, and cannot so well please the observer; this writing by man cannot vie with that pencilling by nature; but, though it be egotism to say so, if some share of pleasure and educating process fall to the courteous reader as was given that morning to the gentle maiden, than the writers will be amply rewarded. They have conducted you on a track which lies through heaps of material piled together in manuscripts, memoranda, newspapers, printed volumes that lie before and around them. They have swerved now to one subject, then to another, conveying you along no direct, but a winding path; but it may be in a highway of narrative that has made clear the events of past years, that were at first jumbled before their minds, but have come into some shape and order as they have gone on. Few picturesque heights of description can they point to, but if some connected view of the times, events, and places through which we have been passing, be given, and any simple expression of your approval be won, than the journey together will be a sunny memory with them, and they will be fully repaid for any pains they have taken to be your companions and guides.

Be this so or not, both writers may testify that their work has been undertaken *con amore*, as being to themselves a pleasing study of God's handiwork, bringing a quickened adoration of Him whose redemptive love is shown forth in human salvation, and inspiring them as they see His works to sing His praise. It is offered to the Wesleyan Church as a memorial of her worthy past, and as a dim prophecy of her grander future. It is placed before the Methodist public as some humble text book for their chorus of praise to Almighty God, and a monument of that Jubilee of joy, thanksgiving, and work which marks this year of grace 1886. "According to Thy name, O God, so is Thy praise unto the ends of the earth: Thy right hand is full of righteousness. Let Mount Zion rejoice, let the daughters of Judah be glad, because of Thy judgments. Walk about Zion, and go round about her: tell the towers thereof. Mark ye well her bulwarks, consider her palaces; that ye may tell it to the generation following. For this God is our God, for ever and ever." Psalm xlviii., verses 10-14.

We could wish the volume to be some legacy to after generations. If our "story" should endear to the Methodist family, the traditions of their Methodist home, and lead to a juster appreciation of its privileges and benefits, and a greater interest in its prosperity, our work will not be in vain. May the dying words of our founder, "the best of all is, God is with us," be our living experience from generation to generation, and "that which was made glorious" in the past, have no glory, by reason of "the glory that excelleth," in our future history.

APPENDIX. TABLE A.

Return of Ministers, Members, Agents, Churches, Scholars, &c., compiled from the Church Records:—

	October 1840	January 1846	July 1851	Conference 1855	Conference 1865	Conference 1875	Conference 1885	Conference 1886
Churches	1	4	18	31	247	373	469	480
Other Preaching places	1		18	40	73	152	274	311
Ministers	1	2	5	15	52	88	109	109
Home Missionaries				1			27	33
Day school Teachers			20	59	137	(a)		
Sunday school Teachers			142	401	2524	3614	4684	4691
Local Preachers	7		39	151	390	559	715	751
Class Leaders	7	19	50		566	717	781	818
Church Members	84	363	712	1955	8088	10,417	15,031	16,095
On trial for Membership		9	45	84	1122	1025	1704	839
Catechumens						382	2022	1741
Sabbath schools			15	41	235	339	475	470
Sabbath scholars			1283	3507	10,741	33,375	40,888	40,459
Day schools			13	37	69	(a)		
Day scholars			699	3007	6677	(a)		

NOTE (a).—Day schools passed into the hands of the State, under "The Education Act, 1872."

APPENDIX. TABLE B.

Number of Wesleyan Methodists, and of the whole population in Victoria, compiled from the Government Census Returns for the years assigned :—

	1841	1846	1851	1854	1857	1861	1871	1881
Number of Wes. Methodists	650	1597	4988	13,982	24,740	40,799	80,491	97,115
Total population of Victoria	11,738	32,879	77,345	236,798	410,766	540,322	751,528	862,346
Proportion of Wesleyans to population (rate per cent.)	5·537	4·86	6·449	5·9	6·02	7·55	10·71	11·26

N.B.—1. The return of Wesleyan Methodists is inclusive of the minor Methodist bodies for the years, 1841, 1846, and 1851, and is exclusive of them after 1851. The Census Returns do not separate them until the year 1854.

2. As the population of Victoria in April, 1886, was estimated at 1,000,000, then, assuming the Wesleyans to maintain the same ratio to the whole population that they did in 1881, we put down the number of Wesleyan Methodists at the present time at 112,610.

3. As the other sections of Methodists numbered, in the Census return of 1881, a total of 11,275, we may compute them in the present ^ear at 13,070. Total estimated strength of the Methodist population 125,680, or about one-eighth of the whole population.

INDEX.

CHAPTER I.　　INTRODUCTORY.　　　　　　　　Page
Rise of British Methodism—Australian and Victorian
Methodism　　...　　...　　...　　...　　9-12

CHAPTER II.　　FOUNDATION.
Early Settlement in Victoria—Mr. Reed—Rev. J. Orton
—Arrival—First Service—Regard for Aborigines—Melbourne Methodism—First class—Sabbath school—Revs.
F. Tuckfield and B. Hurst—Messrs. Parker and Dredge—
First Church—Mr. Orton's Second Visit—First Missionary
Meeting—Rev.W. Simpson's Visit—Mr. Orton's Pastorate
—Treatment of Natives—First Quarterly Meeting—Mr.
Orton's Departure—First Lay Helpers　　...　　...　　12-32

CHAPTER III.　　FIRST ADVANCES.
Inner and Outer Life of Christians—Rev. S. Wilkinson—
Collins-street Church—Mr. Dredge in Geelong—Interior
of Methodist Homes—Rev. W. Schofield—Revival—Rev.
E. Sweetman—Rev. W. Lowe—Messrs. Symons and
Flockart—Newtown (Fitzroy)—Rev. N. Turner—Rev.
J. Harcourt—Sketch of Mr. Sweetman　　...　　...　　32-45

CHAPTER IV.　　TRANSITION.
New Period—Rev. W. Butters—Day schools—First District Meeting—Labour of Local Preachers—Gold Discovered—Immigration—Excitement—Social Convulsions
—New Efforts for New Circumstances—Mr. Butters'
Letter—Commercial Aspects—Second District Meeting—
Immigrants Home—New Churches　　...　　...　　45-61

CHAPTER V.　　GOLD AND CHANGE.
Rev. R. Young— Projected Conference — Arrival of
English Ministers—Third District Meeting—Reports of
Churches—Departure of Revs. F. Lewis and E. Sweetman—Stations—Arrival of other Ministers from England
—Foremost Laymen—Rev. J. Eggleston—Rev. J. W.
Crisp—The Church's Beneficial Influence ...　　...　　61-70

CHAPTER VI.　　EXTENSION.
First Australasian Conference—Rev. D. J. Draper—Rev.
J. C. Symons—Second Conference—Reinforcement of
Minsters—Numbers—Day schools—Officials—Revs. W.
L. Binks and W. P. Wells—Young Ministers—Rev. J. S.

Waugh—Wesleyan Chronicle—Book Depôt—Bazaar for
Wesley College—New Churches—Wesley Church ... 70-81

CHAPTER VII. PRECURSORS OF REVIVAL.
Fresh Ministers, English and Colonial—Other Laymen—
Rev. Dr. Jobson—Rev. E. E. Jenkins—Other additions
to the Ministry—Rev. W. Hill—Death of Rev. W.
Tregellas—Rev. T. Taylor—Rev. J. Odgers—Jubilee of
Missionary Society... 81-89

CHAPTER VIII. REVIVALS.
Those in Other Lands—Influx and Exodus of Population
—Revival at Brighton—In Melbourne Circuits—At Drysdale, Geelong—Rev. Joseph Dare—Revivals, Scriptural,
Reasonable — Mr. M. Burnett — Rev. W. Taylor — In
Wesley Church and other Churches—Revival in Williamstown — Converts — Success amongst Seamen —
Revivals Defended—Mr. E. Stranger — Ministerial
Fruits—Rapid Strides 89-106

CHAPTER IX. CHURCH INSTITUTIONS, MOVEMENTS,
MEMORIALS, (1863-85.)
Formation of Three Districts—Education—State Action
—Wesley College—Rev. Dr. Waugh—Death of Rev. D. J.
Draper—Rev. W. H. Fitchett—Methodist Ladies' College
—Rev. B. Field—Sunday school Union—Wesleyan Home
Missions—Rev. John Watsford—Ministers and Laymen
of Recent Times 106-115

CHAPTER X. SUBURBAN METHODISM.
Williamstown — Brighton — Dandenong — Brunswick—
Coburg, etc.—Former Pentridge Circuit—Kilmore—
Preston and Heidelberg—Emerald Hill—Prahran, St.
Kilda—South Melbourne—Richmond—Hawthorn .. 115-137

CHAPTER XI. GEELONG AND BALLARAT DISTRICT.
GEELONG—First Services—Rev. Mr. Skevington—Messrs.
Smith and Sanderson—First Church—Mr. Dredge—Missionary Meeting — Yarra-street Church — Successive
Ministers—Rev. I. Harding—New Churches—Sabbath
schools—Grandfather Lowe—Elect Ladies—COLAC—
BALLARAT—Early Times—First Class—First Sermons—
First Churches and Officials—Schools—Progress—Rev.
T. Taylor—Quarterly Meeting Records—Rev. Mr. Bickford—Creswick—Rev. J. G. Millard—Rev. Dr. Waugh—
Conference — CRESWICK — CLUNES — EGERTON —
MELTON—SCARSDALE & LINTON—Converts—Reverses 137-160

CHAPTER XII. CASTLEMAINE & SANDHURST DISTRICT.
Forest Creek—Discovery of Gold—First Services—Local
Preachers—Rev. J. C. Symons—Mr. Chapman—Early
Incidents—First Plan and Church—Rev. W. P. Wells
CASTLEMAINE Church—Fryer's Creek—Rev. J. Mewton
—Rev. T. Raston—Rev. W. L. Blamires—Sabbath's
Experience—Training Ground of Ministers—Active Laymen—New Churches—Physical Toils and Hardships—
Tea Meetings—Later Ministers—Strength of Circuit 160-186

CHAPTER XIII. MALDON, MARYBOROUGH AND
ADJACENT CIRCUITS.

MALDON—First Services—Mr. Boots—Mr. Warnock—
Rev. H. Chester—James Jeffrey—Illustrations—Rev. W.
Woodall—Rev. G. B. Richards—Rev. J. Catterall—New
Church — Revival — MARYBOROUGH —Alma—Jeffrey—
Rev. M. Dyson—Rev. B. S. Walker—Local Preachers
—Rev. J. Albiston—Rev. W. Woodall—Progress—Other
Ministers—AVOCA—TALBOT 186-205

CHAPTER XIV. SANDHURST CIRCUIT.
First Agents and Services—Revival at White Hills—
Rev. R. Young—Sandhurst and Eaglehawk Churches—
Officials and Classes—Difficulties—Rev. T. Raston—Rev.
J. Dare—Colleagues—New Churches—Rev. J. Bickford
—Other Superintendents—Junior Ministers—Mr. Hooper
and other Laymen 205-228

CHAPTER XV. KYNETON AND DAYLESFORD CIRCUITS.
KYNETON—Messrs. Mewton, Chester, and Catterall—
Buildings — Laymen — Mrs. Watson — DAYLESFORD—
First Visits—Rev. S. Knight—Rapid Progress—New
Church—Ministers—BLACKWOOD 228-233

CHAPTER XVI. THE DUNOLLY AND TARNAGULLA, AND
INGLEWOOD CIRCUITS.

Mr. Falder—Churches at Tarnagulla—Places Occupied—
Rev. J. Mewton—DUNOLLY—Mr Hansford—Wedderburn—Mr. Bunting—INGLEWOOD—Other Agents ... 233-241

CHAPTER XVII. NORTHERN AREAS.
THE ST. ARNAUD, CHARLTON, ECHUCA & OTHER CIRCUITS.
ST. ARNAUD—First Efforts—Slow Advance—Swift Pro-
gress — CHARLTON — ECHUCA — Kyabram — Kerang—
Raywood, and Elmore 241-247

CHAPTER XVIII. GIPPSLAND DISTRICT.
Comparison, Then and Now—Rev. J. Bickford's Visit—
First Church in SALE—PORT ALBERT and YARRAM
YARRAM—WALHALLA—Upland and Lowland—Home
Missions—WARRAGUL 247-251

CHAPTER XIX. WESTERN DISTRICT.
PORTLAND—Early Settlement—First Methodist—Narra-
wong and Bridgewater—First School and Church—Suc-
cessive Ministers—Rev. F. Tuckfield—New Church—
Rev. J. B. Smith—Drik Drik and Heywood—BELFAST
—Rosebrook—Mr. Watson—Churches in Belfast—Yam-
buk, Koroit, Kirkstall—WARRNAMBOOL—First Laymen
—Ministers—Dennington—Churches, Warrnambool and
Wangoom—HAMILTON—First Visits—First Ministers
—Union Churches—Revs. W. L. Blamires and R. M.
Hunter—Land Racket—Byaduk and John Smith—Active
Ministers and Laymen — MORTLAKE — PENSHURST—
MERINO 251-273

CHAPTER XX. OVENS AND MURRAY DISTRICT.
BEECHWORTH, Town and District—Squatters and Diggers—First Methodists and Services—Mr. C. Williams —Mr. Butters' Visit—Rev. J. C. Symons' Journeys and Pastorate — Subsequent Ministers — Yackandandah— Albury—Growler's Creek—Wangaratta—Benalla and Shepparton 273-285

CHAPTER XXI. NORTH-WESTERN CIRCUITS.
ARARAT—First Events—Fluctuation—Pleasant Creek (STAWELL)—Rev. W. Woodall—Rev. C. Dubourg—Rev. A. Inglis—Mr. Middleton—Moyston and other places —Superintendents—Division of Circuit—Laymen—Rev. R. Hart—HORSHAM—Other Circuits and Stations ... 285-291

CHAPTER XXII. MISSIONS & MISCELLANEOUS.
Missions to Seamen — Suburban Melbourne — Bible Women and City Missions—Mission to Chinese—South Sea Missions—Relations to other Churches—Connexional Finance — Methodist Union — Doctrine—Polity—Laws —Worship—Itinerancy 291-302

CHAPTER XXIII. CONCLUSION.
Methodist Youth and Sunday schools—Other Fertile Topics—Church Doctrine and Polity—Spiritual Life— Influence of Methodism—God's Providence towards Her—Church's Duty and Prospects as to Past, Present, and Future—Jubilee time contrasted with former days —Feeling and hope of the writers in constructing and publishing this work 303-313
Appendix, Table A—Church Returns 314
„ „ B—Statistics of Population ... 315
Table of Errata ... ... END.

ERRATA.

Page	18	line	3, for " Sandridge " read " Lower Yarra."
,,	25	,,	14, for "I" read " We."
,,	31	,,	17, for " the" read " a."
,,	67	,,	10, for " Stephenson " read " Stephinson."
,,	99	,,	27, should begin " to the place of prayer·"
,,	101	,,	16, erase " like " at the end.
,,	107	,,	18, for " prepares " read " prepare."
,,	111	,,	32, for " Cornshmen " read " Cornishmen."
,,	115	,,	7, for " Represetative" read "Representative."
,,	118	,,	21, leave out " then."
,,	132		for " Moorhouse " read " Moorhead."
,,	143	,,	6, for " J " Harding read " I " Harding.
,,	157	,,	19, for " Persley" read " Presley."
,,	167	,,	31, read "amount of £17 was collected."
,,	179	,,	1, for " Tenby " read " Temby."
,,	194	,,	12, for " 1817 " read " 1815."
,,	,,	,,	13, for " 1880 " read " 1877."
,,	213	,,	35, for " Isarel " read " Israel."
,,	220	,,	2, leave out " no."
,,	221	,,	3, instead of " the present site " read " that."
,,	224	,,	4, for " dignatories " read "'dignitaries.'"
,,	,,	,,	31, for " have " read " having."
,,	245	,,	28, for "mentiened " read "mentioned."
,,	248	,,	29, for " was" read " were."
,,	259	,,	15, after " School " insert " house."
,,	265	,,	29, for "Tregellis " read " Tregellas."
,,	269	,,	24, for " Ivan " read " Joan."
,,	276	,,	25, after " Tasmania " insert " and."
,,	287	,,	5, for " Sunday ",read " Saturday."
,,	304	,,	19, instead of " for the Church " read " of the Church."

www.ingramcontent.com/pod-product-compliance
Lightning Source LLC
Chambersburg PA
CBHW030756230426
43667CB00007B/987